GREENHOUSE GARDENING

Miranda Smith

 Rodale Press, Emmaus, Pennsylvania

To my mother, Mabs Clark,
who instilled
all of her love of gardening
and much of her skill,
while neither of us noticed.

Book design by Anita Noble
Book layout by Karen A. Schell
Illustrations by Beth Sachs

Library of Congress Cataloging in Publication Data

Smith, Miranda, 1944–
    Greenhouse gardening.

    Bibliography: p.
    Includes index.
    1. Greenhouse gardening. 2. Organic
gardening. I. Title.
SB415.S657   1985   635′.0483   85-2866
ISBN   0–87857–566–9   hardcover
ISBN   0–87857–567–7   paperback

2 4 6 8 10 9 7 5 3 1   hardcover
2 4 6 8 10 9 7 5 3 1   paperback

CONTENTS

ACKNOWLEDGMENTS

Without the help and support given by many friends, I could never have written this book. Looking backward, from the finishing touches to the first idea, a kaleidoscope of faces passes by, each belonging to someone who made a valuable contribution. Many thanks are long overdue, left from the first writing in 1980–81. Other people helped during the second time around, in 1984.

First, I would like to thank The Memphremagog Group, collectively and individually. As a working group and association of friends, TMG gives a truly unusual amount of respect, trust and support, enabling each of us to learn from the others while following our own paths. This book is a prime example. I've incorporated many things, both technical and attitudinal, that I've learned from other TMG members, but because the process goes so smoothly, it's difficult to ascribe each element to its probable author. So this is a thank-you for the best working group I've yet seen.

Individually, I would like to give a special thank-you to Beth Sachs for her excellent illustrations and for sharing this project through the years. Thank-yous also go to Miriam Klein, for the past ten years of shared horticultural failures and successes; to Sue Alward, for her unwavering and special friendship; to Carolyn Shapiro, for her ability to make the mundane graceful; to Ron Alward, for his gentle perception; to Andy Shapiro, for his relentless curiosity and sensitivity; to Blair Hamilton, for his precision and flexibility; and to Armand Lepage, for understanding my desire to write this book.

And other people helped as well. Bart Hall-Beyer greatly improved the soils information in chapters 6, 7 and 8, while Lydia Allen gave excellent comments on the manuscript from a grower's perspective.

Thanks should also go to the many growers, both amateur and professional, from whom I've learned over the years. Unfortunately, an adequate list would be prohibitively long, so with the exception of one grower, I'd like to offer a general thanks. Linda Gilkeson deserves a special mention, not only from me but also from other American and Canadian organic growers who have been fortunate enough to incorporate her work into their biological pest-control programs.

The second writing of this book may not have been possible without Robert Houriet. Not only did he provide the necessary moral support, but he also taught me some valuable editing techniques.

Babysitters can make or break a project. Christina Studer, Loretta Studer, Suzanne Frizzel and Denise Letourneau enabled me to work without worrying about my daughter Simone.

My children, Tagore and Simone, deserve many thanks and some extra attention for putting up with a highly abstracted mother.

INTRODUCTION

One of my earliest memories is standing, just under bench height, in a two-story domed greenhouse at a lavish botanical garden. Outside, the ground was covered with a dingy, week-old snow. But inside the giant glass building was a warm, moist jungle where banana trees with umbrella leaves stretched to the ceiling and enormous red begonias in pots drooped over benches filled with blooming kalanchoes, calceolarias and primroses. I knew I'd entered a wild, unruly world where plants were only barely restrained from bursting through the glass like Jack's fabulous beanstalk.

My love of greenhouses was born that day. Not that I imagined having one: It was obvious that these wonders were the province only of kings and governments. I categorized greenhouses as unattainable and left it at that for many years.

But times have changed since then. Energy-conserving and solar designs have put greenhouses within the reach of many people. And while these structures are certainly more modest than the 40-foot-tall leaded glass buildings of the 1900s, each has the potential to be a wondrous world. Or, as I so correctly discerned as a child, a wild, unruly jungle of creatures that thrive under glazing.

This book is about a delicate balance—the interplay between wildness and imposed restraint. As an analogy, think of a greenhouse environment as a seesaw. When one end touches the ground, every element of the environment is under artificial and very strict control. There are few surprises. Conversely, when the other end is touching, the environment is completely out of the grower's control. Anything might happen.

As a biological, or organic, grower, neither extreme is acceptable. I try to set the fulcrum of this environmental seesaw for appreciably more control than not. But the invisible and slightly mysterious world inside the artificial bubble is too valuable to give up, on both pragmatic and aesthetic grounds.

Gardening, either inside or out, teaches a respect for the natural world. The more you learn about nature's organization, the more you are awed by its sheer beauty and economy. In scientific terms, this organization is an elegant solution to a terribly complex situation. Every piece has a place. From an aesthetic viewpoint, nothing is more pleasurable than watching the natural world work; and from a practical view, nothing works better.

So this book is about organization, too: the implicit organization of and among plants, insects and environment, as well as the organization that you, as a grower, will impose on both yourself and the greenhouse environment. A solid understanding of the relationships and interactions going on under the glazing gives you the freedom to use "natural" elements of the environment; sterility isn't necessary or even desirable.

In this book I have tried to serve the needs of both beginning gardeners and experienced field growers who are new to greenhouse horticulture. Often the beginning grower has become interested in greenhouses and horticulture as an outgrowth of interest in solar design, while experienced growers usually build greenhouses in response to their need for high-quality seedlings or expanded production. Beginning growers are apt to have solar greenhouses, while field growers, especially those who grow for market, are more likely to have nonsolar, or "traditional," facilities. To make this book useful for *all* greenhouse growers, environmental management techniques for both types of structures are included.

The horticultural information is meant to answer questions from beginning as well as experienced growers. Some of the techniques and information are basic to all gardening activities, inside or out. However, the bulk of the content is directed toward the particular characteristics and requirements of an artificial environment. Even experienced gardeners must develop new concepts and horticultural techniques when they move into a greenhouse.

Experience is my primary "credential" for writing this book. Horticulture, in one way or another, has been a major part of my life for as long as I can remember. My first apprenticeship was to my mother, who sold perennials and bedding plants. She was, and still is, an organic grower. At the time, the 1940s and 1950s, I didn't realize that her growing methods weren't the norm; I simply absorbed the growing style. She taught my brother and me to admire bugs and toads, how to build a compost pile, and occasionally, much to our dismay, how to salt slugs. After such a childhood, my greatest desire was to escape from plants, soils, toads, snakes and bugs.

But old habits die hard. I turned into a "closet" gardener, furtively buying seed packets and building up the soil outside various city apartments for a patch of flowers. Later I moved to a series of country houses, putting in successively larger gardens at each. And then began a long chain of fortuitous accidents leading to a career as a grower.

My first agricultural "job," in 1971, was as an assistant teacher to

John Harrison of Mylora Farms in British Columbia. In response to the swelling "back to the land" movement, John was teaching organic techniques. I may have gotten more out of the experience than anyone else; in addition to some new techniques, I learned that 100 acres of produce, small fruit and cut flowers could be farmed organically. I also discovered that I loved to teach gardening.

Solar greenhouses entered my life in 1975, when I was teaching at an urban gardening project in Montreal. We were supposed to build a large solar greenhouse on the roof of a community center, but because of engineering constraints, had to settle for three small nonsolar greenhouses, eight "crawl-in" solar cold frames, and groups of unsheltered growing boxes. The greenhouses, simple as they were, hooked me. I was astounded at the difference in growth made by two flimsy layers of polyethylene and a heater. And through being introduced to the experimental solar greenhouses at The Brace Institute at MacDonald College, Quebec, I realized that greenhouses were indeed practical, even without government funding.

Since then I've worked as a researcher and a grower in a variety of greenhouses, both solar and traditional, in climates as different as cold, arid Montana and hot, humid Washington, D.C. I've taught and consulted for people at all levels, from beginning growers to commercial farmers. And best of all, I've been extraordinarily fortunate to meet and share information with some of the finest growers and researchers now working.

But certain frustrations, with both myself and the larger world of contemporary horticulture, have tagged along with me through these years. Personally, I am continually frustrated by my ignorance. Despite a happy skill as a good grower, there is much more to learn. And that brings me to the larger frustration: It's difficult to get good information about organic greenhouse systems. Despite the growing awareness of the need for organic methods among farming researchers and consultants, very little attention is given to organic *greenhouse* management. Perhaps because the acreage is smaller or because people believe that "it's just too difficult" or "it's not cost-effective," researchers and educators ignore organic greenhouse growing. Instead, they concentrate on increasingly complex chemical greenhouse systems.

Chemical systems are said to be cost-effective. The chemicals are relatively cheap, and once researchers have figured out the correct ratios of this to that, the grower doesn't have to do much more than follow directions well. However, using cost efficiency as the sole criterion for judging the value of a growing system ignores some important factors. Long-term environmental and personal health and the larger issue of sensitivity and respect for natural systems are not considered. And this most extreme way of growing short-circuits the "art" that most growers pursue in their work.

But despite the research emphasis on chemical systems, increasing numbers of private and professional growers are attracted to organic systems. Some have chosen to forge their own road, while others are inhibited by the lack of good information. Time after time I meet people who talk wistfully of owning a greenhouse, "if only I didn't have to use poisons." "You don't," is my invariable reply. "But," the conversation continues, "friends of mine got such bad aphids (or such a bad fungus on their plants) that they finally had to spray poison on them."

It's impossible to teach organic management in a short conversation. Hence this book. In it, I've tried to pass on the information that enables me to run a greenhouse full of healthy plants and only a few bugs. Some material is conceptual, simply because I discovered a need for it in my own work. Other material is more practical, the "tricks" that make life in the greenhouse easier. But please don't expect to find everything you need to know in these pages; my experiences can't possibly mirror every situation you'll encounter. Instead, use this book as an introduction, a beginning point for your own style as an organic greenhouse grower.

CHAPTER 1
UNDERSTANDING PLANTS IN THEIR ENVIRONMENTS

You probably love plants; most greenhouse owners do. And chances are that you're an excellent outside gardener who provides the right conditions for a multitude of different crops. But many gardeners are so adept at soil management, planting schedules and pest and disease control that they don't have to pay much attention to plants; given the right conditions, plants just grow. Well, they'll grow in a greenhouse, too, but they'll be healthier and more productive if you understand what's going on inside them and how the environment affects them.

Long ago most of us took biology, where we were supposed to learn the basics of plant physiology and processes. At the time, I wasn't very interested in the subject and relegated it to a dusty corner of my mind soon after final exams. It sat there, unused, through many a good growing season while I concentrated on learning about soils, nutrients, pests and diseases. But then I moved into greenhouse horticulture. Within the first panic-stricken week of trying to regulate vents, fans and heaters, I realized that I needed to understand more about plants before I could provide a good environment. Eighth grade biology had come into its own again.

Since then I've taught intensive greenhouse horticulture courses, conducted lots of short workshops, and worked as a greenhouse consultant. And time after time I've learned that people's skill in a greenhouse is dramatically boosted once they know, or remember, the basics of plant and soil science. Horticulture is a balancing game that calls for creativity, decisiveness and good timing. But you have to know what factors are being juggled and what's going to happen if you change just one element. So now I teach the "basics" first. And through the basics I try to communicate an appreciation for the elegance of the natural world—our world where nothing is extraneous and nothing is wasted. That appreciation is as important to a grower as setting a thermostat correctly; a greenhouse is a small world where the natural and the "unnatural" must meet in harmony.

Plant Physiology

Knowing how a plant works is far more important than knowing how it is made. But structure and function are closely related. Being able to visualize plant structures makes it easier to understand processes that are affected by both the environment and your management decisions.

From the Roots Up

Water, gases and mineral ions move between the plant and soil through the roots. Roots allow this passage because, unlike the rest of the plant, their **epidermis,** or "skin," isn't coated with a waxy **cuticle** layer that prevents water and gases from moving in and out. Most of the exchange takes place through **root hairs,** specialized epidermal cells projecting into the surrounding soil, which provide a huge surface area for the exchange of water and other substances. Because they are

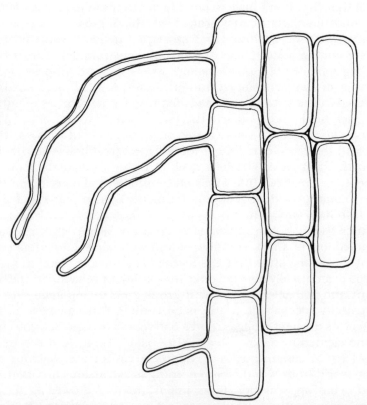

Root Hairs: These tiny, delicate structures are responsible for bringing water and other substances from the soil into the plant.

single cells protected only by the cell membrane, root hairs are tiny, delicate structures.

Everything that enters or exits a cell must be "in solution," that is, dissolved in water. Both soil water and water in the root contain varying amounts of dissolved minerals and gases. Roots generally contain more concentrated solutions of minerals and gases than does the soil water. Consequently, water from the soil is attracted into the root. This movement of water and dissolved substances through a semipermeable membrane, from a lower to a higher concentration, is called **osmosis.** Pressure also helps to regulate water movement. When a plant cell is fully **turgid,** or water filled, pressure from within the cell prevents more water from entering.

Root hairs are extremely fragile. Just imagine them for a moment. They live, die and are replaced quickly, always growing just beyond the tip of the root where new cells are formed and then elongate. They absorb soil water as they grow, and under most conditions keep up with the plant's needs. But if many root hairs are injured all at one time—during a rough transplanting, for example—the plant will suffer. It won't be able to grow new root hairs quickly enough to supply adequate water or minerals. Visualize single-celled root hairs as you transplant seedlings; it helps to minimize losses.

Transportation

Water and dissolved materials must be moved from place to place within the plant. Osmosis occurs from cell to cell, but it's slow. Two other phenomena take up the slack. Water also diffuses into the small air spaces surrounding each cell, allowing faster passage than osmosis. And eventually intercellular water reaches the **vascular bundles,** long

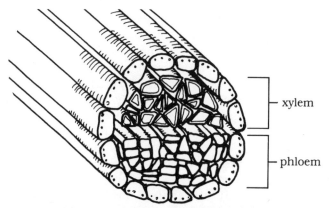

Vascular Bundle: *Xylem and phloem cells make up vascular bundles, the transport channels that stretch from a plant's roots to its top leaves.*

channels that reach from root tip to leaf tip. The vascular system allows for "express" movement of water and nutrients.

Two kinds of vessels make up this system: **xylem** and **phloem.** Minerals and water move from the roots to the rest of the plant through the xylem, while sugars and water move from the leaves to the rest of the plant through the phloem. (Xylem up; phloem down.) There's some mineral movement from xylem into phloem, too. Both kinds of vessels are formed by long chains of single cells. In the xylem, the walls linking adjacent cells dissolve entirely as they mature; it may help to visualize a xylem vessel as a pipe or a hose. Phloem cells are constructed somewhat differently; their cells are called "sieve cells." Adjacent walls, though still present in the mature cell, develop holes that allow large quantities of dissolved sugars to pass from one cell to the next. (Xylem, pipe; phloem, hole-n-'em.)

Xylem and phloem vessels always lie close to each other; hence the word "bundle" is used to describe them collectively. Their location in the plant is telling. In the root, the vascular bundles lie close to the center. If you cut a carrot crosswise, you can sometimes see vascular bundles circling the core. In the stem, they grow close to the epidermis. Look at a cross section of a celery stalk to see a good example. Vascular bundles branch profusely to form the "veins" in leaves and flower petals. Xylem tissue toughens and becomes woody as it matures. Its placement toward the center of the root and the outside of the stem helps to strengthen and support the plant. Knowing the location of the vascular bundles helps you to remember that even a shallow injury to a stem, such as a bruise or a nick, may harm the underlying vascular system and impede growth.

How Plants Grow

New cells are formed in areas called **meristems. Apical meristems** are located at stem and root tips, but meristematic tissue also grows in other, specific, sites in both the stem and root. In the root, meristematic tissue is located near the center, but in the stem it's located in the axils formed where branches meet the main stem. Some plants, such as tomatoes, grow new tissues freely from these **lateral** or **secondary meristems,** but in others the apical meristem produces a hormonelike substance called an **auxin,** which inhibits new growth. Plants with this characteristic, called **apical dominance,** branch only if the apical meristem is damaged or removed. When you cut off the top of an avocado stem or pinch back a geranium, you are removing the production site of the inhibiting auxin, and in response, lateral meristems grow and develop. The plant grows bushier instead of taller. You also see this phenomenon in carrots grown in rocky soil; they branch and form "forks" if their delicate root tip, and accompanying apical meristem, is injured by hitting a rock. Pruning and pinching back are often intended to remove inconvenient (from the grower's point of view) meristematic tissue. For example, removing the "suckers" from the axils of indeterminate tomato plants forces top growth, while pinching the tips of snapdragon stems forces production of more flower stalks.

The Structure of Leaves

Even though we haven't looked at stem or root structure as a whole, it's helpful to look at the leaf this way to understand some plant actions and reactions.

The epidermal layer of leaves is covered with a very thick cuticle. At intervals there are little holes in the epidermis, **stomata,** surrounded by two half-moon-shaped cells, the **guard cells.** When turgid, the guard cells plump up to open the stomate. But when the plant suffers from a lack of water, guard cells collapse and close the opening.

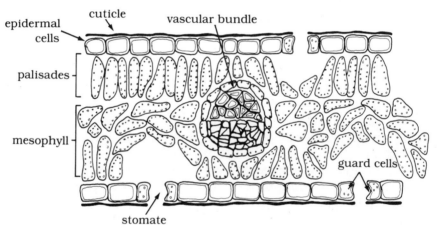

Cross Section of a Leaf: *These structures play an important role within the leaf and ultimately help to determine the health of the whole plant.*

The **palisades,** a group of long, skinny cells, sit just below the epidermis. They contain huge numbers of intercellular structures called **chloroplasts.** Chloroplasts contain molecules of **chlorophyll,** the substance that allows the manufacture of glucose, the basic sugar from which all other plant substances are made. Beyond the palisades is a region called the **mesophyll.** Some of this area is known as the **spongy mesophyll,** and it's aptly named. Cells here contain some chloroplasts, but unlike the palisade cells, they are irregularly shaped, and thus very loosely grouped. A large, continuous blanket of air around and between them allows rapid movement of gases and moisture.

In some leaves another layer of palisade cells sit against the bottom epidermal tissue. The lower epidermis is also punctuated by stomata. In fact, on cultivated plants the majority of stomata are on the undersides of leaves. As we'll see in the following section, leaf structure is important to plant processes.

Plant Processes

As terrarium gardeners can attest, plants release water into their environment. The quantities are amazing. For example, a single tomato plant gives off more than half a gallon of water every day, a corn plant gives off about a gallon, and a tree can give off as much as 150 gallons. It's easy to understand how razing a forest affects precipitation patterns so greatly. If the teak forest still stood in Ethiopia, instead of being cleared for agriculture, there would still be adequate rain for crops and the population would not be starving.

The water that plants release comes from the soil, of course. By osmosis, it enters the root hairs and then moves, by both osmosis and diffusion, until it reaches the xylem. As water travels up the xylem, a tiny portion is taken up and used by the cells along the route for their various activities. But most of the water reaches the leaf's spongy mesophyll. Again, cells in the leaf use some water. But the largest proportion diffuses into the intercellular air. And because air inside the leaf is usually more water-saturated than outside air, it passes out through the stomata. This process is called **transpiration.**

You may have wondered why water in a plant seems to defy the law of gravity by moving up rather than down. Water molecules are cohesive; they're attracted to each other. Remember playing with raindrops on a windowpane as a child? If you can just get them close enough, they rush at each other like magnets to make a big fat drop. The long chains of water molecules inside the xylem act this way, too; they pull each other up the vessel. Factors both inside and outside the leaf determine the speed and quantity.

Molecules of hot air move around more rapidly than those of cool air. More water is also absorbed. This phenomenon controls the fluctuation of humidity. Warm air can hold greater quantities of water vapor than cold air can.

When a leaf heats, air in the mesophyll absorbs more water. Because of its cohesiveness, the faster water is absorbed and released, the faster it moves up the xylem, so a plant's need for water is in proportion to the rate at which water transpires from its leaves. Fortunately, temperature also affects the movement of water into the root and through cell membranes. Heat makes cell membranes more permeable. Soil temperatures are likely to be warm when leaves are also warm, so water movement into roots and out of leaves usually works in concert. When soil is dry or osmosis is inhibited by such things as a saline soil solution, each cell gives up a little water. The plant wilts. As guard cells lose their shape, stomata close, halting gaseous exchange with the outside environment.

Temperature and relative humidity also affect transpiration. When air inside the leaf contains more moisture than air immediately surrounding the leaf, more air passes out through the stomata. Thus, transpiration rates are greater in hot and/or dry conditions than in cool and/or wet ones. Even when it's quite hot, stagnant air retains high relative humidity immediately around the leaf, impeding transpiration. Once you understand the relationship between transpiration and the environment, you know why it's important to minimize water stress and keep air circulation high.

Photosynthesis

Photosynthesis is the name given to the plant process of making glucose (sugar) from water and carbon dioxide (CO_2) in the presence of light in cells containing chlorophyll. In the outside garden you can take this process for granted. It just happens, day after day, without any help. But greenhouse conditions can interfere with photosynthesis; it's wise to understand something about how the process works.

Most of the water used for photosynthesis comes from the soil and moves into the leaves and chloroplasts as already described. Carbon dioxide comes from the air surrounding each leaf. The stomata provide a direct link between interior and exterior air. Carbon dioxide supplies within the leaf are lower than outside, consequently carbon dioxide is attracted through the stomata. Once diffused within the leaf's interior air, CO_2 moves rapidly into cells containing chloroplasts.

The structure of chlorophyll molecules shows why minerals are essential to plants. An atom of magnesium lies in the center of the chlorophyll molecule. Four atoms of nitrogen are connected to the magnesium, and hydrogen, carbon and oxygen atoms compose the rest of the molecule. No one fully understands how chlorophyll works, but generally, it absorbs some parts of the visible and near-visible wavelengths of light. The light energy rearranges the carbon, oxygen and hydrogen atoms from carbon dioxide and water into molecules of glucose. Once again we come to a mineral; this rearrangement can't happen without the presence of phosphorus in the cell. Even though you don't see it in the formula and it isn't a part of the chlorophyll molecule, phosphorus must be present for photosynthesis to occur. The chemical formula for photosynthesis is usually expressed in this way:

$$6\ H_2O + 6\ CO_2 = C_6H_{12}O_6 + 6\ O_2$$

In other words, six water molecules plus six carbon dioxide molecules react to give one molecule of glucose plus six molecules of oxygen.

The "leftover" oxygen is very important to all of us. It moves into the interior air of the leaf and then, because its concentration inside the leaf is higher than that of the surrounding air, moves out into the environment. It's a handy arrangement: Plants use carbon dioxide and give off oxygen while animals use oxygen and give off carbon dioxide.

Each and every compound in a plant (starch, fat, cellulose, lignin, vitamins, enzymes, auxins, and so on) is made from the glucose produced in the leaf. Some compounds contain only carbon, hydrogen and oxygen atoms in different relationships, while others contain minerals as well. You might imagine that each of these compounds is made in the leaf and then transported through the phloem vessels to other sites, but that isn't the case. Only sugars are dissolvable in water, and thus only sugars can move through cell walls.

During the day, glucose is manufactured and accumulated in the leaf as starch (carbohydrates), huge molecules containing only carbon, hydrogen and oxygen in different proportions than found in glucose. At night, enzymes in the cell digest the starch, turning it back into sugar. It moves out into the phloem, travels to various cells and is rearranged and recombined with minerals to form needed compounds. Every organic substance except sugar is manufactured in the cell where it's found.

Respiration

All this rearranging and recombining requires energy. The primary energy source, sunlight, powers photosynthesis. But after water and carbon dioxide have been transformed into glucose, the energy used for that transformation is essentially "tied up." Like some capital assets, it's there, but unavailable. If this energy were to remain within glucose, it could not power other chemical reactions. But life is better organized than that! Some glucose is broken back down into carbon dioxide and water. As this happens, energy within the chemical bond is released and becomes available to fire other reactions in the plant cells.

This activity is called **respiration,** and it can be defined as the process of changing organic substances (those containing carbon) into substances that are partially inorganic. As you can surmise from the definition, compounds other than glucose are also used in respiration.

Look back at the formula given for photosynthesis on page 8, remembering that the process frees oxygen. Logically, when the action reverses itself and glucose changes back into carbon dioxide and water, oxygen is again required. This kind of respiration is called **aerobic,** simply meaning that it requires oxygen.

Anaerobic respiration takes place without oxygen. The products formed in this case are alcohol and carbon dioxide. Plants that prefer boglike conditions normally carry on some anaerobic respiration, as do some fungi and bacteria. Vegetables and most ornamental plants have to respire anaerobically when the soil is waterlogged and their roots can't get enough oxygen. However, they would rather not be treated like skunk cabbage. Most cultivated plants can live through brief periods of anaerobic respiration, but if the condition persists for long, alcohol poisons the plant. You may have had this happen to an over-watered houseplant.

Each cell in every plant respires continuously, day and night. Respiration slows considerably after the first few hours of darkness, but it never completely stops. Photosynthesis happens only during the day or when the correct light wavelengths are striking the leaves. If the rate of respiration were equal to the rate of photosynthesis, there wouldn't be a net gain of glucose; the plant couldn't make anything other than basic sugar. Under correct environmental conditions, plants photosynthesize about 20 times as much glucose during the day as they use over an entire 24-hour period. But some adverse conditions prevent this luxurious production. At these times, plants stop growing. Again, the relationship between a plant and its environment is crucial.

Plants and Their Environment

When gardeners are asked what are the requirements for good plant growth, their typical answer is: slightly acid soil of good texture with adequate minerals in the correct proportions, water, light and air. Greenhouse growers might reply more specifically, adding that a plant needs a certain light intensity for a certain period each day, a certain range of temperature, and air that is neither too wet nor too dry and that contains adequate levels of carbon dioxide. Their different answers stem from differences in experience.

Both sorts of growers are concerned with the quality of the plant's environment, and both instinctively appreciate the principle of the limiting factor. A basic tenet of plant science, this principle postulates that plants continue to grow until one of their requirements becomes deficient, no matter how abundantly their other needs are met. Outdoor gardeners often encounter situations where the limiting factor is water, but rarely where it's carbon dioxide. On the other hand, greenhouse growers don't have to wait for rain but must vent well to keep carbon dioxide levels high enough for good photosynthesis.

Whether or not you consciously recognize the principle of the limiting factor, you'll apply it in conjunction with other basic knowledge. Fortunately, you already act on these other principles, though you may not be aware of them. They are:

- **Environmental factors interact to produce a total environment.** For example, light produces heat, increasing the water-holding capacity of the air, which, depending upon available moisture, either increases or decreases relative humidity.

- **Environment affects all living organisms.** There's no escape. For example, as a day heats, you do, too; in response, you perspire to cool down.

- **Physical processes are interdependent with the environment.** If you and 15 other hot, perspiring people are all sitting in a small, unventilated room on a hot day, the air in the room will become more and more humid as it absorbs the perspiration. Evaporation of your perspiration will slow in response to the increased relative humidity. Evaporating perspiration no longer cools you adequately.

A Day in the Life of a Greenhouse

With these principles, you already understand the basics of managing an artificial environment. Armed with this knowledge, greenhouse gardening is easy—as long as you understand how plants respond and interact with environment. Let's go back to that same hot day, and look at it from the inside of your greenhouse.

Because you know the day is going to be hot, you water early in the morning and open all of the vents. At three o'clock in the afternoon, you go in to pick tomatoes for an early supper. To your dismay, all the tomato plants are wilted. The soil is wet enough, but the plants look as if they're growing in the Sahara Desert. What's going on?

Early in the day, bright light and good moisture levels stimulated the stomata in the tomato leaves to open fully. Adequate carbon dioxide was available, so the plants began to photosynthesize at a great rate. The light striking each leaf raised its internal temperature, which in turn increased both respiration and transpiration. Meanwhile, the root hairs were absorbing water and nutrients and exchanging gases. It was a good growing morning; all processes were keeping pace with each other. But in the hot afternoon, the air became so warm that a great deal of water vapor was absorbed within each leaf. Transpiration was quite high. For a while the humidity produced by the leaves cooled them by evaporating. But the rapid transpiration demanded that the roots absorb an enormous amount of water. They couldn't meet the demand, so the plant gave up a bit of water from all of its cells and began to droop. The guard cells around stomata closed, so the plant gave up less water through transpiration, but its intake of carbon dioxide and thus photosynthesis also decreased.

It's no wonder that your plants are stressed. They're too hot, they don't contain enough water to make full use of the energy produced by respiration and they've slowed glucose production. Their growth is being severely hindered.

What do you do to correct the situation? Water the soil? No, it's still moist from the morning watering. Your immediate response would depend upon other environmental factors, in this case, air circulation and humidity.

In an arid climate where relative humidity levels are low, the best response would be to water the air by using a mister nozzle and spraying above the beds and aisles. If the air is still, you can set up an oscillating fan. By increasing relative humidity and subsequent evaporation, you'll cool the plants. Transpiration rates will decrease as soon as the leaves have cooled, and roots will then be able to supply adequate water. Cells will plump up again, the stomata will open fully and photosynthesis will resume. But you don't want to spend the whole afternoon misting the greenhouse air. A wise alternative would be to wet down the aisles to provide a steady source of evaporating water.

In a humid climate, the response to afternoon droopies is different. It's the same problem: Transpiration is exceeding uptake. But high humidity is partially to blame; raising it only compounds the problem. Instead, rely on a strong fan to pull air quickly past the plants, increasing the rate of evaporation. This usually cools them enough so harmonious rates of transpiration, respiration and photosynthesis resume.

Sometimes these solutions aren't adequate. Despite misting and fans, plants droop day after warm day. The environment is just too hot. Shading is the solution. Depending upon the glazing material in your greenhouse, apply shading compound or install shade screens. Since less light is admitted, the greenhouse doesn't overheat so badly. Even with good shading, increasing humidity and/or air circulation may still be helpful.

If you've done all this and still have wilting problems, it's time to look at the soil for problems and solutions. If it's too wet and/or the texture's too heavy, roots may not be getting enough oxygen. Or the concentration of mineral salts may be so high that osmosis between the soil solution and root hairs is impeded. What do you do in these cases? Unfortunately, you can't do much in a single afternoon. First, hold back on watering to let the soil dry somewhat. Afterward, leach excess salts by watering so thoroughly that water drains freely from the beds. With infrequent but very thorough watering, it's usually possible to get through the growing season. Harvest as soon as possible, and then take the time to adjust the soil mix by lightening it and reducing the concentration of salts.

Looking at this one problem, afternoon wilt, gives some idea of the problem-solving process you'll use in greenhouse gardening. By drawing on your understanding of plant processes, environmental conditions and their interrelationships, it's easy to take remedial action. And it's faster and more effective to work from informed guesses.

Light and Plants

Light is energy. We define it in terms of **intensity** (how much there is), **quality** (what wavelengths compose it) and **photoperiod** (its duration on a daily basis). Each aspect has a profound influence on plant growth. Plant reactions to light include: **photosynthesis, photomorphogenesis** (broadly defined as how the various parts of the plant are formed) and **photoperiodism** (again, broadly, what the plant does when). Photoperiod and photoperiod*ism* should not be confused. Photoperiod is the length of a day; photoperiodism is the rate and sequence of plant growth and development.

Unless you use artificial lights or grow plants well out of their natural seasons, you're likely to be more concerned with light intensity than with quality or photoperiod. Light intensity affects photosynthesis in obvious ways. Without adequate light energy, plants can't manufacture enough glucose. But intensity also affects plant structure. Under full light, plants develop stronger xylem tissues and straighter, thicker stems with shorter distances between their branches (internodes). Their leaves are smaller and thicker, while stomata are smaller and closer together. Cells contain fewer chloroplasts, but the chlorophyll content of each chloroplast is higher. Both the cell walls and cuticles are thicker. The leaves on "hairy" plants grow more "hair."

These environmental adaptations of the growing plant make sense. Light acts to form an auxin that slightly inhibits growth. When you forget to rotate houseplants on a windowsill, stems grow toward the glass because cells on the shaded side elongate more than those in light, forcing the stem to bend. This **phototropic** reaction is a warning signal that the plants don't have enough light for good growth. Another plant adaptation to light intensity, a thickened cuticle, helps to retain water and has the important side benefit of giving more resistance to fungal attack.

High light intensities increase the interior heat of the plant, particularly the leaf, with its large surface area. As light energy is converted to heat, both respiration and transpiration speed up. The extra hairiness that develops on certain leaves helps to cool them. The hairs block air movement and thus conserve moisture so that it can evaporate from the leaf surface. Hairiness is a blessing in normal field conditions where there are continual breezes, but inside, it can cause problems by creating too much humidity around the leaf. Growers use forced-air circulation to break up the humid **boundary layer** of air around leaves.

Light intensity also affects the photoperiodism of plants. For instance, tomatoes don't flower or fruit well under low-light conditions, no matter how long their photoperiod.

Specific light wavelengths trigger specific reactions. Red and blue light are necessary for photosynthesis, while far-red light stimulates flowering and fruiting. Natural light contains all the wavelengths necessary for good growth, of course. If your plants see nothing but the sun, they'll receive enough of each wavelength. However, if you use artificial lights, you'll need to think about light quality. Depending upon the crop, different sorts of artificial lights are appropriate. You'll find a more detailed discussion of artificial lighting in the next chapter.

It's easy to understand how the length of the day could affect photosynthesis. But for many plants, daylength also determines the time of flowering, budding or dormancy. Plants are called "short-day" or "long-day," depending upon their preferred photoperiod. Although some plants, such as tomatoes, aren't very particular about daylength and will perform well under a wide photoperiod range, others—such as chrysanthemums, poinsettias, onions and melons—won't produce well under the wrong daylength. Most greenhouse vegetables are grown close enough to their natural season so there's no need to worry about whether they're long-day or short-day plants. Those that grow well in cooler winter greenhouse temperatures can continue growing, though more slowly, with shorter daylengths. But you'll have to pay attention to photoperiods if you grow many flowering ornamentals or start early-spring vegetables and bedding plants. For example, it's wise to start petunias under lights, since a 16- to 18-hour daylength stimulates their earliest and most profuse flowering. However, you will need to shield marigolds from the petunias' supplementary light because their greatest bud set occurs under a 12-hour day. You will find the photoperiod preferences of specific plants in chapters 13, 14 and 15, which deal with popular greenhouse crops.

Air

A living plant contains 80 to 90 percent water. But if you dried and analyzed plant material, you'd see the importance of gases. Plants incorporate so much carbon and oxygen into their tissues that 45 percent of their dried weight is carbon, while oxygen accounts for another 43 percent. These facts alone should make you regard the air in your greenhouse with new respect.

Air is composed of approximately 78 percent nitrogen, 21 percent oxygen, 1 percent argon, 0.03 percent carbon dioxide and 1 percent miscellaneous gases. Moisture content varies between 1 and 3 percent. The air also carries dust particles, pollen and microorganisms that hitchhike on handy particles. Of all these substances, the concentrations of carbon dioxide and moisture are the most important to greenhouse growers.

In tightly constructed greenhouses, carbon dioxide is the most common growth-limiting factor. To keep supplies high, new air must be introduced into the greenhouse environment. Many commercial growers augment CO_2 levels for maximum production, but you can certainly achieve good crop yields if your greenhouse has adequate ventilation.

Moisture content in the air is measured as either relative or absolute humidity. Absolute humidity is the *total amount* of water vapor present, while relative humidity is the *percentage* of water vapor present at a certain temperature compared to the potential moisture level at that temperature. Warm air holds much more water vapor than does cold air; every 20°F increase in air temperature doubles the air's moisture-holding capacity.

As air cools, relative humidity rises. At about 100 percent relative humidity (which meteorologists call the dew point), the air is so saturated that water vapor returns to liquid form by condensing. You'll see this happening in your greenhouse in the evening and early morning. Depending upon the interaction of temperature and moisture content, humidity rises sharply and condenses on the glazing and even on the plants. Fall, winter and spring are the seasons when condensation is greatest; if the outside air is below freezing, dew forms on the glazing at a relative humidity as low as 35 percent. Condensation on the glazing acts to retain some heat. However, plants are more susceptible to fungus diseases when they are constantly moist. To help sidestep problems, protective measures are discussed in the next chapter.

Relative humidity affects a plant in several ways. Many plants mature too quickly if transpiration is high and relative humidity is low. They may bloom and bear fruit so fast that their quality is adversely affected. Both leaves and fruit are apt to be small and tough. On the other hand, constantly high relative humidity levels induce too much vegetative growth and delay fruiting and flowering. The plants look "sappy"—soft and pliable.

After a few years of greenhouse consulting, one of the most common "problem" patterns became clear to me. In late June or early July, people would call with complaints that their tomatoes and cucumbers weren't setting enough fruit. Through conversation with these people, I would analyze each element of the environment: Is there enough light? Are nutrient levels high enough? Are flowers being pollinated? Are temperatures so high that pollen is sterilized? Is watering thorough? Is air circulation high? Most people reported that each factor was well controlled. Finally I learned to ask at the beginning of the conversation about relative humidity levels. In most cases this was the operative factor. Once ventilation and interior air circulation were stepped up, the problem plants began to bear. However, in some cases the remedial action came too late and the plants never produced well.

Temperature

Both air and soil temperatures determine how a plant grows. As we saw earlier, air temperature affects all plant processes by increasing internal temperatures. Most plants are fairly particular about temperature ranges; quality, crop maturity and fruit set are all affected. Lettuce and tomatoes provide good examples. In a cool spring, lettuce grows admirably, but once it's hot, the crop may be bitter or flower and go to seed prematurely. Tomatoes don't grow well in a cool environment. If temperatures stay below 50°F for any length of time, tomato pollen loses viability. But in a hot environment—over 90 or 100°F—pollen can be sterilized.

Some fluctuation between day and night temperatures is desirable. Plants have evolved to live within natural temperature variations. Many can't germinate, grow well or set fruit without a 10 to 20°F difference between day and night temperatures. To aid germination of tricky perennials and herbs, some greenhouse gardeners set the thermostats on soil heating cables about 10°F lower at night. During most seasons, greenhouses cool off more than enough at night. In fact, without excellent thermal storage and/or an energy-conserving structure, it's usually necessary to add supplementary heat just to maintain a small enough temperature difference to keep the plants from being stressed by cold.

Soil temperatures are important, too. Even when the air temperature is a bit lower than recommended, plants with warm roots can grow well. At night many commercial greenhouse growers save on heating bills by heating the soil rather than the air.

At soil temperatures below 50°F, roots slow their rate of respiration. Without respiratory energy, they can't grow and absorb minerals at an optimum rate. Similarly, osmosis from soil solution to roots slows down, since cell walls are less permeable when they're cold. And since the operative enzymes do not form or fail to act, some seeds won't germinate in cool conditions.

The microorganisms that are so important in a healthy, living soil also require specific environmental conditions. Soil temperature affects both their populations and their rates of activity. When warm, micro-organisms decompose organic matter from compost or other sources, making nutrients available to plant roots. But below 50°F, many mi-croorganisms die or go into a dormant phase. This adaptation enables microbial populations to withstand wide climatic fluctuations. But it's difficult to maintain soil fertility without active populations. In a year-round greenhouse, a brief midwinter period of cold soil won't harm crops—other environmental elements at this time of year aren't con-ducive to active growth, either. But remember that it's useless to add organic fertilizers to cold soil. A balanced nutrient supply can't become available until the medium warms.

Soil can be too hot for microbial life as well. As a matter of fact, some plant pathogens can be killed either by freezing or by "baking." But the effect of hot soils shows up first on plants. Evaporation in-creases dramatically and soil water is rapidly depleted. Overheated roots need more moisture just when it's being lost to the air. In the summer greenhouse, cucumbers, peppers and eggplants appreciate warm soils, but tomatoes may need to be mulched with a light-reflective material to keep temperatures cool.

The first step in successful greenhouse growing is understanding how plants are affected and how they interact with their environments. The next is learning how to use your greenhouse and accessory tools to provide the best possible growing conditions. We'll look at this next step in chapter 2.

CHAPTER 2
CONTROLLING THE GREENHOUSE ENVIRONMENT

Greenhouse plants are completely dependent upon the greenhouse environment: temperature, air quality, relative humidity, moisture levels and light availability. And environmental conditions are regulated by the greenhouse gardener. Managing an artificial environment may seem daunting at first. But like other skills that require the coordination of a number of factors at once, it just takes practice. Remember learning to drive? It seemed as if there was too much to do at once. But before long, you could harmoniously integrate the clutch, gear shift and accelerator. Your reflexes had taken over. So it is with learning to manage the environment in your greenhouse.

Managing greenhouse environments doesn't usually include training new physical reflexes, but it does demand that you exercise mental and sensory responses. At first it's difficult to balance environmental elements. For example, on an overcast spring day, it's sometimes hard to determine a good mix of heating and venting. In deference to tomato, melon and cauliflower seedlings, an "optimum" daytime temperature for the spring greenhouse is 70°F. But 70°F isn't *always* appropriate. For example, on a humid, cool, cloudy day, photosynthesis slows in response to the low light levels. At the same time humidity is likely to be too high, and in a closed greenhouse, carbon dioxide (CO_2) levels will be too low. Venting takes care of humidity and CO_2 but means extra heating time to bring temperatures back up to 70°F.

So what do you do? In the beginning most people would spend a few minutes scratching their heads questioning whether to vent and then heat or save on fuel bills by leaving the greenhouse closed. With experience you'll be able to solve this kind of problem without having to ponder all the options. You'll know that keeping interior temperatures at 70°F under such circumstances stresses the plants and makes them more susceptible to fungus diseases. In a spring greenhouse under cloudy conditions, you'd know that 60°F is more appropriate than 70°F. Accordingly, you'd lower the heater thermostat, move tender

17

plants close to the heat, turn on an interior fan and water only the bone-dry flats. If your schedule permitted, venting would wait until the warmest part of the day. A few hours before sunset, you'd turn the heating thermostat back to 50°F, switch off the interior fan if humidity was 60 percent or less, and saunter off without a worry. After the right reflexes are in place, environmental management becomes fairly routine.

Getting Started

The first step in successfully managing your greenhouse environment is to train yourself to perceive the environment from a plant's point of view. Pay attention to soil, air and light. In this chapter we will cover air and light. Soils, soil mixes and fertilizers will follow later.

Light, temperature, relative humidity, carbon dioxide levels and air circulation are the standards by which plants measure a growing day. Outdoor gardeners can take some of these things for granted, but in an artificial environment each element must be controlled and balanced.

Every greenhouse is a unique microclimate. Interior environment results from the combination of design, materials, construction, arrangement, auxiliary systems and management. The greenhouse climate also responds to the climate outside. I once visited two greenhouses of similar design and construction in the same geographic area. One was tucked into a protected niche on a sunny south-facing slope. The other stood in an open field. The owners used quite different management regimens to achieve the same optimum conditions. The open-field greenhouse required more auxiliary heat, especially during windy weather, while the protected greenhouse needed extra ventilation.

As you start to learn how to handle the greenhouse environment, experiment with your management tools. The primary systems for manipulating the plant's world are vents, heaters, fans, shade materials and accessories such as heating cables and artificial lights. Thermometers and other sensors keep track of environmental conditions, but the most important monitoring devices are your own senses.

Remember that a greenhouse is a coherent system of checks and balances. The gardener must assume the role of a conductor, synchronizing each element into a harmonious orchestration.

Greenhouse Design

A full discussion of greenhouse design is beyond the scope of this book. The Bibliography lists some excellent design and construction sources that you can consult for more information. But it's impossible to discuss environmental control without at least a cursory look at basic greenhouse design.

The two basic design types are generally termed "traditional" and "solar," differentiated by their use of light energy. All greenhouses are partially heated by sunlight, but unlike their predecessors, solar structures store energy for heating during the night and on cloudy days.

Traditional greenhouses have no provision for storing excess heat. They also have other characteristic features:

- Auxiliary heat (combustion, electrical or waste heat) for use during cool or cloudy weather.

- Glazing on the roof and all sides (except for lean-tos designed with one opaque wall). Most have just one layer of glazing, but recently many are being built or retrofitted with two layers.

- If freestanding, the longest sides face east and west. This orientation gives maximum light exposure in a completely glazed greenhouse.

- Vents of the same dimension on both the ridge (the top or peak) and the kneewall or bottom of the long sides.

- Intake vents and fans installed on the short sides.

- Most commonly shaped as even-span rectangular or Quonset huts. Some smaller structures are square or round, even octagonal.

Solar greenhouses depart from the traditional design in several important ways:

- Heat gained during the day is stored in rock, water or the building mass.

- Heat from sources other than the sun is used sparingly or, in some cases, not at all.

- Frequently, only the south side is glazed. The glazing is usually installed at an angle to allow maximum light penetration during the winter. Exceptions are found in northern latitudes where light is reflected from a constant snow cover.

- The north side and a portion of the roof are insulated. In some designs, either one or both of the east and west sides are insulated to retain heat. An opaque roof area blocks direct light when the midsummer sun reaches its zenith.

- Interior opaque walls and glazing supports are painted white to reflect, rather than absorb, incoming light.

- The greenhouse is sited so that its longest sides face north and south. This ensures good penetration of direct light during the winter when the sun travels low.
- All translucent walls are double-glazed to retain heat.
- Ridge, or top, vents are larger than those on the kneewall or bottom to create greater airflow, or passive ventilation, than is possible with equally sized vents.
- Solar greenhouses are usually rectangular and longer than they are wide.

Obviously, not all greenhouses neatly fit these categories. Many traditional designs are double-glazed; some have a means of storing heat. Many solar greenhouses with insulated north walls and angled glazing lack adequate heat storage and depend on supplementary heating. But obviously, energy-conserving features make solar greenhouses more economically practical than their traditional counterparts. Their rapid development and popularity are due in part to rising fuel and utility costs.

From a strictly horticultural standpoint, traditional greenhouses are somewhat easier to manage. Results are not necessarily better; it's just easier to get good results. Because they aren't built so tightly, more outside air infiltrates, lowering humidity and raising CO_2. Forced ventilation is very effective in drawing air across the plant canopy between the intake vent and the fan opposite it. Total glazing offers more uniform exposure to light than is usual in many solar greenhouses. But,

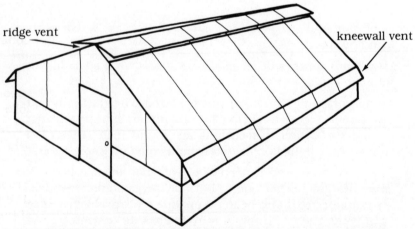

Freestanding Greenhouse: *This "traditional" design does just what its name implies—it stands alone.*

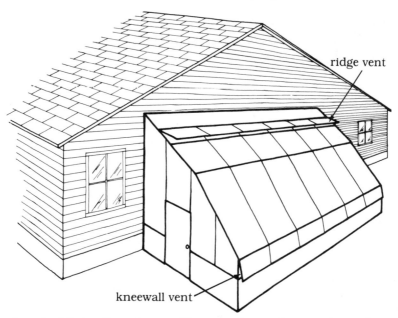

Attached Solar Greenhouse: *This greenhouse design adjoins the house through window and door openings.*

while you must always worry that a traditional greenhouse will collapse under a 12-inch layer of wet snow or that plants will freeze during a power outage, solar greenhouses offer great security. You can sleep soundly through a blizzard and wake confident that the solar greenhouse has not only survived but has maintained its environment.

Both solar and traditional designs are also characterized as freestanding, attached, lean-to or pit.

- **Freestanding** greenhouses, as their name implies, stand alone. Even when they're close to another building, they don't share a common wall.

- **Attached** greenhouses adjoin a house through window or door openings. Air movement between the two spaces can be controlled or not.

- **Lean-to** greenhouses share a common wall with a building but do not exchange air with it.

- **Pit** greenhouses are dug into the ground. Commonly, only the roof and a foot or so of sidewalls are glazed and sit aboveground. Pit greenhouses may be attached or not, but because so much of the area is buried, they have built-in insulation thanks to the surrounding soil. Limited light exposure is also common.

How you manage the environment of each of these design types differs slightly. Attached, pit and lean-to greenhouses tend to be warmer and require less auxiliary heat than freestanding structures. Because they're tightly built, they require more diligent ventilation. In attached greenhouses, both relative humidity and carbon dioxide levels are easy to manage; as air is exchanged with the living space, relative humidity decreases while CO_2 rises. But summer temperatures can create problems unless the ventilation system is designed to rapidly dump excess heat. Lean-tos can be fitted with intake vents and fans, of course, but pits are generally vented by lifting or removing a glazing section. Unlike the others, freestanding structures usually have excellent light levels because they can be situated independent of existing buildings. However, depending upon design and construction, winter heating may be a major undertaking.

Every greenhouse has its problems and advantages. A little experience tells you which environmental factors require your particular attention during each season of the year. And while it's difficult to change overall design, most people make it easier to provide the best possible environment by refining a few design elements, accessory tools and planting schedules.

Air Temperature

Plant growth proceeds best within a fairly small temperature range. Warm-weather plants, such as tomatoes, cucumbers and melons, prefer daytime temperatures between 65 and 85°F and night temperatures not much lower than 60°F. Cool-weather crops such as lettuce and other greens do nicely in daytime temperatures between 50 and 75°F and night temperatures no lower than 45°F. Although there is some latitude, most growers find that staying within these ranges produces healthier and better-tasting crops. You'll find specific ranges for each of the major greenhouse food crops given in chapters 13 and 14.

To decrease heating and ventilation needs, most people grow only cool-weather plants during the winter months and warm-weather plants in summer. But even when plants are well scheduled according to their temperature needs, unmanaged greenhouses overheat on some days, even in winter, and cool too much at night or on cold, cloudy days.

Hot and Cold

Providing adequate heat is usually the major task in traditional greenhouses, and ironically, cooling is often the most difficult environmental feat in a tightly built solar structure. But regardless of design, it's helpful to understand why a greenhouse overheats so easily, why it cools down so quickly and what you can do to control the temperature.

Light and heat are essentially the same thing—wavelengths of radiation. The difference between the two is simply wavelength size. Light wavelengths are shorter than heat wavelengths.

Glazing material allows roughly 80 to 90 percent of the sun's radiation into the greenhouse, primarily as light waves. Most light waves striking plants and other materials pass through or bounce off, but some are absorbed and converted into heat. The quantity of absorbed light varies between materials; leaves let more light pass through than do rocks or metal. Color is also influential. More light is reflected, or bounced off, white objects than black ones. If sheets of black and white metal were placed side by side, the black ones would be hotter on a sunny day. The more light an object absorbs, the hotter it gets.

Heat doesn't just stay inside a warmed material. Some is released, or reradiated, back into the environment. This is the principle behind heat storage, of course. Water, rocks and masonry have good heat "gain" and "storage" capacities. They absorb a great deal of light and reradiate it as heat, warming the environment.

Hot air rises. Outside, it just moves upward, but in an enclosed space its movement is restricted. Solid walls, especially when well insulated, trap hot air. Even glazing materials trap heat; while they allow relatively free passage of short-wave radiation, they are less "transparent" to the longer heat wavelengths.

The "closed car syndrome" is a good way to think about heat generation and transmission. Imagine opening your car after leaving it closed in a sunny parking lot. Inside, it's sweltering because:

- Windows allowed free entrance of light.
- Seats and dashboard absorbed some light.
- Absorbed light was converted to heat.
- Heat was reradiated into the air.
- Glazing and solid walls prevented hot air from escaping.

If you had left some windows cracked, the car would have been slightly ventilated, and some heat would have been able to escape.

All greenhouses are designed with an understanding of light and heat. But solar greenhouses take it one step further. Each of their characteristic features (orientation; double glazing; opaque, insulated walls; well-caulked seams and joints; and heat-storage materials) retains heat. It should come as no surprise that solar greenhouses, unless their design is excellent, overheat more easily than their traditional counterparts. But *all* greenhouses overheat in bright light conditions.

Ventilation Systems

Ventilation systems work according to a very basic principle—they admit cool air while exhausting hot air. **Passive** ventilation occurs naturally because of differences in heat between adjacent areas. An example is the air movement through openings between the greenhouse and an attached house or the outdoors. **Forced** ventilation is accomplished with fans, which push air one way or the other.

Ventilation systems may include vents on the top and bottom of the long sides, vents and/or fans on the short sides, openings into another building, air-to-air heat exchangers and interior fans or blowers. Few greenhouses need *all* of these elements. But you'll find that management is easier with a means for both fast and gradual release of excess heat.

In most greenhouses, bottom and ridge vents provide primary ventilation. Outside air, which is relatively cool, moves in through the lower vents to replace warm air rising and exiting through the upper ones. This continuous air movement cools the greenhouse. Designers have learned that air movement increases when ridge vents are larger than bottom ones. This creates a "chimney effect"; the top vents allow hot air to exit rapidly, which in turn increases the rate at which cooler air enters through the smaller bottom vents.

In structures lacking ridge and bottom vents, ventilation is usually provided by a louvered vent opening on one short side and an exhaust fan on the opposite end. As the fan blows warm air out, cooler air enters through the intake vent. This causes air to travel from one end of the greenhouse to the other. Exhaust fans are almost always installed with an automatic thermostat. Their normal "on" pattern is sporadic; they don't run full-time unless the greenhouse is seriously overheating.

Ventilation requirements differ in response to weather, infiltration of outside air and the crops being grown. Infiltration and passive ventilation are difficult to calculate accurately because they depend upon wind conditions and differentials between inside and outside temperatures. However, it's reasonable to assume that infiltration accounts for at least half to one complete air change every hour, even in a tightly built greenhouse. As for passive ventilation, under normal conditions a well-designed structure generally provides three to five complete air changes an hour (ACH).

In hot, humid weather, passive ventilation doesn't always cool the greenhouse adequately. If overheating problems occur during the summer months, you'd be wise to add an exhaust fan and intake vent. These accessories are also blessings if you're away from home during other seasons. When you leave for work on a spring morning, it may be too cool to open the vents. But, as the day warms, the greenhouse may overheat unless an automatic exhaust fan can ventilate as needed.

Commercial growers install systems that provide 8 to 11 complete ACH. Home growers need not be so scrupulous; their diversified crop schemes and somewhat relaxed growing schedules allow more flexibility. As a general guideline, most home greenhouses do well with a ventilation capability of 3 to 5 ACH. However, a freestanding home greenhouse may perform better with capabilities of 5 to 8 ACH.

To decide how much air the ventilation system should move, first calculate the volume of air inside the greenhouse. It's easiest to divide irregular dimensions into manageable shapes. For example, in a 10-by 20-foot structure with an 8-foot peak and a 3-foot kneewall running down the long side, first calculate the volume of the bottom rectangle: 3 feet times 10 feet times 20 feet equals 600 cubic feet. Then treat the triangle above as a square by multiplying 5 feet by 10 feet by 20 feet to get 1,000 cubic feet. Halving this last number gives you the volume of the triangle, or 500 cubic feet. Add 600 and 500 to get 1,100 cubic feet, the volume of air in the greenhouse.

For every air change, 1,100 cubic feet of air must be moved. Fans are rated by the cubic feet of air that they move in a *minute* (cfm). To choose the correct cfm rating for the fan, first divide the volume of our sample greenhouse, 1,100, by 60 minutes in the hour. A rate of 18.3 cfm gives one air change an hour, but let's assume that five ACH are needed. Multiplying 18.3 by 5 shows us that an exhaust fan with a 90 cfm rating would be appropriate.

These calculations should give you a good idea of how to determine the size fan you need, but if your situation is more complicated than this simple example, ask advice from the people who sell exhaust fans. They are practiced at the necessary calculations, and I've always been pleased by their recommendations.

Greenhouse exhaust fans and intake vents are available with louvered shutters that open automatically during operation. The shutters are meant to restrict incoming cold air when the fan isn't operating. But an appreciable amount of cold air does infiltrate, even through closed shutters. Many greenhouse growers make their own insulated and weather-stripped covers, similar to insulating window plugs, for use at night and on cold days. Designs and suggestions for making window plugs are frequently found in publications about energy conservation. Plugs are inserted *only* when the exhaust fan won't be operating. If you leave a greenhouse unattended during the day, remove the plug in case the sun shines enough to heat beyond the thermostat setting. Otherwise, you risk having the greenhouse overheat.

Cooling the Greenhouse

It's surprising how hot a closed greenhouse can get on a cold but sunny winter day. Outside, the temperature may be hovering at −20°F, but if the sun is out and light is also reflected from a snow cover, it can overheat before 10:00 A.M. The greenhouse design and construction determine both the extent of heat gain and the management techniques you use to bring the temperature down.

Winter Cooling

Attached solar greenhouses are a blessing during the winter. Cooling is accomplished by opening the doors and/or windows into the adjoining house. Excess greenhouse heat migrates into the home, cutting utility bills. Passive air movement between the house and greenhouse often gives satisfactory ventilation. However, in some designs, a small fan is installed to blow warm air from near the ridge into the home. An intake vent low on the shared wall brings cooler air into the greenhouse and encourages air to move in a circular pattern. It's a treat to share air between the greenhouse and living quarters; plants love the extra CO_2, and people love the extra humidity, oxygen and lowered heating bills.

Tightly built solar greenhouses attached to superinsulated homes provide the only exceptions to this management technique. A house

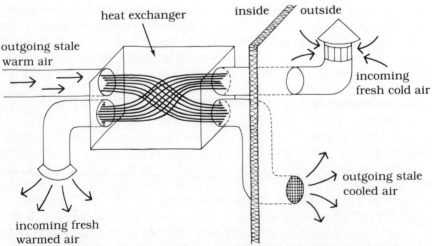

Air-to-Air Heat Exchanger: *This schematic illustration will help you see how this system expels stale interior air through one set of channels, while it pulls in outside air through the other set. In the process it prewarms fresh air at no extra expense.*

that's been built to conserve energy can retain uncomfortably high relative humidity levels from ordinary activities such as cooking, bathing and even breathing. Airborne pollutants from gas stoves and furnishings also add to air-quality problems. If you simply recirculate air between the home and greenhouse, both areas suffer. To reduce humidity and pollution, you must introduce outside air.

In many cases the most energy-conserving way to improve interior air quality is an air-to-air heat exchanger. This device prewarms fresh air at no extra cost while expelling excess humidity and airborne pollutants. Several designs are available, but a basic model is usually composed of a heat-exchanging core, two fans and ductwork leading to areas within the home. Inside the core, two distinct groups of channels allow air passage. A fan blows stale interior air through one set of channels while outside air is pulled in through the other set. The two airstreams are separated by very thin membranes that allow heat transfer: about 70 to 80 percent of the heat in the outgoing air transfers to the incoming stream. In heat exchangers made with moisture-impermeable channels, humidity is not exchanged.

Owners of superinsulated homes with attached greenhouses often install a heat exchanger so that it has a stale-air pickup in the greenhouse. Prewarmed incoming fresh air is sometimes dumped into the greenhouse as well. However, check with a manufacturer or distributor to determine the best location for your particular house/greenhouse design.

Because of their expense, heat exchangers are most practical in greenhouses attached to homes with moisture or air-pollution problems. However, heat exchangers are also useful in freestanding greenhouses that experience serious problems with relative humidity. At The Ark, a now defunct research greenhouse operated on Prince Edward Island, Canada, both fish and plants were grown. Greenhouse managers had difficulty regulating winter relative humidity levels because of the moisture evaporating from the open fish tanks. After an air-to-air heat exchanger was installed, researchers saw a sharp decrease in winter crop loss due to fungal infections.

Freestanding greenhouses that overheat during the winter call for a different set of management techniques. If you're at home to respond to changes in temperature, you can slightly crack bottom and ridge vents during the warm part of the day. However, if you're usually away during the day, install an exhaust fan and intake vent. Despite the increase in utility bills that fans and heating outside air can bring, it's worth keeping the greenhouse cool for the sake of your harvest. Crops grown with a large temperature fluctuation aren't as healthy and may even taste bitter.

To safeguard the health of your plants, never expose them to cold drafts. If passive ventilation provides most of the winter cooling in your greenhouse, elevate pots above the top of the intake vents. Set beds about a foot away from vents to give the incoming air a chance to mix with warmer air before it hits the plants.

In a forced-air system, place a "wind" screen in front of the intake vent to protect plants. If it's slightly angled to direct incoming cold air to the ridge, it helps to destratify the greenhouse air. Even without a screen, leave at least a foot between the vent and the closest plants. Be sure to put only the hardiest plants at the intake end.

Summer Cooling

Cooling during late fall and early spring is handled as in winter. But, as early spring turns to early summer, cooling needs escalate. In most climates, cooling doesn't become difficult until the point in the season when warm-weather crops have been planted in the outside garden. Only heat-tolerant plants are being grown inside, but even melons and cucumbers can't produce well if daytime air temperatures exceed 85 to 90°F. Tomatoes produce best within a slightly lower range; their preferred daytime maximum is 70 to 75°F.

If you're late in venting on a sunny morning, don't be surprised to see interior temperatures soar as high as 120°F. Once summer has really arrived, most people leave the vents fully open from early morning until late at night. In the South or during hot spells in other regions, growers leave vents open all through the night as well.

Heat from an attached greenhouse is certainly not welcome in the main house during mid-July. But with the proper arrangement, a greenhouse can help with summertime cooling. Set up a fan to blow hot air from the house into the greenhouse, where it will exit through the ridge vents. Remember to leave a door or window in the house open to create a good airflow through the house as well as the greenhouse. Not only will this keep you cooler, but the constant airflow will help cool the plants, too.

Owners of freestanding greenhouses with a forced-air ventilation system often face high electricity bills during the summer months. To cut costs, some southern growers remove a section of the glazing (if possible), usually on the end wall opposite the exhaust fan and/or door, and substitute a screen. This allows greater airflow through the greenhouse.

Although venting and directing the airflow can help, shading is usually the most practical solution to summer overheating. One way to keep the sun out is to paint shading compound on the exterior glazing to decrease light and consequent heat levels. Whitewash is the traditional shade paint for glass houses, but it damages other glazing materials. Check with the distributor of your particular glazing to determine the correct shade paint.

When shade paint is impractical, notably with polyethylene houses, use shade cloth. A black or green plastic mesh, shade cloth is rated according to the degree of shade (normally 30, 40, 50, 70 or 80 percent) that it gives. Check with other growers in your area or with the local extension agent to determine the right value for the crops you're growing.

Shade cloth is hung from inside rafters or suspended on frames above particular beds or growing areas. In a solar greenhouse, place shade cloth on south glazing; if the greenhouse is traditional or has an east-west orientation, you may need to install it on the west side for protection against afternoon sun.

You'll find that shade cloth is most practical when it's set up to be used only when necessary. The arrangement can be quite crude; I staple shading material to a long dowel. Big hooks screwed into the rafters support each end of the dowel. If the shade cloth setup isn't too un-wieldy, one person can roll the shade cloth up or down as the weather decrees. For example, a string of cloudy days may occur just as your tomatoes are ripening and need strong light. It's great to be able to roll up the shade and let maximum light into the growing area.

Greenhouse suppliers are accustomed to making custom-designed shade curtains for large greenhouses, but they're often unwilling to sell small lengths of cloth. Sometimes they do have remnants and will keep your order on file. Since commercial shade cloth can be hard to get, it's good to know that commercial shade curtains don't work any better than homemade ones. Burlap, loosely woven muslin, bamboo screening or cheesecloth give nice shade.

When you're making your own shading devices, you can hang the material from a dowel, as described earlier, or stretch it across small frames. Shade cloth hung along the length of the sunny side of the greenhouse cools the whole area. Small shade frames protect only one area but have the advantage of being easier to move to where they're needed. For example, you can use a frame to shield several flats of seedlings or summer greens from bright light. Small frames are usually the most practical system for solar greenhouses. During the summer it's unusual for a solar greenhouse to receive too much light, especially in the rear.

Heating Systems

Heating systems, and their attendant operating costs, are the bane of the commercial industry. It takes an amazing amount of heat to keep a glass building warm on a cold, starry night. People who run single-glazed houses don't joke about utility bills. They don't even like to talk about them.

Standing inside an unheated, single-glazed, traditional greenhouse on a cold night, you can almost feel the heat being sucked away. Glazing cools in response to the outside temperature. Greenhouse air that touches cold glazing also cools, giving up its heat to the glazing and, eventually, to the cold outdoors.

Solar greenhouses are designed to retain heat, of course. In many climates, depending upon both design and construction, little auxiliary, or backup, heat is needed to maintain the desired winter temperature ranges (60 to 70°F during the day and 45 to 50°F at night).

But in harsh, cloudy climates, even tightly built solar structures with good heat-storage capacity sometimes require auxiliary heat. In attached solar greenhouses, you can provide supplementary heat by opening doors and/or windows. This may be enough to maintain good growing temperatures, but a portable heater provides a double backup. Freestanding greenhouses, even solar designs, almost always require auxiliary heat.

Guidelines for Planning a Heating System

Greenhouse heating systems range from small electric or combustion heaters to elaborate systems used in commercial and experimental greenhouses. Researchers are working to develop energy-conserving systems such as in-soil, solar-heated water pipes, but most of these are still in the design stage. For now, most home growers choose portable electric or combustion heaters to ensure a warm winter environment. To help you plan a safe, efficient heating system for your greenhouse, here are some guidelines.

Determine Your Heating Needs

Regardless of outside temperatures, a heater should be capable of maintaining desired temperatures inside the greenhouse. Plan for the worst possible weather and take your design into account. Obviously, single-glazed, freestanding greenhouses without heat storage require larger heaters than insulated structures with 3 gallons of water storage per square foot of glazing area. Attached greenhouses may have minimal auxiliary backup needs if heat from the main house is used, but buy a little heater for emergencies anyway.

Because each greenhouse is so different, it's impossible to give a general heater sizing formula. With new structures, the designer should recommend a heater as part of the design package. But if you've inherited an older greenhouse, begin by making whatever energy-conserving repairs you can before choosing a heater. (Practical conservation measures are discussed in the following section.) After tightening the greenhouse, a much smaller heater should do the trick. If you're uncertain about heating needs, ask the assistance of a local designer, a home energy extension agent (from your local Cooperative Extension Agency) or even a knowledgeable salesperson from a good building supply house.

Plan Good Heat Distribution

Heat should be distributed as uniformly as possible throughout the growing area. Because the cost of heating systems with distribution capabilities can be prohibitive, small forced-air or radiant heaters are normally used in home greenhouses. You should place these heaters a few feet away from the nearest plants; a blast of hot air is as lethal as a cold draft! Try to arrange the heater so that hot air has a chance to mix before the plants feel it. Good distribution is sometimes tricky; you may need to try several arrangements before you find the right location. In solar greenhouses, most people put the heater on the floor toward the north, or unglazed, side. In traditional greenhouses, it's usually located in the middle of the house. One grower whom I visited set his heater at one end and used a fan high on the same side to direct rising warm air back down to the plants.

Automate the System

To make your life simpler, the system should be automatic. Thermostats are reliable and don't demand constant attention. Some people rely on a small wood stove to keep the greenhouse warm. When they're well vented and stoked, wood stoves work very well. But, for the sake of your sanity, don't install a stove that can't keep a fire all night. I'd recommend adding an automatic heater as backup because I've seen too many freeze-outs with wood stoves. If your luck is like mine, you're certain to get stuck in a snowbank miles from home just as the greenhouse is plunging toward disastrous temperatures.

Guard Against Fumes

Heaters *must not* give off noxious fumes. According to the product literature, they all burn cleanly. But I've seen some mighty strange-looking seedlings in houses with unvented burners. Leaves twist and pucker and sometimes look anemic. Be especially careful with older heaters; as they age they operate less efficiently. At the first whiff of fumes, vent to the outside or buy a new heater.

Fumes come from other sources, too. I get several calls a year from people with integrated livestock/greenhouse structures. They all report the same strange phenomenon. Overnight (usually the first cold night of the season) the greenhouse plants have turned so white they look bleached. It's eerie to see plants that were once so green look so ghostly.

There's a perfectly logical explanation for why this happens. Animals give off good heat and CO_2, but they also release lots of urine. No matter how deep the litter or how vigilant the mucking, ammonia poisoning is almost inevitable without a forced-ventilation system. Whitened leaves are a symptom of ammonia poisoning. Air-to-air heat exchangers are the most practical solution since they conserve heat while expelling the gas.

Energy Conservation Measures

Energy conservation techniques for a greenhouse are similar to those used in other buildings. The same basic principles apply: minimize infiltration of outside air as much as possible, add insulation and decrease heat loss from glazed areas.

Begin with infiltration by checking all joints and seams for cracks. Hold a lit match or candle in front of joints; if the flame flickers, air is moving past it. Recaulk all leaky spots with good-quality caulk and repaint it. Then check weather stripping on doors and vents to make certain that it's still good. Replace or add it as necessary.

Most solar greenhouses are insulated to the proper specification for the local climate because they are relatively new structures. But traditional greenhouses with only one layer of glazing lack insulation of any sort. With these structures, a second glazing skin is needed to cut heat losses. You can use it on either the interior or exterior of the greenhouse, but it's usually easier to add an interior skin. (Any good greenhouse construction book can give you pointers on how to do this; see the Bibliography for some suggested books.) Construction grade 4- or 6-mil polyethylene is the least expensive material. Both of these thicknesses are strong enough to resist tearing, and construction grade provides adequate light transmission during the first year. After a winter in the greenhouse, take the polyethylene down and use it to cover cold frames or garden areas. A second skin works only if it's airtight; be sure to tape all seams and the inevitable small rips with poly tape.

Many people build insulating panels for traditional greenhouses. Foil-covered Styrofoam sheets can be used to form a "kneewall" area from the ground to plant level. Sidewall panels with cutouts for fans, intake vents and door areas reduce the glazing area significantly and cut down on heat loss. Use them on both sides unless light from a south sidewall is imperative.

Even if a greenhouse isn't designed to be solar, you can still store heat in rocks or water. Fifty-five-gallon drums make very good "legs" for benches. Look around the greenhouse for space to add some heat-storage capability. Even a little bit helps.

Insulating curtains are sometimes used over glazing areas. Although their initial cost is high, well-designed curtains pay for themselves within a few years. Greenhouse conservation specialists recommend numerous materials, including aluminized mylar bonded to black plastic film, Styrofoam panels, aluminum-painted burlap and thick quilts with a water-repellent layer sewn onto the side facing the greenhouse. A flexible curtain is easiest to use. I've yet to meet anyone who liked Styrofoam panels for more than a week or two; it's hard to find convenient storage space and it's time-consuming to move them twice a day. But, no matter what the material, remember that insulating curtains must be sealed at all edges to keep warm air from escaping behind them. If you're interested in purchasing some or making your own, good designs for insulating curtains are found in publications about greenhouse design and construction.

From a horticultural viewpoint, it's important to keep curtains from blocking precious winter sun. Raise or remove them at first light. For some reason, most people install insulating curtains so that they are stored near the ridge. In midwinter the sun is so low that stored curtains don't shade beds, but once spring arrives, they cast a big shadow. Stored below plant level, a rolled curtain won't cause shading problems. And with a small pulley system it's just as easy to roll *up* as *down*.

Insulating curtains are not always appropriate. If you can't seal the edges, they won't work. And the difficulty and expense of making curtains for a traditional greenhouse could dissuade even a rich, persistent genius. But fortunately, curtains for the glazing aren't the only way to retain nighttime heat. Small insulating covers over beds and benches are just as effective and much less expensive and bothersome to make. Even a polyethylene sheet retains some heat, but it's better to use one of the materials suggested for big curtains. Because transpirational moisture condenses on the covers, make sure they don't touch plants. Suspend the covers on frames that allow 4 to 6 inches of headroom. The bottom of the cover should extend at least a foot below soil level. Again, remove covers early in the day and put them back at twilight.

Bed curtains must allow heat from auxiliary sources into the growing area. Enclose the heater or a duct from it; otherwise, heat will migrate out of the greenhouse without warming the plants. Place small heaters at the head of each bench. Or you might find it more practical to have the cover enclose both a heater and several beds. More and more growers are using heating cables or mats under insulating covers to cut costs. Because the warm air is trapped so well, these small devices are often adequate.

One other heat-conserving technique is worth mentioning. In greenhouses with a fairly high peak, warm air tends to collect well above plant level. A fan, suspended from the top rafters, can be adjusted so that it creates turbulence and doesn't let interior air stratify. Overhead fans are especially useful during marginally cool, humid weather since air movement helps prevent fungus diseases.

Innovative Heating Systems

Researchers are presently exploring new ways to heat commercial greenhouses economically. Traditionally, the most common heating systems in large facilities have been overhead propane heaters with forced-air distribution systems or piped steam heat from a large combustion furnace. Neither system is cost-effective at today's fuel prices, so research on energy-conserving systems is proceeding rapidly. One of the most exciting new systems involves burying hot air/water/steam pipes in growing beds. With warmed soil, growers conserve heat generated by a furnace because they can maintain lower air temperatures.

Some innovative market gardeners use their compost piles for supplementary heat. Pipes are laid close to the bottom of the pile where it's hot and then led into the greenhouse and buried in bed areas. The distance between the compost pile and greenhouse entry is kept as short as possible, and any exposed pipe is insulated well. Heat-retention curtains are usually draped over the beds.

Controlling Relative Humidity

The first thing to know about managing humidity in your greenhouse is that relative humidity levels should range between 50 and 70 percent. When humidity is consistently well above or below this range, plants grow poorly, mature too early or late and are susceptible to disease.

In a well-heated and -ventilated greenhouse, relative humidity levels are generally within a tolerable range. But sometimes, especially during cool periods, humidity gets too high. Only in arid climates is it often lower than desired. But humidity is easy to control in any climate as long as you understand how it works.

Everyone who gardens in artificial environments should memorize the following principle: Warm air has the capacity to carry larger quantities of moisture than cool air. It's not surprising that relative humidity levels go down with ventilation; incoming air is generally cooler and thus contains less moisture.

Remember, too, that plants create their own humid environments. As we already learned in chapter 1, they release a tremendous amount of moisture through transpiration. The boundary layer surrounding each leaf is more humid than the rest of the atmosphere.

In bright, dry conditions, the boundary layer is a protective device. Outside, where plants are exposed to breezes, it's quite necessary for their survival. But in a stagnant environment such as a greenhouse, this humid air layer can interfere with growth. Because it's denser than surrounding air, the boundary layer doesn't just float away. It hugs the leaf and tends to block access to fresh air containing new supplies of carbon dioxide. It may also lead to fungus diseases, which are dependent upon high moisture levels for spore germination.

Managing this problem is a snap—or, more commonly, a switch. When it's too humid, use an interior fan to blow boundary layers away from leaves. Be especially watchful during the evening when air is cooling. Even if plants don't need carbon dioxide at twilight, they should be protected against fungal diseases. You should also use interior fans during humid periods when outside venting is minimal.

Both outside ventilation and interior fans are used to adjust humidity levels. The following examples describe solutions to common humidity problems in the greenhouse.

Problem: It's an evening in early spring. Greenhouse air temperature is hovering at 55°F while outside temperatures are 35°F and falling. Earlier, interior temperatures were 75°F and humidity was high. Beads of moisture are condensing on the glazing, threatening to drip onto tomato, cucumber and melon seedlings on the top benches. Some plants have had fungus diseases already this season, and you're afraid many more may succumb.

Solution: Vent, or preferably, use the exhaust fan to blow warm, moist air out of the greenhouse. After a complete air change, turn the heat on until the night low of 50°F is achieved. Use an interior fan during heating and for some time afterward.

Problem: It's the dreariest part of winter. A succession of cold, cloudy days have gotten everything but the heating bill down. Even though the auxiliary heater has been running frequently, interior air is quite damp. Your common sense rebels at the thought of exhausting humidity by introducing and heating outside air.

Solution: Use the interior blower to disperse humidity around the leaves. Remember that it can be left on all night. Don't water unless absolutely necessary.

Problem: It's been a muggy mid-July week. The vents are fully open and outside air is as humid as inside air. Some plants are showing the first signs of fungus problems.

Solution: Again, the interior blower comes in handy. You can't lower relative humidity, but you can keep air from becoming stagnant. Use it day and night during these conditions.

Counteracting Low Humidity

Arid climates can be as troublesome as humid ones. When outside humidity levels are peaking at 20 to 30 percent, it takes work to keep greenhouse humidity high enough for good growth. Mist the air during the morning and, when possible, again in the early afternoon. Keep aisles and other surfaces watered so moisture can evaporate.

Some people set a series of open water containers in front of intake vents. Incoming air may pick up some of the water and carry it into the greenhouse. Water from open buckets set around bed areas will evaporate as well, slightly increasing local humidity levels. The increase may not be much, but even a slight rise in humidity is an improvement.

To provide more moisture around plants, mulch beds with a layer of light-colored, water-retentive material such as hay or straw, and keep it moist. You can also set individual pots on pebble trays as described in chapter 4, under Watering Systems.

In winter, low humidity is less likely to occur because a closed greenhouse retains transpirational water. In fact, growers accustomed to an arid climate are often surprised to encounter excessive humidity levels. These should be handled as described above in the series of problems and solutions.

Controlling Carbon Dioxide

Fresh outside air contains about 300 parts per million (ppm) of carbon dioxide. Not surprisingly, this level is adequate for good growth; it's been working well for a long time now!

But carbon dioxide levels change in response to other elements in the environment. For example, air that is polluted with combustion fuel by-products usually carries high CO_2 levels, while air in a closed area filled with photosynthesizing plants may contain less.

In a home greenhouse, only one rule about CO_2 applies: The more CO_2, the better. Levels over 300 ppm increase growth, especially if other environmental factors are favorable. Commercial growers often augment CO_2 to increase production. Pressurized tanks emit a measured amount throughout the daylight hours. But this equipment is expensive and unnecessary for home growers. If your greenhouse has at least three to five air changes an hour, plants won't suffer from CO_2 deprivation.

As we learned in chapter 1, plants use CO_2 only during the day when they are photosynthesizing. At night, as they respire, they release it. By morning, CO_2 levels can reach 500 ppm in a closed greenhouse. When the early morning sun hits the plants, photosynthesis begins again. After only a few hours, air in a closed greenhouse can contain as little as 200 ppm. When CO_2 levels drop, photosynthesis slows until fresh air is introduced.

Problems with CO_2 levels are common during the winter. Owners of tightly built, freestanding facilities are often mystified by poor winter growth. As a consultant, I've learned to ask about ventilation rates right away. When growers are having problems, ventilation is usually too low to keep up with the demand for CO_2. It's ironic, but heat-guzzling environments with lots of infiltration have few problems with CO_2—it comes in with all the cold air. Attached greenhouses are the best CO_2 providers of all. Carbon dioxide from all of the living, breathing inhabitants feeds the plants in the growing area.

In the greenhouse the plants' needs and the environment often work together to maintain a healthy balance. Plants use CO_2 in relation to light and warmth. The brighter and warmer it is, the more CO_2 the plants use. This means that plants need fresh supplies of CO_2 under the same conditions that cause you to open the vents for cooling. But even if it isn't warm enough to warrant cooling, introduce fresh air by midmorning every single day. Add supplementary heat if necessary.

An interior fan can't add CO_2, of course, but it can permit greater access to it. On particularly cold days when ventilation is kept to a minimum, use the interior fan to blow boundary layers of air away from leaves. Fresh air laden with CO_2 will move in to take its place.

Novel Ways to Boost CO_2

Small-scale growers have experimented with inexpensive methods of augmenting CO_2 levels. Some people compost in the greenhouse because the gas is released by an active pile. Others who've composted inside report trouble with traveling pests and even diseases promoted by high humidity. If you do compost inside, be scrupulous about managing the pile; haphazard efforts will certainly bring problems. Balance the materials so that the ratio between carbon- and nitrogen-containing materials is close to the optimum of 25 to 1; otherwise, volatized ammonia will poison the plants. (Composting is discussed in more detail in chapter 7.) Surround the pile with window screening to minimize pest migration, and vent as often as necessary to dump excess humidity. If you're not an experienced composter, you might want to make a pile *outside* the greenhouse and use a screened forced-air duct to bring in the air released by the pile. An outside pile permits flexibility; if too much ammonia is being given off or if fungus diseases are suddenly thriving, you can simply block the duct. Ill effects from an interior compost pile aren't quite so easy to eliminate.

Animals, especially rabbits, are often promoted as good winter greenhouse inhabitants because they give off CO_2 as they respire. But I've seen too many sick rabbits to blithely send them to this fate. Rabbits are very sensitive animals; they can't tolerate sudden shocks, excessive humidity, poor sanitation or high temperatures. They become neurotic very easily and literally get heart attacks from unexpected noises. More than one mother rabbit has eaten all her babies rather than expose them to a world she considers unfit. In my opinion, only experienced rabbit growers should install rabbits in a greenhouse because only they really understand the urgency of daily cleaning, high ventilation and cool temperatures. Rabbits must never be thought of as year-round denizens of the greenhouse. In the spring they must be removed to a cool, shaded spot because they can't possibly endure greenhouse temperatures.

And then there are chickens. Combined chicken coop/greenhouse operations give as many potential problems as any other combined livestock/plant operation. From the plants' point of view, excess ammonia is the usual culprit, while excess humidity is the chickens' complaint. Creating a whole biosystem is lovely in concept but difficult to pull off in reality. Be absolutely certain that niches within the ecosystem suit both the plants and animals before embarking on it.

Letting in Light

Traditional greenhouses leave no doubt that their designers meant to get as much light as possible into the structure, but owners pay for this advantage in heating bills. In a spirit of reform, solar engineers design heat-conserving structures and add roof shading for protection against summer overheating. But in some solar greenhouses, particularly those designed in the early 1970s, too much light was thrown out with the heating bill.

Shady areas can be frustrating. Just when seedlings and light-loving summer crops need maximum light, the rear of the solar greenhouse is shaded from about noon until two or three o'clock. In warm climates, summer vegetables are usually grown outside and rear shading helps to protect a crop of flowering greenhouse ornamentals. But in regions where frosts strike in June, August and sometimes come as a surprise in July, good indoor light is crucial. Frost-tender crops such as tomatoes and cucumbers need summer protection, and because they are tall, they are generally placed along the north side. Fruiting crops require at least six to eight hours of strong light to bear well, hence the frustration if they're shaded.

I've suffered through several summers in facilities with too much shade. In desperation, I once counted and weighed each tomato from every plant to determine yield loss from shading. I knew the situation was bad, but the results startled even me: unshaded plants on the south side yielded four times as many tomatoes as shaded north-side plants. The best remedy in this particular greenhouse was outright surgery: a 3-foot-wide area was cut and glazed along the length of the north roof near the ridge. The next year, there was summer light and plenty of tomatoes.

Surgery is certainly in order if your greenhouse is too dark. Glaze at least the east wall and a portion of the roof. To prevent winter heat loss, make insulated Styrofoam plugs for the extra glazing. The sun is so low in winter that the plugs can stay in place during the entire heating season.

Northern growers who are designing a greenhouse should check sun angles for June 21 to ensure that *direct* light will reach all growing areas. Publications about solar design and construction give directions for this computation.

And finally, remember to wash the glazing frequently. Light doesn't pass through dirt very well, but dirty glazing is as easy to ignore as dirty eyeglasses.

Tools to Monitor the Greenhouse

Before you can manage your greenhouse environment, you need to have some facts at your disposal: What are the air and soil temperatures? How much moisture is in the air? What are the light levels in different areas? Gathering this data is easy with the proper tools.

Thermometers

Three thermometers are all you need to monitor the temperature in a home greenhouse—one to measure interior temperatures, one for exterior temperatures and a soil thermometer. If there are automatic devices, such as exhaust fans or auxiliary combustion or electric heaters, they will have thermostats.

Inside Thermometer

To get the most accurate readings, take the time to shield the thermometer. Mount a min-max thermometer on a piece of solid insulating material, such as Styrofoam, that is attached to a wooden stake. The stake should be pointed on one end so that you can drive it into a greenhouse bed and thus record temperatures at plant level. Place it so that it faces north in a solar greenhouse. This orientation gives you the best ambient readings because direct sunlight can not hit the casing materials, causing the thermometer to overheat. This placement is also good in a traditional house, although, to be certain that the thermometer is not registering too high, some people make an insulated and ventilated box, as described for outdoor thermometers later in this section.

The placement of a thermometer within the greenhouse is as important as insulation and shielding. Every greenhouse has different temperature zones resulting from proximity to the glazing, the heater,

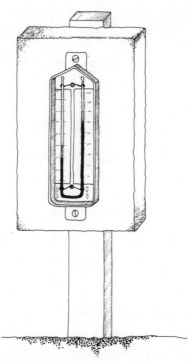

Mounted Thermometer: *A min-max thermometer mounted on a block of Styrofoam will give you the most accurate readings. Locate it so that it records temperatures at plant level.*

the ridge or the intake vent. Often these differences are more extreme in solar greenhouses than in traditional ones. Nonetheless, if you monitor any greenhouse carefully, you will find significant differences in temperature from one location to another.

You may have seen drawings of solar greenhouses indicating that the temperature is higher at points close to the ridge and on the south side than near the floor or north side. This description is generally true, but it's helpful to know the approximate areas of the zones in *your* greenhouse as well as the normal temperature differences between them.

To determine zones, place a thermometer at plant level in various locations, first on a sunny and then on a cloudy day. Try setting it on the top rear bed, on beds in the middle area and on beds closest to the glazing. Check the areas close to the end walls, too. When the indicator stops moving, relocate the thermometer. Work quickly so the information isn't made invalid by a change in outside conditions. By charting the temperature of different areas, you'll find temperature zones.

Zones differ from season to season. During the first year of operation, go through this procedure at least once every season. By the beginning of the second year, you'll know where to plant various crops and where to place the thermometer during the year for day-to-day monitoring.

Ideally, the thermometer you check for daily readings should register the *average* inside temperature. If you place it in a "hot spot" or an unusually cold pocket of air, you may think that the greenhouse needs more ventilation or heating than is actually necessary. Use your zone chart to find an "average" spot for the thermometer.

If you use more than one thermometer, check to see that they agree. Thermometers have uncanny habits of registering accurately at one temperature and inaccurately at another. Place them side by side to spot-check them at various temperatures. If you find a sharp difference, choose one as a reference and mark the difference on the other (for example, "registers − 1°F at 50°F; + 2°F at 85°F"). By doing this, you'll have a clearer idea of the actual difference in temperature between one area and another through the growing season.

Outside Thermometer

Knowing the greenhouse response to outside wind and temperature conditions makes predicting heating and cooling needs easier. Keep a record of daily wind speed and high and low temperatures. Mount another min-max thermometer outside the greenhouse, preferably on the north side. But no matter what the location, make an insulated and vented box to shield it from direct light and excessive heat buildup. Venting can be assured if you cut holes into the sides as well as the top of the box. If a magnet is used to reset the thermometer, keep it handy by tying it securely to the casing. I've spent more than one frustrating afternoon pawing through children's toy boxes in search of a magnet strong enough to use on a thermometer.

Soil Thermometer

Many people run home greenhouses with little knowledge of soil temperatures. But soil is as much a part of the plants' environment as air, and its temperature should be monitored as carefully.

Soil temperature is affected by air temperature, bed depth, moisture content and mulching materials. Temperatures below 45 to 50°F stunt plant growth by slowing metabolic processes as well as preventing microorganisms from breaking down nutrients. High temperatures cause their own problems—when the soil is warmer than 80°F, plants' metabolic rates increase beyond a desirable point.

A soil thermometer can indicate necessary management steps. If, for instance, beds are registering under 50°F, a dark mulch, such as black plastic or compost, should raise the temperature. If that doesn't work, you can increase night heating and, when possible, install deeper beds.

Clear plastic mulch also adds heat to the soil. When a bed needs to be sterilized, lay clear plastic over it for a week of sunny weather. Many pests and pathogens will be killed by the high soil temperature.

When you need to cool the soil, use light-colored mulches. These lower soil temperatures by reflecting light. Tomatoes are one crop that really appreciates cool soil and reflected light; summer mulching with hay or straw often improves their yield.

A waterproof soil thermometer with a round dial attached to an unbreakable metal probe is the most practical. Glass probes break too easily. The dial should read by increments of one or two degrees. Soil probes come in various lengths. The most common is 6 inches long, but if you can find one 8 to 12 inches, buy it immediately. Not only is it useful for monitoring soil temperatures, but it's great for a compost pile.

Soils also have different temperature zones. Soil on the surface of a bed is more immediately sensitive to air temperatures than soil at lower depths. Spend some time probing into a bed at varying depths. A graph of the results would show sharper differences between 1 and 4 inches than between 5 and 9 inches. At night the graph would show that the top couple of inches cool rapidly, but below 4 or 5 inches, there would be little, if any, difference between day and night temperatures. It takes many days of consistent temperatures to affect soil in lower zones.

Thermostats

Thermostats are always set in reference to temperatures at plant level. A heater or exhaust fan should switch on when the air *around the plants* is a certain temperature. But thermostats are rarely in the same temperature zone as plants. If simply set at 45°F, for example, they'll activate equipment at temperatures inappropriate for the plants.

Begin by shielding the thermostat from direct light. Depending upon its orientation, make a small insulating cover. Strips of Styrofoam held together with tape work very well. Duct tape will attach the cover to the heater or fan casing. Remember to add vent holes to this shield, too.

Even shielded, you have to fiddle with the thermostat setting. To adjust a fan thermostat, sit in the greenhouse on a warm day. Watch the temperature reading on the min-max thermometer at plant level. When it reaches the maximum desired temperature (usually 75 to 80°F), turn on the fan by moving the thermostat dial. The reading for the thermostat may be slightly below or, more likely, above the temperature registered by the min-max, but it will be responding to the plant environment.

Set the thermostat for a heater in the same way. Spend some time in the greenhouse on a cold night. As soon as the min-max registers the desired low, activate the heater by turning on its thermostat. In this case the reading may be closer to the temperature experienced at plant level.

Check thermostat settings against min-max readings every few weeks. Not only do they drift, but changes in season may warrant a change in setting. Whenever two thermostatically controlled devices are used, they must work in harmony. If they've been set as described, the heater won't be on while the fan is operating. But pay attention— settings can be inadvertently moved.

Monitoring Relative Humidity

There are occasions when relative humidity levels should dictate your management decisions. Two different tools, varying in price and accuracy, measure relative humidity. A hardware store hygrometer costs very little, but it may read as much as 15 to 20 percent high or low. A sling psychrometer is much more accurate and is appropriate for use in a home greenhouse. (You can buy one of these at any scientific supply house.) It has two thermometers—a conventional dry-bulb mercury thermometer and a "wet-bulb," which is covered with muslin. To use, wet the muslin with distilled water, swing the entire apparatus in the air for almost a minute, and note the difference in readings on both thermometers. Thanks to a handy chart that comes with the psychrometer, you can figure the percentage of relative humidity from the two readings.

Buy a sling psychrometer if your plants are showing signs of humidity-related problems and you are uncertain about correct ventilation and heating rates. I don't use one because I work in a consistently humid climate and I've trained my nose to tell me when to ventilate.

Monitoring Light

It's sometimes useful to measure interior light levels with a good photographic light meter. However, remember that plants are the best light meter ever invented. In low light, plants grow toward the glazing or have excessively long internodes, thin stems and enlarged and thin leaves.

On a bright day, sunlight hitting the earth's surface measures about 10,000 footcandles (the unit of measurement for light intensity). Vegetables can grow in minimum conditions between 1,500 (for low-light crops such as leaf lettuce) and 2,500 to 3,000 footcandles (for high-light fruiting crops). Levels slightly higher than the minimums produce better results, of course. Some ornamentals require more than 3,000 footcandles for good flowering or leaf coloration.

Given the numbers cited above, it could seem that light would never fall below tolerable ranges, but it does happen. To correct a poorly

lit area, change the glazing pattern or install artificial lights as described in chapter 4.

Making It Easy

Environmental management gets easier as time goes by and you
get used to thinking about vents, heaters and fans. In the beginning
you may need to consciously develop habits. Check the thermometer
every time you go into the greenhouse. Stick your finger in the soil.
Sniff the air for humidity. Notice if the air feels stagnant. Pretend you
are a plant and just feel the environment. Before long, you'll develop
unconscious guiding senses.

CHAPTER 3
DESIGNING
THE INTERIOR

"Form follows function." It's an old and practical adage that we all tend to ignore. Even though this little saying may seem banal, dust it off and mutter it under your breath while you plan the interior layout and fittings for your greenhouse.

A greenhouse serves several functions. It's an environment for plants, a workplace and, for most home growers, a recreational area and quiet place of refuge. The interior design can affect operation as much as the venting configuration, glazing angles or capacity for thermal storage. Environmental control is not independent of layout; a greenhouse works as a whole system. But it's easy to make mistakes. For example, incoming air from kneewall vents can be seriously restricted by solid beds covering the openings. A mass of cucumber vines growing over the side intake vents can produce the same result, although to a lesser extent.

Like a kitchen or other workshop, a greenhouse must be arranged for convenience and efficiency. If you can't reach the back of a growing bed, you might not notice an expanding aphid colony. And you're likely to avoid adjusting a thermostat if you need to stand on a stool to reach it.

Safety is a major concern. Place heaters far enough away from flammable materials so they can't possibly start a fire. Suspended fans must be securely attached to their moorings; you don't want to worry that they will jar loose and fall on unsuspecting heads. Protect all electrical connections and appliances against inadvertent watering or dripping condensates. Fans, both heavy-duty exhaust fans and small oscillating ones, must be completely screened with fine mesh hardware cloth to protect small, exploring fingers.

My greenhouses tend toward the utilitarian. I don't waste precious space on groupings of chairs and coffee tables. When I want to sit down to admire the plants and enjoy the sun, I perch on an overturned bucket. However, I do have more hedonistic friends who design layouts with a proper appreciation of lounging space. From their designs I've seen that it's not necessary to sacrifice growing area to make a sitting area. My favorite layout has a wooden deck at bed height over a section of aisle; leisurely weeding from a semiprone position is just as effective as weeding from a standing position. Other friends have set up string hammocks over aisles and low growing beds. Even if you don't find these options attractive, you might move a couple of folding chairs into the greenhouse. And the next Sunday morning when it's bright and cold outside, prop up your feet on the edge of a growing bed, lean back and enjoy the sunshine.

Planning the Layout

Some people are gifted with an ability to accurately imagine all of the possible variations of a given environment. However, most of us can't visualize quite so well, and forget to account for one factor or another. As a result, it's wise to plan the interior layout on paper. If you're fortunate enough to be involved in the overall design of your greenhouse, plan the interior as the greenhouse shell is drawn and redrawn. If you're moving into an established greenhouse, make a complete interior layout plan before bringing in so much as a philodendron.

Unlike all of the engineers I know, I simply can't visualize dimensions. But my profession has required me to plan layouts in numerous greenhouses for myself and other people. Consequently, I've developed a system that saves time and helps to avoid terrible mistakes. Graph paper is the secret of planning for nonvisual people. It generally takes at least a package of the stuff before a design seems suitable. Begin by drawing a map of the floor area that indicates the location and dimensions of all permanent fixtures: vents, windows, doors, electrical outlets, water faucets and, in the case of solar greenhouses, areas of heat storage. Make additional maps of walls that could give problems.

Checklist for Planning the Interior

As you work with the map of your greenhouse interior, ask yourself these questions about each element you want to add or move around.

- How does the element affect environmental control?
- How does it affect light availability?
- How does it affect temperature control?
- How does it affect air circulation?
- Is this a convenient working arrangement?
- Is this arrangement safe?

And then take advantage of modern technology. Graph paper is drawn with blue lines that won't photocopy on most machines. However, few machines object to graph paper used in place of photocopying paper. With care, you can align the original map so that the lines appear at the right places on the graph paper. Unless you are a practiced designer or engineer, make a stack of maps, take them home, and settle in for a long design session.

Designing Growing Areas

An enterprising person could invent a board game to design the best configuration for greenhouse growing areas. Points would be given for each square foot of growing area, and penalties would be accrued for every inconvenient feature. It's not a bad idea to initiate this game during your planning process. Give your family and friends a copy of the floor plan and let them help design the layout. Remind them that all growing areas must be easily accessible. Most people can't reach more than 3 feet comfortably; beds that sit against the glazing or a wall should be no wider than that. If aisles surround a bed, a 6-foot width is fine. Floor-level troughs can take more area only if stepping-stones or footboards are placed in permanent positions every few feet within the bed. (Remember to deduct points for the areas under stepping-stones or boards, since they won't be available as growing space. I would give penalties for having to work in a stooped position, but that's arbitrary; some people don't object to cramped quarters.)

Many layouts make the use of carts or wheelbarrows difficult to nearly impossible. A small cart fits into a 2-foot aisle, but most wheelbarrows require 3 feet of space to maneuver. Even if you don't plan on using carts, aisles should be at least 2 feet wide. Plants always grow over bed edges; you'll be surprised how narrow they can make a 2-foot aisle. Three-foot aisles are mandatory for people working from wheelchairs.

Watering patterns are always important considerations in determining the layout. Under no circumstances should a hose be drawn across a growing bed. Even if you have to use an extension rod, it should be easy to water all areas without moving the hose from the aisle. In a large facility, the layout should provide easy traffic patterns. Home greenhouses are rarely large enough to give problems, but trace likely paths just to be certain of the layout's convenience. It's nice to put a potting bench close to the propagating area, for example.

To give you a starting point for your own greenhouse design, here are some sample bed layouts for both a 12- by 24-foot attached solar greenhouse with water barrel heat storage and a 12- by 24-foot free-standing traditional greenhouse with no heat-storage area.

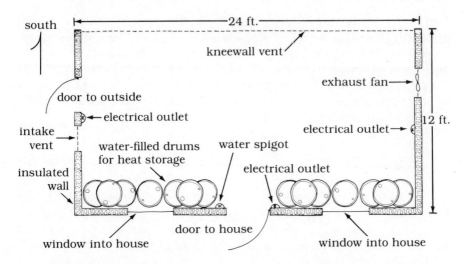

Attached Solar Greenhouse Floor Plan: *This basic floor plan shows that there are 264 square feet of usable floor area.*

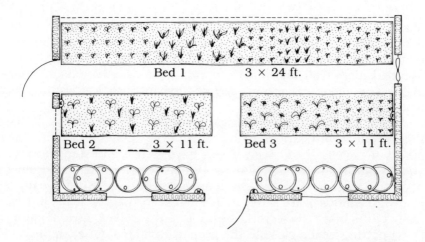

Attached Solar Bed Layout 1: *This bed arrangement is fairly common. All aisles are 2 feet wide and all beds 3 feet wide. The grower can move freely in this space. Growing area in the beds measures 138 square feet.*

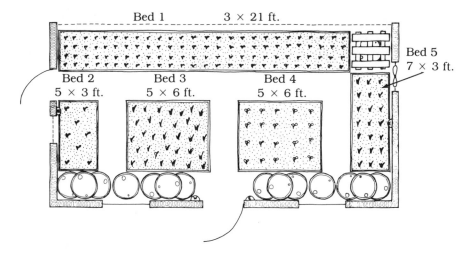

Attached Solar Bed Layout 2: *This bed layout is less common. It offers the advantage of 21 more square feet of growing area in the beds, and it provides discrete areas for different crops. The area at the southwest corner would be inaccessible if it were made into a bed. Instead, a barrel covered with boards can collect and store heat and make a cozy area for a flat of seedlings. The 2-foot-wide aisles allow easy movement.*

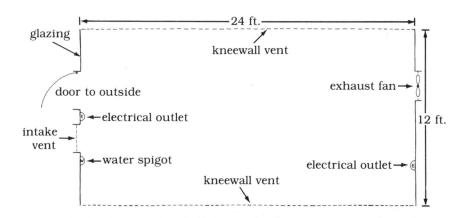

Freestanding Greenhouse Floor Plan: *This basic floor plan shows that there are 288 square feet of usable floor area.*

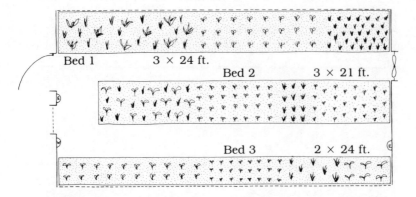

Freestanding Bed Layout 1: *This common layout gives the grower 183 square feet of growing area in the beds. The extra foot of aisle space near the door provides enough room to bring a wheelbarrow or large cart into the greenhouse.*

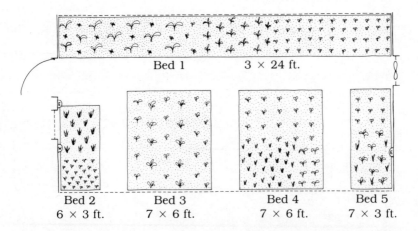

Freestanding Bed Layout 2: *This less conventional layout allows for more growing area in the beds. The design provides 195 square feet of bed area, an increase of 12 square feet over the more traditional layout. Depending on the crops that are grown, this layout might be more practical than Layout 1. However, if the crop scheme calls for many hanging baskets, Layout 1 would be preferred since the overhead baskets would be more accessible. All aisles are 2 feet wide, except for the 3-foot aisle near the door.*

Bed Design

Once you know where growing areas are going to be located, you have to decide what kind of beds to use in each location. Depending upon the crops you'll grow, the climate and the greenhouse design, you can choose from three basic types: troughs dug into the floor, deep containers (or beds) that sit on the floor or are raised above it, or benches on which pots and other containers are placed.

Troughs

Troughs dug into and extending slightly above the floor level of the greenhouse conserve space. Because the root zone is below the floor line, topgrowth can become quite high without being difficult to reach. One drawback does arise because the floor and the underlying ground are the coolest areas. If your greenhouse is located in the North or has an uninsulated foundation, troughs may be too cold an environment for plants during the winter.

Because of potential shading problems, use troughs only in greenhouses that are glazed to the ground. In solar greenhouses with opaque north walls, plants in a south trough may give shade during winter when the sun is low on the horizon. In this case, plant only low-growing crops in a south trough during the fall and winter. Troughs on the north side of a solar greenhouse aren't usually practical because plants don't get enough light when they are small. Build beds or benches for the north side of a solar greenhouse.

The water table under the greenhouse is an important consideration when you're planning troughs. If groundwater is high during any part of the year, excess moisture is likely to migrate into the growing area. Roots may be deprived of oxygen, and humidity may be hard to control. Under these conditions, plants are likely to languish and they're more susceptible to diseases.

Build troughs only if conditions are optimum for them. The greenhouse foundation should be insulated, glazing must reach to the ground, the water table must be low and drainage under the greenhouse must be excellent.

Many very good greenhouse growers like troughs. But troughs are my least favorite kind of growing area. For one thing, it's much more difficult to dig out the soil in a trough than in an aboveground bed. You may never have to go through this tedious operation. However, there is always the possibility that your growing medium will host harmful nematodes or an insidious disease such as late blight or clubroot. When this happens, the most practical solution is to remove the soil mix and put it through a very hot compost pile. Emptying a bed is bad enough; the thought of digging out a trough makes me shudder.

And while it is possible to completely empty a container and sterilize it thoroughly, a trough can never be completely cleaned. Chemical fumigation is about the only way it could be done. But fumigation is dangerous; the chemicals are lethal to people, too.

Building a Trough

Making a good trough is not as simple as turning over the greenhouse floor. If the soil under your greenhouse is in top-notch condition, you may be tempted to plant directly into it. However, few field soils have all the necessary attributes of greenhouse growing media: high and balanced nutritional content, deep topsoil, good drainage, excellent texture and structure, and absence of disease and pest organisms. Even if you're sitting on a treasure like this, it's unlikely that it will remain healthy after a few seasons as part of an enclosed environment. Outdoors, field soils can be covercropped and green-manured. The rain brings nitrogen, while the yearly cycles of freezing and thawing, moisture saturation and drying serve to hold pest and disease organisms in check, to leach excess salts and to break down the bedrock. This doesn't mean that it's easy to maintain a field soil, only that a field soil is more easily maintained in the open rather than under cover. If you do begin by using just the soil under your greenhouse shell, be prepared to dig it out within a few years for construction of a more sophisticated trough.

To provide good drainage and rich soil, a trough must be as carefully built as any aboveground container. Begin by digging a trench at least $2\frac{1}{2}$ feet deep. This depth accommodates a minimum of 6 inches of drainage material and 2 feet of soil mix. When troughs are placed against a wall or the glazing, most people limit the finished width to 3 feet for easy access. People with very long arms or a willingness to work while stepping on small boards can make the growing area wider. Troughs that are accessible from both sides can be a full 6 feet wide without causing any inconvenience.

In very compacted soils, it may be possible to let the sides of the trench serve as trough walls. But even so, it's wise to reinforce the top foot of each wall. To distinguish growing area from aisles, the soil level should be raised a bit as well. Partially bury several layers of bricks, cinder blocks or rocks to reinforce the sides and form a small wall. You can also make walls out of boards as described below.

In uncompacted soils, trough walls should be reinforced to hold the medium in place. In my opinion, wood is the most suitable material for belowground trough walls. Cut 1×6 or 1×8 boards to the dimensions of each side. The boards must be held in place with wooden 2×2 stakes driven into the bottom of the trench at intervals along each wall. Use smaller stakes along the outside edges of the wooden walls to give additional support. The top board on each side should extend at least 4 to 6 inches above the level of the greenhouse floor so that unwary visitors don't inadvertently step into the bed.

To avoid using a preservative or if migrating moisture is a concern, line the sides of the trough with 6-mil construction grade polyethylene. Staple it onto the boards and bring it up over the top edge of the bed. Don't line the bottom; drainage is essential. Water will still seep through staple holes and any rips in the plastic. This method doesn't give as much protection against decay as preservatives do, but it should be adequate.

Good drainage is always important. In a trough, the most practical drainage system is a 6-inch layer of gravel or mixed gravel and sand. Some gardeners cover the gravel with several layers of fine-mesh nylon screening to hold the soil mix in place. This isn't necessary, but saves time if you need to remove the soil at some future date. With screening you can leave the drainage materials in place while you replace the medium.

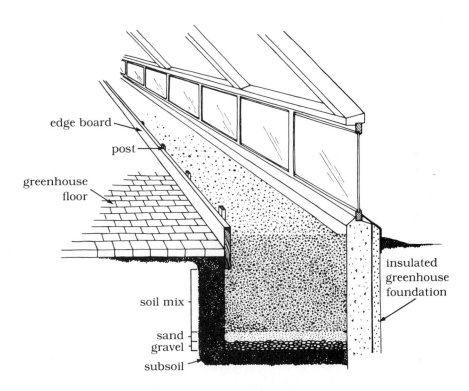

edge board

post

greenhouse floor

insulated greenhouse foundation

soil mix

sand
gravel

subsoil

Inside Look at a Trough: *This view gives you a good idea of how to construct a sturdy trough that will provide plants with a good growing environment.*

Soil mix is the last thing to go into a trough. Prepare the soil mix as for other types of greenhouse beds. You'll find directions on how to do this in chapter 6.

Deep Beds

Deep beds are my favorite growing areas for greenhouse vegetables. Unlike troughs, beds don't allow excess groundwater to move into the growing medium. They sit high enough so that roots are in a moderately warm zone; they allow enough space both horizontally and vertically for good root growth; and if well constructed, they are easy to maintain. You can make deep beds from lumber, cinder blocks or even rocks. The important considerations are adequate depth and adequate drainage.

Though many people use containers that hold only a foot of soil, a 2-foot depth is far more versatile. Soil this deep doesn't dry out quickly, nor does its temperature fluctuate greatly. Roots have enough space to grow well, so plants are rarely container-bound. But some interior layouts require a few shallow beds. Try to keep them at least a foot deep and plant only shallow-rooted crops in them. You'll have to be sensitive to the plants' increased needs for maintenance, too. (Lettuce, parsley and spinach are some shallow-rooted crops you might want to try.)

Bed design determines drainage design. If beds sit directly on a soil floor, don't give them a bottom. Instead, excavate under each bed and add a layer of gravel. The depth of the drainage material varies with the native soil type. On sandy soils with good drainage, 3 inches of gravel should provide enough protection. However, if the beds sit on a heavy clay soil, 6 inches of sand and/or gravel would be more appropriate.

Elevated wooden containers usually allow for drainage and air circulation with slat bottoms. Use pressure-treated lumber or paint the slats with a preservative. Bottoms tend to rot more quickly than the sides. (For more pointers on using wood preservatives, see the box, Tips for Long-Lasting Wooden Structures.) When you build a slat bottom, leave about ½ inch between each board to allow for expansion once the wood absorbs moisture. Even when they're this widely separated, slats alone do not provide enough drainage. Drill ¾-inch-diameter drainage holes about 6 inches apart in every direction across the bottom. Because soil mix can escape through these large holes, staple fine-mesh nylon screening over the bottom of the box. A 1- or 2-inch layer of sand or a sand and gravel mix below the soil medium gives plants even more protection from soggy conditions.

Sidewalls can be made from well-seasoned boards. Some people use plywood, but I don't think plywood containers last long enough to

Tips for Long-Lasting Wooden Structures

Naturally durable woods such as cedar and cypress or lumber treated to resist decay can prolong the life of wooden structures. Pressure-treated lumber is often used in greenhouses. Since it has been treated with arsenic compounds, the safest way to use it is as part of the structural frame. Don't use it for containers that will come in direct contact with the soil. Cedar and cypress, which naturally resist decay, are the best choices for growing beds. These woods can be expensive, but perhaps you can locate other growers in the area who would be willing to join forces to place a large order that would qualify for a reduced rate.

If you can't locate these woods, or if they're not available, you can use a wood preservative to treat beds and containers. The safest preservative is copper naphthenate (sold under the trade name Cuprinol). It is very effective, and while it poses no harm to plants or people, copper naphthenate does kill soil fungi and bacteria for a brief period of time after application. It also releases volatile toxic solvents as it dries. When you use copper naphthenate on lumber for beds, let the boards weather outside for a few weeks before exposing them to soil.

Try not to use paints or preservatives inside the greenhouse when plants are growing there. If you must do so, wait until a week when the weather is warm enough to leave the greenhouse open all night. Vent as completely as possible during the entire time that the paint or preservative is drying . . . and then add a few days for extra measure.

While I'm insistent upon treating all wooden parts of a greenhouse structure with preservatives, I use beds made from untreated wood lined with plastic film. These beds might rot a few years before preserved wood will, but they pose no threat to soil life. I use 6-mil construction grade polyethylene stapled to the sides of the beds or to any wooden containers. I never use it to cover the bottoms because that would prevent water from draining away.

warrant their expense. Soil mixes are damp enough to make them warp and lose their strength within a couple of years. Boards for deep beds should be preserved or covered with 6-mil polyethylene. Because only one side of the wood is in contact with soil, you can leave exterior surfaces in their natural state, oil them or paint them with a matte-finish clear plastic paint or a water-based latex paint. Of course you'll allow plenty of time for the paint to cure before you plant in the containers or bring them into a closed greenhouse.

Containers with bottoms should be elevated several inches above the floor to facilitate drainage and air circulation. The bottoms of the

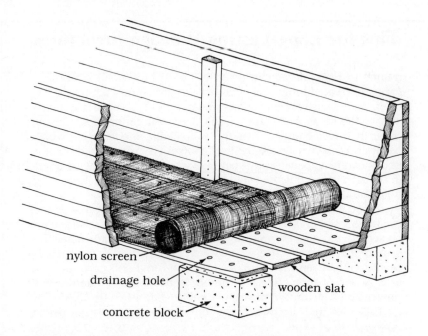

nylon screen
drainage hole
concrete block
wooden slat

Deep Growing Bed: *You must provide plants with good drainage and air circulation. In this bed the open-spaced slats, drainage holes and concrete blocks all ensure that water will escape and air will circulate.*

boxes will also last longer if one side is allowed to dry. Scrap blocks of wood, bricks or cinder blocks make good legs. The height should take the position of the intake vents into account. The tops of the beds should be slightly below or level with the bottom of the intake vents. With this arrangement, incoming air will blow through the plants. You may find it necessary to lower the floor of the greenhouse to position deep beds correctly. In greenhouses where this isn't feasible, leave about a foot of space between the vents and the bed so that incoming air will not be restricted. With this arrangement northern growers must remember to use the forced-ventilation system on cold days. Otherwise plants closest to the vents will be injured by cold drafts.

Benches

Benches are most useful in greenhouses or areas devoted to seedling or potted ornamental production. The traditional bench design looks like a long, slatted-board table with a 2- or 3-inch lip. Slats allow excess water to drain. Nonetheless, protect wooden benches with a preservative.

I prefer to make benches from wooden 2 × 4 frames covered with bench mesh, a strong metal screening available from greenhouse suppliers. It's wonderful material: strong, lightweight, easy to sterilize and nonshading. Good wire cutters or a welding torch are the only tools that will cut it. You'll need U-shaped nails to attach the mesh to the frames. Turn the benches so that projecting 2 × 4s form a lip. If you plan to use heavy pots on a wire bench, add cross-supports at 3-foot intervals.

The most stable and versatile legs for benches are wooden 2 × 4 sawhorses. But almost anything else will work as well. Some people use a couple of plastic or wooden crates while others pile up cinder blocks. Height is determined by convenience; benches aren't solid enough to interfere with air circulation. I like to work with benches about 3 feet off the ground. At this height the root zone is quite warm, and besides, my back doesn't hurt after a long day of potting or transplanting.

Almost every greenhouse can use at least one bench. Many herbs and ornamentals grow in small pots as well as or better than they do in a bed. Benches also make very good starting areas for seedling flats because it's so easy to transform them into propagating chambers. The space under a bench is a handy storage area. Fill it with boxes of pots,

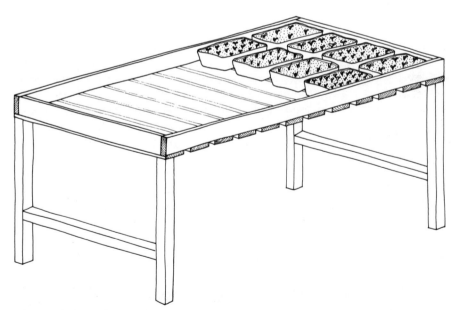

Slatted Bench: *This greenhouse workhorse is a great place to locate seedlings and potted ornamentals. The slats allow water to drain away.*

buckets of soil mix ingredients, and jugs of liquid seaweed and fish emulsion. In the fall it's easy to clear all of the pots off a bench and use it for a drying rack for onions or a curing area for winter squash. Draped with a sheet of polyethylene, benches make good vegetable and herb drying areas.

Hanging Pots

Hanging pots expand your growing area significantly. Besides making use of normally idle space, many herbs, ornamentals and dwarf vegetable crops are healthier when grown toward the ridge where it is bright and warm.

The easiest way to hang pots is from a cable system as described under Plant Supports in chapter 4. Pot placement depends upon several factors: light availability, watering convenience and headroom. Foliage plants need filtered light or shading for part of the day. Light-loving herbs and flowering crops need brighter conditions. But don't forget the plants in lower beds; a dense row of pots can shade them for many hours. Watch light patterns and readjust the arrangement if light-hungry crops are shaded for more than a couple of hours. Pots, especially those in bright light, require watering more frequently than beds. You'll want to be able to water pots with an extension rod; don't ask yourself to drag a stool around every day. Plants hanging over an aisle must be high enough so that the very tallest of your friends and family can ignore them. It's no fun to walk into a heavy 12-inch pot.

I love the contrast of green leaves in a white pot. Some ornamentals, such as blue lobelia with its sparkling white centers, beg for white containers. But a word of caution is in order. Only the best white plastic pots are thick enough so that light doesn't penetrate into the root zone. Many plants object to having their roots lit, so ensure healthy growth by using only top-grade white plastic. You can't see light through good-quality pots. If you want to buy less expensive pots, choose a dark color that doesn't admit as much light. This caution is especially relevant to small nonhanging pots. If you don't believe this, set up an experiment. Plant the same crops in several thin white and dark pots and watch their general vigor for a season. You'll find that the difference is surprising enough to make a believer out of you.

Propagation Area

Players in the greenhouse design game should get extra points for adding a specific propagation area. In the spring almost every square foot is devoted to seedlings and cuttings, but a small area is adequate

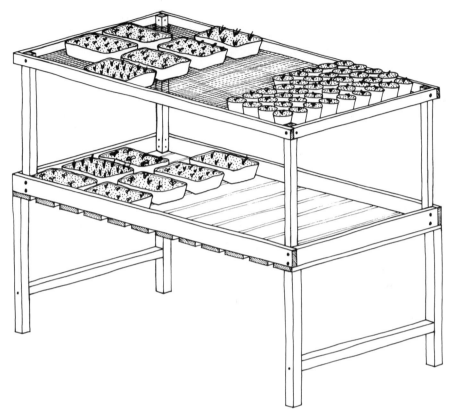

Double-Decker Bench: *Add a second story to a bench and you've instantly doubled the space available for trays of seedlings.*

through the rest of the year. Thanks to the equipment discussed in chapter 4, propagation areas don't need prime growing space. You can transform a bench or shallow bed into a cozy spot for starting seeds or rooting cuttings. Freestanding propagation areas are another option (these are discussed in more detail in the next chapter).

Seedling time is frustrating. No matter how large the greenhouse, there's never enough room. Rather than cut back on the number of seedlings or wish for a bigger greenhouse, it's time to take advantage of vertical space. I like to use benches covered with bench mesh that bolt, double-decker style, over other benches or deep beds. With this arrangement it's important to watch shading patterns. Give the top area to high-light plants such as tomatoes, cabbage family crops and melons. Lettuce, parsley and other greens can grow well on the lower level as long as they get filtered light for about eight hours a day. Don't pack the upper level; leave enough room to shift flats for greater light availability below. In a greenhouse that has strong rafters or glazing bars, you can also hang benches. Make sure that hanging benches have a good 2-inch lip so that pots won't slide off. Be certain, too, that no one can accidently bump into them.

Potting Area

My greenhouse fantasies include having a potting area with a sink, a good mixing board, storage space and a smooth potting table. It would, of course, be adjacent to the finest propagation area imaginable. Although I dream about it, a luxurious potting area isn't essential to a good operation. You don't even need a permanent spot; a wide board set over a high bed or bench works perfectly well.

Given a choice between mixing soil in a bucket or on a board, I'll opt for the board every time. It's easier to make a homogenized mix when you can lift and scrape and mash lumps with a sharp-edged plasterer's trowel. While a lip at the working edge of the board would be inconvenient, a 4- to 6-inch lip on the sides and back will contain the mix. A clean, smooth surface is mandatory. I paint mine with several coats of plastic or enamel paint and sterilize it with a 10 percent solution of laundry bleach before every use.

Storage Space

Somehow, somewhere, you'll need to store materials. A list of the items that most growers keep on hand is not intimidating—until you calculate their volume. Soil mix components such as peat moss and vermiculite are so much cheaper in bulk that you'll buy 3 cubic feet at a time. You'll probably store compost and topsoil for spring seedling production, too. A small, uninsulated but raintight shed close to the greenhouse is the ideal place for off-season storage of bulky items. If this is impossible, you'll need to develop some very creative storage systems, especially when you don't have enough space under benches. Use a wide board to cover a row of plastic or galvanized garbage cans that hold soil mix ingredients. The board can serve as a shelf for a group of pots. In a solar greenhouse with water barrel storage, it might even be worthwhile to sacrifice a barrel or two for storage area.

Items that are used every day should be accessible. I use small shelves to house nozzles, fertilizers, a few pots and flats, small tools and record books. Seeds are stored in labeled plastic refrigerator containers while I am actively seeding. Afterward, I move them to a dark, dry drawer or the freezer, where they'll remain viable.

In a solar greenhouse, shelves can be hung on the north wall. In a fully glazed greenhouse, build low shelves that won't impede incoming light and set them where they least interfere with your activities.

Hoses must be stored above the floor to prevent the growth of fungal organisms. When you allow hoses to sit on the ground, fungi breed in the puddles that collect under the hose end, and even on the nozzle itself. If possible, hang an L-shaped bracket near the spigot. Freestanding caddies will hold hoses where brackets aren't feasible. It's wise to store hoses in a wound position; they last longer and are less annoying if they haven't developed kinks.

Some Final Thoughts

After your interior design is complete, go back over it again. Make certain that there is enough room to work, that you'll be able to fill and seed pots comfortably, that materials will have a home, that visitors will be safe and that environmental control isn't hindered. If you've cajoled other people into the design process, thank them for their efforts with the first ripe tomato, a freshly picked spinach salad or a winter bouquet.

❧ CHAPTER 4 ❧
EQUIPPING THE GREENHOUSE

My first greenhouse was minimally equipped. I had been so impressed with the cost of the overall structure that I was stingy when it came to buying tools and equipment. My supplies were limited to a hose with a squirter nozzle, a bucket or two for mixing nutrient solutions, an old dishpan for mixing soils, a couple of forks and a dented set of aluminum measuring spoons. But it didn't take long to understand that I had fallen into the trap of a false economy. Little by little, I equipped myself with tools that could save me time while improving the quality of my plants. Good equipment is not an "extra" expense; it pays for itself many times through the years.

Most growers enjoy being creative—it comes with the avocation. Some gardening activities, such as planting the forty-fifth row of lettuce, don't require much innovation. But choosing, installing and inventing equipment for the small greenhouse provides wide scope for invention. You are likely to discover that some of the tools that would make your greenhouse more efficient aren't available. The market has not yet caught up with the needs of the small greenhouse. Even in those instances where it has, you may prefer to custom-build equipment anyway.

Equipment should suit the crops, the climate, the greenhouse type and the grower's needs. For example, expensive drip irrigation systems may be unnecessary for most greenhouse gardeners. However, if you live in an arid region, grow ornamentals in small pots and are frequently away for several days at a time, you would probably consider drip irrigation essential. Each greenhouse situation should be handled individually.

For good ideas about equipment, visit other greenhouse growers in your area. Many small growers have developed practical systems, but even large commercial greenhouses are fitted with accessories that can be modified or scaled down. And it's never difficult to start a conversation about equipment; most growers remain fascinated with the topic. After all, there's always a better tool or technique just waiting to be discovered.

Watering Systems

Handwatering is practical for home greenhouses. By "handwatering" I don't mean a watering can and the kitchen sink, however. Running back and forth gives you a lot of exercise, but you'll end up cursing the job. It's also likely that none of the beds will be watered thoroughly enough at one time. Repeated partial watering is disastrous; excess salts are never washed out of the soil medium and can accumulate until they reach toxic levels.

Watering cans are a mixed blessing. Only the best are fitted with good nozzles and well balanced enough so you can easily control the flow. The nozzle, or rose, should break the water into many fine, small streams. But no rose is gentle enough for tender seedlings. Once a seedling has been knocked over, its stem is bruised, allowing disease organisms to penetrate the cuticle. Protect your seedlings from an untimely death by using watering cans only for sturdy, mature plants.

A good watering system should be easy to use and gentle to the plants. Most people install hose systems because they are practical and relatively inexpensive. The best systems carry warm water, reach every area, and can be fitted with a variety of nozzles for different uses.

Water temperature should range between 65 and 90°F. At these temperatures, water feels cool to lukewarm. For plants, water temperature is critical. Roots take in more moisture when they are warm; cool water lowers the soil temperature, and thus water absorption. During the winter and early spring, water from the cold tap can drop to as low as 35°F. If you add it to the soil, roots cool and plant growth is slowed. Tender plants and seedlings may be permanently damaged by cold irrigation.

Few gardeners can afford to install a separate water heater. Those with attached greenhouses have the luxury of choosing to lead both hot- and cold-water pipes from the main system into the greenhouse or to fit the nearest spigot with an attachment that accepts a hose.

Freestanding greenhouses can present real problems with water temperature. If the greenhouse is used only during the spring, summer and fall months, a hose can be led to the greenhouse from the nearest outside spigot on the house. But this system can be time-consuming, especially in the spring. On cold nights you must drain the hose and store it in a warm place to keep it from freezing and cracking. In the morning it's best to preheat water for tender seedlings by filling the hose and letting it sit in the sun for a few hours before watering time.

Few of us have the patience or the time to be so fastidious. Instead, we are likely to use the water at whatever temperature it comes out of the hose. Most plants survive under this regimen, but young seedlings should be watered separately. Fill a couple of buckets and let them sit for a day in the greenhouse to warm up. This extra attention will be

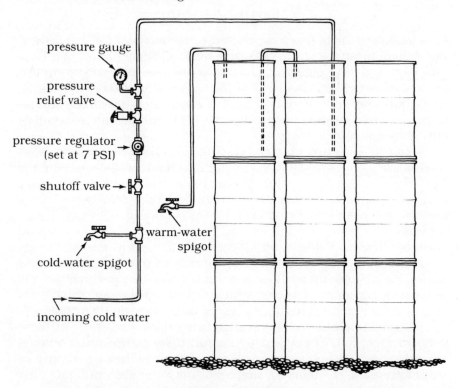

pressure gauge

pressure
relief valve

pressure regulator
(set at 7 PSI)

shutoff valve →

cold-water spigot

warm-water
spigot

incoming cold water

Economical Way to Heat Water Year-Round: *This variation on the heating system developed for the NCAT greenhouse will provide enough warm water to tend the plants in a 288-square-foot greenhouse. Here the top left and center barrels that form the system are supported by other water barrels used for heat storage. Cold water piped into the top center barrel will rise as it's warmed by the sun, and move into the top left barrel, where it's ready to draw from the spigot.*

repaid by the increased health of your seedlings.

A year-round freestanding greenhouse must have a year-round supply of water. An ingenious low-cost system for providing warm water was developed by Andy Shapiro and Ron Alward when they were designing an experimental solar greenhouse for the National Center for Appropriate Technology (NCAT) in Butte, Montana. They built a sturdy platform near the top of the greenhouse and placed four 55-gallon water drums on it. Piping from the faucet below fed cold water into the first barrel. Small pipes connected each barrel to the next. Water was drawn off from the last barrel in the system. Because the barrels were about 9 feet above the floor, gravity exerted enough force to keep the water pressure reasonably high.

The principle behind this system is simple. As the water in each barrel heats in the sun, it rises. Still seeking to rise, it then moves into the pipe connecting it to the next barrel. As water moves along the series of barrels, it becomes increasingly warmer. The large volume of water storage allowed this system to work equally well during cloudy and sunny weather. The 450-square-foot greenhouse required approximately 10 to 15 gallons of water at each irrigation; the barrels gave adequate year-round supplies at an average temperature of 75°F. If you try this system in your own greenhouse, be sure the barrels don't contain potentially injurious residues. And, to be entirely certain that the system is safe, install a pressure indicator as shown in the accompanying illustration.

Nozzles

Nozzles are one of the best investments a greenhouse grower can make. Every grower should have three nozzles: a spray gun, a water breaker and a Fogg-It. A rigid, curved extension rod and a shutoff valve between the hose and nozzle can also make watering easier.

Buy sturdy brass or steel nozzles from greenhouse equipment suppliers. The aluminum and plastic versions sold in some hardware stores are only fractionally less expensive, but break so easily you'll end up spending more by replacing them. Unfortunately, the only extension rods on the market are aluminum. They bend easily, so store them carefully to prolong their usefulness.

Keep all nozzles in a clean, dry area and wash them periodically in a 10 percent solution of laundry bleach. Under normal circumstances, sterilize nozzles, attachments and the metal fitting on the end of the hose every week or so. When you know that disease organisms are in the greenhouse, sterilize watering equipment before and after every use. It takes only a moment to dump them in a bucket, swish them around and rinse them off in clear water.

A standard spray-gun nozzle delivers a very hard spray that is really too rough for watering plants. Instead, use it to wash the glazing and interior surfaces of the greenhouse. The spray is hard enough to help mix nutrients into solution, and can also be used to wash off aphids or spider mites from *mature* foliage. Don't just turn the hose on a plant; support each leaf by holding it against your hand while you spray.

Water breakers have a large flat surface perforated with about 400 holes, which break up the water into a gentle stream. This nozzle is well suited for most watering jobs. Although gentle, water breakers deliver quite a bit of water at once. I don't use them on tender seedlings. Wait until plants are sturdy before watering with these nozzles. Water breakers work best with beds and potted plants.

Fogg-It nozzles deliver a very fine mist gentle enough for seedlings and newly planted flats. If you need to add humidity to the greenhouse air, this is the nozzle to use. Three versions—regular, fine and super-fine—are available. I have used both the regular and the fine and have found very little difference between them.

Seedling nozzles are also available. Their spray pattern is like a donut, empty in the center, but they deliver more water than a Fogg-It. Some people must like this nozzle, but I find the spray pattern disconcerting. I would much rather use a Fogg-It nozzle on my young plants, even if it takes a bit longer to water them.

Watering Accessories

Fertilizers are sometimes sprayed directly onto the leaves of a plant. This practice, called foliar feeding, can be done with a hand-held plastic mister when only a few plants are to be fed. However, when the greenhouse is full of seedlings or when foliar feeding is an essential part of the fertilizing program for a mature crop, a manually compressed air sprayer makes the job easier. These sprayers are called "manual" because you pump a plunger until interior pressure builds enough to deliver a steady misting stream.

Greenhouse and garden suppliers sell compressed-air sprayers that hold 1½ gallons of liquid. The end of the narrow hose is fitted with a misting attachment that is appropriate for all soluble nutrients. However, if you use materials such as Epsom salts or Sul-Po-Mag (a ground rock used as a fertilizer), the nozzle may clog. Prevention is the best remedy; don't add anything to the tank unless it's completely dissolved. Add questionable materials through a sieve lined with several layers of cheesecloth or a paper coffee filter. If the nozzle does clog, remove it and flush under a hard stream of water. I use a compressed-air sprayer for foliar feeding outside the greenhouse, too. It's easy to carry to a crop of young seedlings in a cold frame or even in the field.

A proportioner is a small gadget fitted to a water outlet, which mixes a certain proportion of liquid fertilizer into the water stream. Proportioners are quite expensive, but a device called a Hozon does the same thing and costs less than five dollars. The Hozon draws liquid from a bucket placed below the faucet and mixes it at a predetermined rate with the water stream. Coupled with a Fogg-It nozzle, you can also use a Hozon for foliar feeding.

Automated Systems

Watering systems in large greenhouses are often automated, simply because there are so many plants to water. In arid climates or when the home grower is too busy to water plants, these systems can be

useful in smaller greenhouses. Soaker hoses, spaghetti tubes and moisturizing mats are all options that may be appropriate. But don't make
an investment in automated watering equipment without doing a very
thorough investigation of the systems installed by other growers in
your area. In most cases a good medium in a deep bed will retain enough
moisture so that mature plants don't need fancy equipment. Small
homemade water-retention devices such as pebble trays are easy to use
and will generally take care of problems during the seedling period
when roots are small. Perhaps the only people who should seriously
consider going to the expense of installing an automated watering
system are those who are away from the greenhouse for days at a time.

Soaker hoses are laid along the soil surface between rows of plants.
Water gradually seeps out of the hose, keeping the medium constantly
moist. Traditionally, soaker hoses were made of a single layer of water-
permeable canvas. The newer plastic or rubber ones are constructed
with a single or double perforated wall. The double-walled hose is generally a better-quality product.

Soaker hoses must be used with some care; it's easy to overwater
a bed in a windless environment. With the exception of greenhouses
in extremely arid locations, the most sensible way to use a soaker hose
is for germinating very small seeds in beds. However, it's much easier
to drape a sheet of clear plastic over a newly seeded bed and mist the
medium as required.

Spaghetti tubes are probably the most common watering system
in commercial greenhouses. Skinny, spaghetti-sized tubes lead from
a main, or header, pipe to individual pots. Commercial growers like
spaghetti tubes because they save so dramatically on labor costs. Soluble nutrients can be fed at a consistent rate, and a turn of a dial can
take account of changing weather conditions. However, the best plants
are not mass-produced; an observant waterer always does a better job
than an automated system. Again, consider spaghetti tubes only if you
are forced to be away from the greenhouse at crucial times or if you
are moving up to commercial production and can no longer take the
time to handwater your plants.

Moisturizing mats water pots and flats from below by capillary, or
wicking, action. A regulated water supply coming from the greenhouse
hose system keeps the mats uniformly moist and increases humidity
levels around the plants. This system is wonderful for starting seedlings
or rooting cuttings. Cuttings require extra humidity levels to protect
them from excessive transpiration while they are forming roots. A mat
measuring 3 feet by 150 feet costs about 50 dollars, but few home
gardeners need such an extensive rooting or seed starting area.

Fortunately, it's easy to make an inexpensive facsimile of a moisturizing mat, which some people call a pebble tray. Fill a large tray
with gravel, place pots on the gravel and fill the tray with just enough

water so that the bottoms of the pots are only slightly submerged. If you want to increase humidity without adding moisture to the growing medium, see that the water level is slightly below the pot bottoms. In either case, drape a plastic sheet over the pots to create an area of high humidity. The plastic will interfere with normal air-circulation patterns, so you may need to vent this enclosure during the sunny part of the day to keep temperatures within tolerable ranges. Don't seal the bottom edges of the plastic; you'll need to lift them for venting. Small holes along the top surface can increase air circulation just as they do in the greenhouse itself. Even when vented, humidity levels within this enclosure should be high enough to protect tender cuttings or germinating seeds.

Equipment for Air Circulation

Air circulation in even the best-designed greenhouses is rarely adequate during some seasons of the year. Both passive ventilation and exhaust fans keep a minimum amount of air moving, but both rely on pulling outside air through the greenhouse. When the outside air is too cool to introduce, growers may still need to keep interior air moving. Good air circulation protects plants from fungal diseases and also conserves heating energy by preventing stratification of hot air near the ridge.

Fans are a practical way to move interior air. You can arrange small oscillating fans so they move the air at plant level to disperse humidity from around the leaves. To destratify interior air, suspend a fan from a central position along the greenhouse ridge. Hang it so that hot air collected at the peak is blown back down onto the plants. Make certain that the suspension wires are strong enough to withstand the vibration of the fan. Like other electrical appliances, fans should never get wet. Protect overhead fans from dripping condensates by making a plastic or metal shield to cover the motor.

It's unlikely that you'll need to use the ridge fan and plant-level fans simultaneously. Properly set up, the ridge fan should take care of air circulation during the sunniest parts of cold days when stratification occurs. The fans at plant level are used during humid or hot periods when plants are in danger of contracting fungus diseases or suffering from the heat.

You'll find that interior blowers make good destratifying devices. They can move a large volume of air, but they differ from oscillating fans in that the outgoing airstream flows in only one direction. You can suspend a blower from the greenhouse ridge and fit it with a polyethylene tube to direct the warm air back onto the plant canopy. Perforated polyethylene tubes are available from greenhouse suppliers,

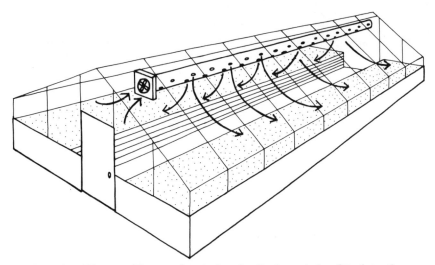

Interior Blower: The perforated polyethylene tube fitted to the blower in this greenhouse directs warm air back onto the plant canopy. For support, the tube must be suspended with wires along the ridge or sidewalls.

but if you require only a short length, you can make your own. Just tape a 1- to 2-foot width of 4- to 6-mil polyethylene together with polyethylene tape. Then cut 3- to 4-inch-diameter holes at intervals of about a foot along the length. Tape the far end shut and seal the tube to the blower with polyethylene tape. Suspend the tube with wires along the greenhouse ridge or the sidewalls. The air pressure from the blower will direct air all along the length of the tube.

In the same NCAT experimental solar greenhouse with water barrel heat storage mentioned earlier, researchers ran a homemade tube behind the second level of barrels on the north wall, placing perforations in the spaces between barrels. This not only increased the air circulation at plant level, but it also added some heat to the barrels.

Propagating Equipment

You may never need anything more elaborate than a couple of flats, a roll of plastic wrap and some soil medium to propagate your greenhouse plants. Most vegetable crops grow so easily that almost anything else is overkill. But propagating equipment is valuable for rooting or germinating fussy ornamentals and when you're starting vegetable plants well before the greenhouse has warmed in the spring.

Soil Heating Cables

Seeds are perverse about temperature requirements. They germinate most easily when the soil around them is about 10°F higher than the air temperature preferred by the mature plants. They will sprout at lower temperatures, of course, but seeds always germinate the fastest in a warm starting medium.

For many years my house was decorated each spring with rows of germinating flats on every radiator or heat register. When I had a furnace room, it held piles of flats and trays of pots. When I moved up in the world and had wood heat, I set the flats around the stove. My daily routine included watering trips to every propagating area and hasty rearrangements as seeds sprouted and needed light. Each time one flat showed green, I seeded another and moved it into place.

No matter how many times I go through this springtime ritual, it's always surprising to me how many plants can be produced in a small, warm area over several months of diligent care and constant rearrangements. If you don't mind water dripping on the floor, inquisitive babies and cats pose the only problems with this sort of germinating system. Flats are irresistible playgrounds and litter boxes. After a good many frustrating springs spent guarding my plants, I made a wise investment: heating cables. These cables and the new plastic heating mats work as well as the best of radiators and have the added advantage of being portable. Seeds can be germinated well away from all of the small creatures in your house.

Heating cables are plastic-clad wires that carry electrical heat. Most are thermostatically controlled. Cables can be used directly under flats or buried in a soil mix. If you use a cable directly under flats, arrange it in a serpentine pattern, leaving about 4 inches between the loops. Put a metal tray without drainage holes over the cable and use this to hold the flats or pots. Watch the soil temperatures in the flats; it's easy to kill some germinating plants if temperatures exceed 90°F. Most seeds germinate well when the thermostat is set at 70 to 75°F. Cucurbits and some tropical ornamentals prefer warmer temperatures of 80 to 85°F.

If you choose to bury the cable, lay it out on a growing bed as described before. Cover it with about an inch or two of soil medium. To avoid problems when it comes time to transplant, seed in flats or pots rather than directly in the warmed soil. Burying the cable helps to protect the plants against overheating because the surrounding soil absorbs some of the heat.

Propagating mats are plastic mats that are heated throughout their surface. They, too, are thermostatically controlled. In my opinion, they're too expensive to use in a home greenhouse because even the smallest one is larger than most people need at any one time.

One of the best new greenhouse technologies is a semirigid plastic mat with copper wires running through it. Unlike traditional propagating mats, these can be sized to suit your area. You can set pots directly on this mat without fear of injuring it or overheating the growing medium. A choice of several different heating configurations is available. Some mats are banded with continuous wires to heat flats uniformly, while others have heating elements at 3-inch intervals so that pots can be heated economically. These plastic mats are inexpensive to buy and cost less to use than traditional heating cables or propagating mats. You shouldn't have any trouble finding them because most greenhouse suppliers are stocking these mats.

Artificial Lights

Artificial lights aren't generally thought of as propagating equipment. However, considering the way they're used by most gardeners, they certainly fit into that category. Fluorescent lights promote good seedling growth at any time of the year, either by themselves or in combination with other propagating equipment. They have the added advantage of stretching the greenhouse area. If it's too cold to start plants inside the greenhouse, you can set up lights in a warm spot in your house. Once the plants are well established, you can move them into the cooler greenhouse environment.

When you're growing plants under lights, fluorescent, rather than incandescent, lighting is mandatory. Incandescent bulbs don't give off enough of the red and blue portions of the light spectrum required for good growth. They do add heat, however, so you can use them in conjunction with fluorescent lights for that purpose.

Seedlings and leafy green crops do well under cool white fluorescents in combination with warm white or daylight tubes. Fruiting and flowering plants need more light waves at each end of the spectrum. "Plant lights" are fluorescent tubes that emit a wide light spectrum. Although more expensive than fluorescent tubes used for general lighting, they're absolutely necessary if you're growing mature fruiting or flowering plants under artificial light.

Fluorescent tubes degenerate over time, and become less effective at promoting good plant growth. Don't use the same ones for more than a season of daily illumination. If you don't have other fluorescent fixtures around the home, give the used tubes to a school or other institution. The bulbs will still provide many hours of lighting.

Some greenhouse growers use high-intensity lamps for supplemental lighting. These lamps have some very attractive features: they have moisture-resistant fixtures, last 20 to 50 percent longer than fluorescent tubes and take half the wattage to produce the same light.

However, high-intensity lamps do produce heat, and they require special wiring, fixtures and switching equipment. I can't make any personal observations on how these perform since I've never had occasion to use them.

Garden supply houses sell fancy, and expensive, plant light fixtures and shelves. If those seem beyond the scope of your budget, inexpensive fixtures are available from electrical supply houses. Contractors who raze or renovate old buildings may have them for sale. Look for 4-foot fixtures fitted for at least two 40-watt bulbs.

Artificial lights won't do much good if the plants are set too far away from them. Keep plant tips approximately 5 inches from the bulbs for the entire time that they're growing under artificial light. Mount either the light fixtures or the plant supports so they are easy to adjust as the plants grow.

Extending Daylength

Artificial lights aren't used only to increase light intensity; they can also prolong a short photoperiod. Even when seedlings and cuttings are strategically placed to receive maximum sunlight during winter days, they may need additional time under lights. For example, in northern Vermont we have good midwinter light from about 8:00 A.M. until almost 4:00 P.M. That means our photoperiod is only eight hours long. Seedlings of many plants, especially perennial ornamentals that must be started early in the season, require more than eight hours of light.

Artificial lights and an automatic timer solve the problem. Use the timer to turn on the lights as the natural light fades and to turn them off after the required illumination period. In my greenhouse, lights for most crops are set to switch on at 4:00 P.M. and run until 8:00 or 9:30 P.M. Farther south, where the natural photoperiod is longer during the winter, lights don't need to be on until later in the afternoon. Set your timer according to the photoperiod in your area.

Some people make the mistake of thinking that if a little light is a good thing, constant illumination would be even better. Photoperiods longer than 12 to 16 hours weaken many plants. To make sure you don't overdo it, refer to the recommended photoperiods for specific plants given in chapters 13, 14 and 15.

Few people grow fruiting plants during the winter because of heating and lighting costs. If you decide to try it, remember that mature fruiting crops grown in cloudy areas during low-light seasons should be illuminated both during the day and early evening. High-intensity plant light bulbs can be permanently installed from the rafters. Suspend fluorescent fixtures with a strong, movable pulley system so you can easily adjust them to the correct height above the plants.

Propagating Enclosures

Propagating enclosures are little plastic houses fitted with an automatic misting system. These enclosures are normally placed over a greenhouse bench so that interior light levels will be high. As you might expect, manufactured propagating enclosures are quite expensive because of the automatic misting system. If you root large numbers of ornamentals for sale, these enclosures pay their own way in healthier plants. But it certainly isn't necessary to buy a propagating enclosure. With a little know-how you can make one yourself.

Make a 2-foot-high wooden frame to fit over one of the greenhouse beds or benches, hinging one of the long sides. Tack and tape clear 4- to 6-mil polyethylene over the frame, making certain to use a separate piece for the movable side. This side provides ventilation when it is

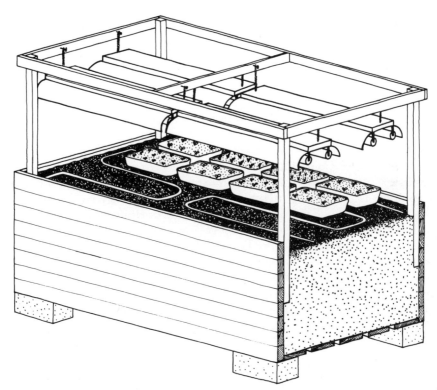

Propagating Enclosure: *Build a frame to cover a bed, fit it with fluorescent lights, install a heating cable and you're all set to start seeds or root cuttings. Although it's not shown here, a sheet of polyethylene large enough to cover the frame will retain beneficial humidity levels and still be easy to vent.*

opened and also allows easy access to flats and pots. Slow, steady ventilation can be provided by small holes punched near the top and bottom of the sidewalls. If you'll be using the area for rooting difficult cuttings, you can install a misting system. Greenhouse suppliers carry a number of suitable automated misters, or you can make your own with a misting nozzle on a short length of hose. No matter whether you use a commercial or homemade mister, you'll need to connect it to a timer.

If you're using a propagating enclosure for rooting cuttings, you must maintain high humidity levels when the enclosure is placed in bright light. Cuttings don't have roots, so high light stimulates them to release more water through transpiration than they can acquire through their stems. Rooting proceeds quickly in bright light because the plants can photosynthesize nutrients at a rapid rate. But without high humidity, the plants may die from lack of moisture.

A misting system is rarely necessary. Most plants root successfully in a rooting medium placed on a gravel tray filled with water. The high temperatures inside the enclosure guarantee that the water will evaporate quickly, keeping the area humid. When you use this setup, guard against diseases by sterilizing the tray and gravel between each new group of cuttings. If you're unable to keep the humidity high inside the enclosure, place it in moderate shade or drape cheesecloth over it during the sunniest parts of the day.

Carbon dioxide (CO_2) levels should be high for good rooting. There's an easy trick you can use to increase CO_2 within a small area. Set small custard dishes filled with water, a tablespoon of baker's yeast and a pinch of sugar (food for the yeast) inside the enclosure. The yeast releases CO_2 as it grows. Remove the dish after the mixture has stopped bubbling. The yeast organisms have died and will begin to decompose.

In northern Vermont as well as other northern areas, a second kind of propagating enclosure is very often needed in the early spring. Spring in this climate is often nothing more than a date on the calendar and a state of mind. It's not unusual to start seeds when the outside temperature is hovering near zero and the sun is obscured, day after day, by miles of opalescent clouds. A greenhouse can be entirely too cool for any self-respecting tomato seed.

The most practical solution to this problem is a heated and well-lit area. Many people build a freestanding set of shelves similar to a bookcase that's sturdy enough to support fluorescent lights attached to the underside of each shelf. They attach a timer to the lights to regulate the photoperiod and set a small, thermostatically controlled electric heater under the shelves to add heat. A sheet of polyethylene completes the structure; it helps to retain both heat and humidity. Dishes of yeast can add CO_2 to this enclosure, too.

Temporary Propagating Area: *It may not be elegant, but it works. Build a set of freestanding shelves wide enough to accommodate lots of seedlings. Attach fluorescent lights to the undersides of the shelves, put an electric heater below and drape the whole thing with a polyethylene cover.*

Plant Supports

Inside a greenhouse, you must provide vertical support for tall and vining crops, otherwise they'll take over the whole area. Disease resistance is also increased when plants are trained upward and held where each leaf can "see" light and benefit from good air circulation. But conventional garden stakes just don't work in a shallow greenhouse bed filled with a light soil mix. Instead, most gardeners use a modified trellis, an overhead wooden framework or a cable and string arrangement.

Wooden or wire trellises are often bolted to the side of wooden beds or to an adjacent opaque wall. These supports can be set up or removed as necessary. But they support only those crops grown at the edge of the bed. Another drawback is that fruit can be injured if it presses against wire as it grows. To avoid this, place several layers of soft material between each developing fruit and any adjacent wire.

You can custom-build overhead wooden frameworks to fit your beds. To give them a firm foundation, bolt frames to the bed by their side supports. Lengths of twine hung from each of the overhead pieces serve as plant supports. Properly built, this system is quite strong. However, depending upon light levels and location within the greenhouse, an overhead framework may shade the growing area. (The same is true with trellises.)

In my opinion, cables provide the best support system. They're quite strong, completely versatile, and don't shade the crops. You should install cables as part of the interior finishing details. Securely attach heavy eye screws to the side glazing bars or walls and to each of the glazing bars along the length of the greenhouse. Space the eye screws

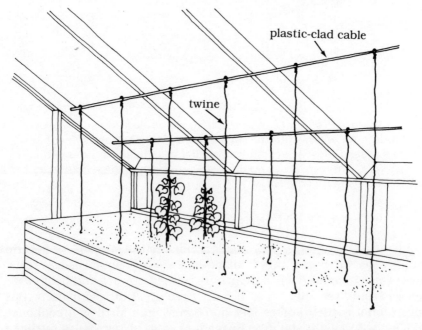

Cable Trellis: *Take advantage of vertical space by installing a trellis system for vining crops. Run plastic-clad cables above growing beds, and loop pieces of twine over the cables to provide support for upwardly mobile plants.*

so that plastic-clad wire cables can be strung at 12- to 18-inch intervals over each bed or area where you'll be growing vining crops. If there's an area where you plan to grow only cucumbers, space the cables more widely to accommodate the greater area needed between rows. (See Cucumbers in chapter 13 for more specific spacing directions.)

At the beginning of the season, tie or loop pieces of strong twine over the overhead cable and let one piece dangle over each stem that will require support. As the plants grow, you'll wind the stems in a clockwise direction, around the twine. More detailed instructions for training vining plants are given in chapter 13. Dispose of the twine at the end of each growing season to avoid spreading old diseases to new crops.

Screens

Greenhouse screens are controversial. Some people are violently opposed to them, while others wouldn't build a greenhouse without them. Screens prevent insects, slugs, rodents and even cats from migrating into the greenhouse from the great outdoors. Those people who do not screen vent and door openings have experienced valuable invasions of pest predators and parasites, along with the migration of less desirable insects. They argue that balanced pest and pest-control populations are easier to achieve if insects can have ready access to the greenhouse. Advocates of screens are equally convinced that they are right; it is easier, they say, to control insect activity in a screened facility. My opinion? I would not come to blows over the subject of screens, but I admit to having strong prejudices. I use screens in all greenhouses except freestanding spring seedling areas.

Screens are helpful in attached greenhouses and in any that are used year-round. If beneficial flying insects such as lady beetles or wasps are a crucial component of the pest-control program, screens will keep them in the greenhouse. Given the choice, beneficials are likely to decide that the aphids browsing on the lamb's-quarters outside are more appetizing than the weak specimens available in your greenhouse. Enslavement may be the most practical course.

Screens also keep problems on the outside. One morning I watched an army of slugs relentlessly crawling up the kneewalls of a friend's greenhouse. Only two of the vent openings were screened. We posted ourselves over the open vents and gingerly grabbed every invading slug as it crested the sill. It goes without saying that each of these marauders was dumped into the proverbial can of water topped with a film of gasoline. By lunchtime the invasion was stemmed, but we had completely lost our appetites. The afternoon was devoted to building vent screens.

And then there are larger visitors—namely mice and cats. Mother mice devote themselves to providing their children with a warm habitat close to a nutritious food source. They may summer outside, but in the fall they scurry inside again. Mice are quite intelligent; they realize that a mixed crop of seedlings or winter greens will sustain them through unseasonable times. Screens are certainly more effective than mouse poison. Cats aren't interested in finding a winter home or eating your crops (aside from uninvited mice), but they do appreciate the pseudo–litter box and sunning facilities they find in greenhouses. Again, screens will prevent disruptive visits from neighborhood felines.

Greenhouses used only to start spring transplants don't really need screens. The season is still cool enough through most of this period so that aphids and whiteflies remain dormant. Active pests are content to feed on winter host plants. But when the weather warms enough to transplant tomatoes and cucurbits, aphid populations look for summer hosts. That's the point when they usually invade the greenhouse. Diligent mechanical or insecticidal control measures will keep populations low enough to prevent serious damage. And you'll be pleasantly surprised to see that indigenous predators and parasites such as syrphid flies, lacewings and predatory wasps follow the aphids into the greenhouse.

Small Tools and Supplies

You won't need a rake or a hoe in the greenhouse, but you will need some small tools. Most of these can come from your kitchen or the hardware store. The following is a list of the items I use most frequently:

- Dibble sticks or pencils
- Hand cultivator
- Labels and waterproof pencils or pens
- Large and small spoons
- Plastic film or wrap
- Pots and flats
- Quart misting container
- Scissors and paring knives
- Table forks
- Tools for greenhouse maintenance: screwdrivers, hammer, caulk, caulking gun, polyethylene tape, nails, screws, bolts
- Trowels
- Twine and twistie ties or strips of old cloth

❧ CHAPTER 5 ❧
UNDERSTANDING SOIL

Greenhouse growing media are made by combining soil and various materials in "ideal" proportions. Once you know what you're doing, you've got amazing control. If a plant requires slightly alkaline conditions, for example, it's easy to add extra lime or bone meal to its pot. You can increase specific nutrients as the need arises. Drainage is rarely a persistent problem because you can fine-tune the amount of water-retaining materials. This extraordinary control is one of the factors that makes greenhouse gardening easier than outdoor gardening.

But greenhouse growing media also present special problems. The lack of subsoil in combination with constantly warm temperatures, top-watering and intensive cropping means that nutrients are used and washed away more quickly than they would be in the garden. To make up for this, fertilizers are added. But too much fertilization is as bad as too little: excess fertilizer salts can accumulate and injure roots.

Recipes for growing media are widely available. Most of them work quite well at first, but you run into problems by expecting a mix to stay the same for very long. All growing media, even those in a greenhouse, are dynamic: materials change and must be adjusted periodically. It's common to add some nutrients throughout a growing season and then test and remix beds at every major crop change.

Some people get by without knowing very much about soil types, soil amendments or nutrient requirements. But ignorance can be frustrating. If you don't know what factors to regulate, you might be tempted to throw out a whole growing mix, when adding specific amendments would be just as effective. As with anything else, understanding leads to greater control, efficiency and pleasure. Since soil is the backbone of greenhouse growing mixes, we'll examine its relevant characteristics. Directions for making growing mixes are given in the following chapter.

Soil Composition

Good topsoil contains approximately 45 percent inorganic minerals, 20 to 30 percent air, 20 to 30 percent water and 5 to 8 percent organic matter. The inorganic minerals are rock particles that have been broken down mechanically and chemically into tiny fragments. Wind, water, temperature fluctuations and growing roots literally wear rocks down, while by-products from plants and animals are responsible for chemical breakdown. Organic matter comes from dead plants and animals that have been decomposed by microorganisms and soil animals such as earthworms and nematodes. Soil characteristics are determined by the interaction of local climate, rocks, plant and animal matter and, of course, agricultural practices.

Soil Texture

Soil texture influences the availability of air, water and nutrients to all soil life. The ratio of the solid portions of soil—sand, silt, clay and organic matter—determines its texture. Sand is made of relatively large rock particles, silt is characterized by somewhat smaller particles and clay by even smaller, flattened ones.

Sand particles don't attract water, and so give soil a porous quality. Even when watered well, sandy soils don't retain moisture for long. Clay soils are heavy and have poor drainage because clay particles attract water. Their size and shape also inhibit air from entering soil where they are dominant. Although their problems are different, both sandy and clay soils benefit from the same treatment: the addition of organic matter. Microorganisms, soil animals and even plant roots excrete sticky gums that bind tiny soil particles together into irregular formations called aggregates. Spaces between these aggregates hold both air and water, improving structure.

Most soils are made up of all three kinds of rock particles. For container growing, the "ideal" soil type is a loam composed of 40 percent sand, 40 percent silt and 20 percent clay. But few people are fortunate enough to have a steady supply of loam. Growers must learn to identify soil types to amend them correctly.

A few simple tests reveal a great deal about soil type. Take some moistened soil in your hands and try to shape it into a ball. If it crumbles and won't form a ball, the soil is too sandy. If you see a shiny film on your fingers, adequate silt is present. Rub a thumb across the ball; if it polishes slightly, there's enough clay present for good soil texture. Little tracks across the polished surface indicate sand, but if the ball polishes very easily and shows few sand tracks, there may be too much clay. Next, roll the soil between your hands to make a "worm." If you can bend the worm into a circle, the clay content is definitely too high. Now form it into a ball again and hold the ball in the palm of one hand and hit it sharply with the edge of the other. If the soil flies apart in all directions, the texture is good. Even a predominately clay soil with adequate levels of organic matter reacts this way. A clay soil that's short on organic matter won't fracture—it just dents. And a soil that's far too sandy won't make a ball.

Microorganisms

The most effective way to sustain and improve soils, whether in the field or in the greenhouse, is by creating conditions in which soil microorganisms prosper. Bacteria, actinomycetes, fungi, algae and viruses are all vital parts of the soil system. Each provides nutrients to other plants or animals. Some decompose complex organic materials and convert them into usable forms while others capture gaseous nitrogen and make it available to plants. Aggregates formed by sticky exudates increase a soil's capacity to hold water, air and nutrients. Microbes' home is the topsoil, where organic materials are deposited. Roots exude substances they need, so microorganisms are most numerous in the area surrounding plant roots.

Microbial populations and levels of activity are governed by several factors: types of available organic matter, the availability of water and air, soil temperature and acidity. If their minimum requirements aren't met microorganisms either die or go into a dormant phase.

Each species of microorganism has its own niche, attacking specific types of organic material and providing different by-products. Organic matter can be roughly divided into four primary materials: carbohydrates, proteins, cellulose and lignin. Decomposition proceeds in that order, too: carbohydrates first, lignins last. The end product of thorough decomposition is a relatively stable material called humus, the dark, crumbly, earthy-smelling stuff you find in a well-aged compost pile. Humus decays, too, but much more slowly than raw organic matter.

Microbes That Specialize

Some bacteria are "decomposers." They release enzymes that chemically decompose particular organic materials. The bacteria then absorb and metabolize by-products of that process. Once the first decomposer dies, other organisms can use the changed compounds.

Other bacteria consume atmospheric nitrogen, changing it into organic nitrogen within their bodies. There are two broad classifications of nitrogen-fixers. **Symbiotic** bacteria form colonies on the roots of legumes, such as peas and clover. The nitrogen they fix moves directly into root cells. Other nitrogen-fixers are called **free-living** because they don't have a particular plant association. Free-living nitrogen-fixers include some fungi and actinomycetes as well as bacterial species. After these nitrogen-fixers die, a series of microorganisms change their nitrogen compounds into forms that can be used by plants: nitrites and, to a much greater extent, nitrates. In very wet conditions, some bacteria also convert nitrates back into atmospheric nitrogen.

Actinomycetes are extremely numerous in a good soil. The characteristic "soil" smell is actually the smell of actinomycetes. If you make compost, you've probably seen them—huge gray-colored colonies that form in bands about a foot under the surface where it's only moderately warm. Actinomycetes attack some cellulose and lignin after bacteria have worked on more easily digested materials.

But actinomycetes don't decompose all of the tough cellulose and lignin. They're followed by different types of fungi. Fungi are extremely diverse; they're part of a big family with lots of strange relatives. Some tolerate very acid conditions and concentrate on decomposing tree leaves and old wood. Others prefer more succulent fare and cause damping-off and other plant diseases. To combat destructive fungi, some growers apply fungicides to their soil. These chemicals are *too* powerful. Not only do they kill harmful fungi, but they also kill beneficial species.

Mycorrhizae are fungi that grow adjacent to or directly inside specific plant roots. They live symbiotically with the plant, absorbing some manufactured nutrients while supplying minerals such as phosphorus and magnesium. Plants are healthier when substantial mycorrhizal populations are present. By keeping the soil slightly acid (a pH of 6.5) and adding compost to it, you'll encourage mycorrhizal growth. In the near future, it may even be possible to buy specific species to add to the soil. Researchers are working to culture mycorrhizae in laboratory conditions with an eye to selling them in premixed starting soils.

Algae are plants rather than animals. Certain species are able to produce chlorophyll. You often see colonies of these chlorophyll-producing algae on the surface of very wet soil or on growing media with a high percentage of perlite. Some species are blue-green algae that derive a portion of their nutrients by fixing atmospheric nitrogen. Other algae live under the soil surface, feeding upon both living and dead material. Like all other forms of life, algae provide food for other organisms.

Viruses feed on living organisms. Nasty as they seem when you're the host, viruses keep other microbial populations in check. Every time they eat something, nutrients are recycled.

Encouraging Soil Life

All agricultural systems, except totally sterile hydroponics, are dependent upon microorganisms. Even when chemical nutrients are used, soil life must be encouraged. Without it, a soil "dies" and loses the capacity to hold water, air or nutrients. Organic systems are particularly dependent upon soil life, of course, because they rely on natural decomposition and conversion of both organic and inorganic materials. But this reliance provides some security for a grower; counting on soil life for good nutrient balance and availability is much safer than adding dribs and drabs of chemical fertilizers. Instantly soluble nutrients make it too easy to overdose or throw a soil out of balance. Using chemicals makes me nervous. I'm always worried that my soil test or my math isn't quite right. It's much easier to be an organic grower. Microbial decomposition may take awhile, but it gives more latitude for error.

Fortunately, it isn't hard to "grow" a good-sized population of soil microorganisms; if you can grow a head of lettuce, you can certainly grow bacteria. Adding compost or aged manure to the medium assures a good "seed" population. Keeping microorganisms flourishing is just a matter of maintaining good growing conditions and adding compost or aged manure periodically.

Soil Animals

Soil animals also contribute to soil health. Out of all the hundreds and thousands of creeping, crawling things living in the soil, growers are primarily concerned with nematodes, earthworms and a few insects. All of these play an important role in the overall health of plants.

Nematodes

Nematodes are microscopic, nonsegmented worms. Some feed on decaying organic matter, some on microorganisms (including other nematode species) and a few feed on plants. The last group is the one you've probably heard the most about. Even though they're the least numerous, injurious nematodes are the ones people notice. Unchecked, they can produce a substantial crop loss by infesting roots and robbing plant nutrients. Root-knot nematodes are one of the first problems you look for with an ailing tomato crop, for example. If infested, roots show small lumps, sites where the nematodes are colonizing and parasitizing. For more complete information on nematodes, and how to prevent and control them, see Nematodes in chapter 11.

Earthworms

Earthworms are some of the best friends a gardener can have. They eat both inorganic minerals and organic materials. After earthworms have metabolized the nutrients they need, by-products are mixed with inorganic minerals and enzymes and passed out in a form called castings. Castings contain concentrated levels of calcium, magnesium, potassium, phosphorus and balanced trace elements. As you can see, they are truly a superb fertilizer. In high-quality agricultural soils, as much as 16,000 pounds per acre of castings are deposited every year. Earthworms also bring subsoil and the minerals it contains to the surface, while building channels for air and water. To top off the list of their good works, earthworms produce copious amounts of gums, which help form good soil structure.

In some communities, earthworms are being used to decompose sewage sludge. They are efficient at this work, but researchers have discovered a curious side effect. Earthworms concentrate cadmium in their bodies. This heavy metal is toxic to most animals in any but trace amounts. When cadmium-laden earthworms die or are eaten by other animals, high cadmium concentrations are made available to the rest of the food chain. This research has relevance to those people who use sewage sludge as a fertilizer. Even if the cadmium level is quite low, earthworms shouldn't be used in the growing beds. They will accumulate the metal that might otherwise drain away into groundwater.

Even if you don't add earthworms to growing beds, there are legitimate concerns about the safety of using sewage sludge. When cadmium or any other heavy metal becomes available in high concentrations, plants often absorb too much. Lead, mercury and cadmium are all serious health hazards. The body accumulates these metals and is eventually injured in one way or another. In my opinion, only a few sludges are free enough of heavy metals to be used directly on food crops. Ideally, we should be removing these elements at the source rather than recycling them through treatment plants. But in lieu of that, most composted sludges should be used as fertilizers only on turfs or forested areas. As a society, we must learn to conserve this nutrient-rich resource without creating more hidden problems.

In the greenhouse, earthworms are a valuable addition to deep growing beds. You can add garden worms or buy red wrigglers from a commercial worm grower. Whatever the choice, worms need something to eat. Compost or aged manure in the mix is often sufficient, but organic mulches or mixtures of used coffee grounds, dry leaves and crushed eggshells supplement their diet. Place worm food at specific sites on the beds. I use hidden corners or back edges and lay it down no more than an inch or so deep to keep it tidy.

Every year or so, the population of earthworms in the beds may become too dense. Before worms die out from overcrowding, transfer some to the garden. To do this efficiently, wait until a crop change and then place shovelfuls of the growing mix on a smooth board under bright light. Wait a few minutes; soon you'll see the worms escaping from light by moving to the bottom of the pile. While keeping an eye out for small, oval, reddish to brownish egg cases, brush successive layers of the pile away. As you find them, place worms and egg cases into a bucket of cool, damp soil. Release the worms in a somewhat shaded area of the garden where they can quickly burrow into the soil.

If you've separated egg cases, gently set them in a cool, shady spot and cover with an inch of loose soil.

Miscellaneous Insects

Numerous insects and other arthropods live at or near the soil surface. A few, but only a very few, are harmful to plants. Of all insects, approximately 1 percent are harmful, about 8 percent are beneficial and close to 91 percent are benign. Beneficial insects help decompose organic matter, improve soil texture and prey upon their destructive fellows. Those most involved with decomposition processes include springtails, mites, centipedes, millipedes, beetles, snails, slugs, ants and sow bugs. Some of these are not to be trusted around plants and will be discussed in chapter 11, which deals with pest control. As for the great majority of animals that you see in the soil, check a good reference book before killing them; the lives you save may be your plants'.

How Nutrients Pass from Soil to Plants

There's a fascinating choreography that goes on between soil nutrients and plant roots. But to understand how this works, we need a quick review of some simple chemistry.

Particles of clay and humus have a huge surface-area-to-weight ratio and their surfaces carry a small electrical charge. They are said to have **colloidal surfaces**. Many chemical compounds, including plant nutrients, carry a charge as well. Charged elements are called ions. Cations are positively charged while anions are negatively charged. Cations include calcium, magnesium, potassium, hydrogen, zinc, manganese, iron, copper, cobalt and aluminum. Anions include phosphate, nitrate, sulfate, borate and chlorine. Both cations and anions move through the soil solution (the water between soil particles). Because clay and humus are negatively charged for the most part, they attract and hold positively charged cations. But nothing is static; a cation isn't captive forever. When another, more attractive cation happens along, the first cation is exchanged for it. If we could see this process, it might look something like a big game of musical chairs. Plant roots also give off cations, primarily hydrogen, and exchange them for other cations from both the soil solution and the colloidal surfaces that root hairs touch.

By and large, anions aren't attracted to colloidal surfaces, but move freely through the soil solution. For this reason, they are easily washed away, or **leached**, particularly in a greenhouse bed. Not only is the medium top-watered, but it must be purposefully leached every month or so. Plant roots take up most anions directly from the soil solution. This is one reason why it's so important to have plenty of organic matter in the growing media. Soils with a high humus content retain more water, hence anions are more readily available.

No matter what the concentrations in the soil around them, roots take up only so many cations and so many anions. But when there's an excess of particular kinds of nutrient ions, roots may absorb them to the partial exclusion of others. For example, an excess of calcium can cause a potassium deficiency; an excess of potassium, a magnesium deficiency. Similarly, an excess of chlorine can cause a nitrogen deficiency; too much nitrogen, a phosphorus deficiency. It should be quite evident from these examples that balance matters.

Soils vary in their **cation-exchange capacity** (CEC) as the percentage of clay and humus varies. Some clays have a higher CEC than others, but humus outdoes them all. Too low a CEC makes it difficult for roots to acquire minerals. If it's too high, balancing soil nutrients becomes more difficult because so many cations are held on colloidal surfaces.

If your plants seem healthy and a conventional soil test indicates that nutrients are in balance, a test for CEC is certainly not necessary. But if there are signs of nutrient deficiencies, a CEC test is a useful diagnostic tool. (Private laboratories test for CEC; ask your local extension agent for the name of laboratories in your region.) Greenhouse growing media, because of their composition and small volume, are easy to correct. To increase the CEC, add vermiculite or well-aged compost or manure; to decrease it, add sand or perlite.

Soil pH

The pH level is a measure of the soil's acidity or alkalinity. This level affects both soil life and nutrient utilization. To a large extent, soil pH is determined by the number and availability of hydrogen ions. The more hydrogen, the more acid the soil. Hydrogen enters the soil in water, but plant roots give it off, too. As hydrogen moves through the soil solution, it attaches to colloidal surfaces, displacing other cations. As a result, plants in an overly acid soil may have trouble getting the necessary nutrients.

Soil pH is measured on a scale of 1 to 14. Neutral is designated by the number 7, while numbers lower than 7 indicate acidity and higher numbers indicate alkalinity. To figure out the significance of a change in pH level, for every full point change, multiply by 10. For example, a soil pH of 4.5 is 10 times more acid than one of 5.5 and 100 times more acid than one of 6.5.

Most plants and soil organisms prefer an environment that measures 6.0 to 6.8. Minerals dissolve more readily in slightly acid soil, but at a pH lower than 5.5, many nutrients are unavailable. In an overly acid soil, iron, manganese and aluminum combine with phosphorus to make insoluble compounds, and deficiencies of both phosphorus and iron may develop. Aluminum and/or manganese become so soluble that plants may absorb toxic quantities. Except for some fungi, the growth of soil microorganisms and animals is also inhibited, further limiting nutrient availability. Alkaline soils are just as disastrous, because they make most trace nutrients unavailable.

You should test all soils and mixes for pH. Any soil test laboratory, including that of a State Extension Service or a Provincial Department of Agriculture in Canada, can do this test, but you can also buy a small kit to test pH at home. Because of the frequency of both leaching and fertilizing in the greenhouse, it makes sense to test pH every month or two. You'll find information on how to adjust pH in the next chapter.

Soluble Salts

Just as too much salt in your food is injurious, excessive salts in greenhouse soils harm soil life. Soluble salts are water-soluble compounds that conduct an electrical current. Mineral ions used as plant nutrients form salts. If too many are applied at one time or allowed to accumulate, salt levels may become too high. Salts hold soil water very tightly; when salt levels are excessive, plants can't absorb enough water.

Laboratory tests can measure salt content, but they're rarely necessary if you're observant. When you spot white incrustations on soil particles or see white rings at soil level on pots, salt levels are too high. Other good indicators of salt buildup are plants wilting in moist soil and browning leaf tips.

Because they are soluble, you can literally wash salts out of the soil. To keep unused nutrients from building up to injurious levels, you should leach both beds and pots periodically. Unless a bed has been overfertilized, leach about once every five to six weeks. If you see white incrustations on the soil, leach more frequently and decrease fertilization. To leach, water the container until it drains copiously. Be prepared—it takes quite a bit of water to wash salts through a bed. Schedule this procedure carefully; you don't want to leach during a humid, cloudy period when plants may be susceptible to diseases.

You can prevent salt buildup to a certain degree by practicing good watering techniques. Water *thoroughly*; don't wet just the top layer. Water until the whole medium is moistened. While the soil surface should dry slightly between waterings, don't let lower levels dry out.

Other safeguards include good drainage, a mix that's rich in humus and judicious fertilization.

When you're mixing and adjusting growing media, a basic understanding of soils is invaluable. If, as you gain experience, your curiosity is aroused and you want to know more, refer to some of the books listed in the Bibliography at the end of the book.

❦ CHAPTER 6 ❧
GREENHOUSE SOIL MIXES

Every gardener has a favorite soil mix. And recipes for mixes, always highly recommended, are a dime a dozen. But in my opinion, blanket prescriptions are often misleading. Soil forms the base of an organic mix, and soil types are too different to be treated as identical. For example, if Joe is starting with sandy loam and Mary has a clay loam, the same recipe won't give them the same kind of mix. Joe's may drain better, but Mary's will probably have a better exchange capacity, meaning the plants will have better access to nutrients. So I'm quite stubborn about working from the soil type. With that starting point, as well as an understanding of the properties that each amendment adds, it's easier to develop a mix with the right characteristics for your plants.

Greenhouse growing media are necessarily different from field or garden soils. Without exception, media must have better drainage and higher levels of humus. Even so, it's hard to maintain a good balance between moisture content and aeration over a long season. Top-watering compacts soil and eliminates many of the larger pore spaces through which water drains and air enters. Populations of soil animals are often lower, so fewer new pore spaces are made. In beds and other containers, water can drain only through specific holes, rather than through the entire lower depth. And salt levels can be so high that too much water is retained in the mix.

In addition, the nutritional content of greenhouse growing mixes becomes unbalanced more quickly than does the content of garden soils. Nutrients are depleted rapidly because cropping systems are very intensive, and beds are rarely given a rest under a cover crop. And conversely, the consistently warm greenhouse environment can make some nutrients, particularly nitrogen, *more* available, so there's the risk of an overdose for plants. Given the way most greenhouse growing areas are prepared, there's rarely subsoil from which worms and weeds can bring up nutrients. And finally, the nutrient balance can be upset by periodic leaching.

No matter how good they are, unadulterated field or garden soils don't work well in containers. At the very least, you must lighten these soils to increase drainage and aeration and amend them with nutrient-carrying materials.

Most people work with a combination of peat moss, vermiculite, perlite, sand, and compost or aged manure. Although they work in very different ways, each of these amendments affects both the nutrient-carrying capacity of the soil and its aeration and drainage. Once you understand their different properties, it's easier to work with them.

Sphagnum Peat Moss

Sphagnum peat moss is a partially decomposed moss found in boggy regions. It increases aeration and improves drainage in heavy clay soils, but aids moisture retention in sandy ones. While its surfaces attract some mineral ions, peat moss doesn't add any minerals or tie them up to any great extent. It's relatively stable, lasting a long time without further decomposition. Once incorporated into the soil mix, it doesn't rise or settle. Due to these attributes, peat moss is often used to "bulk" a mix. It has a curious side effect, too: peat moss carries antibiotics that inhibit the growth of some fungi, particularly a few of the species that cause damping-off disease.

When you buy peat moss, pay attention to its "nationality" and grade. Depending upon its point of origin, the pH can measure from less than 4.0 if Canadian or German, to 6.0 or even 6.5 if American. If you have a choice, buy American peat moss when amending an acid soil and Canadian for an alkaline one.

Three grades of peat moss are commonly sold. Poultry grade is composed primarily of large lumps of material, up to several inches in diameter. True horticultural grade has more variation; some particles are small, but there are also big lumps. A uniformly small grade is also sold under the name horticultural peat moss or milled sphagnum peat moss. While this grade is excellent for seedling mixes, a more varied mixture is better for deep beds.

Dry peat moss absorbs so much water that it "steals" from moist materials in the mix. Saturate peat moss before incorporating it into a mix or using it to cover a flat. Warm water is almost essential because it's more easily absorbed. To saturate, put the peat moss in a large container and water it, mixing thoroughly, until it *all* seems wet. With a good system, count on about half an hour of concerted work to water and mix a large bale of peat moss.

Perlite

Perlite is volcanic glass, expanded by a heat process to form a sterile lightweight aggregate. It improves aeration and drainage by literally shedding water. The pH is about 7.0 to 7.5. Perlite weighs only 8 pounds a square foot, in contrast to the normal weight of soil, which ranges from 60 to 95 pounds. Because it's so light, perlite migrates to the top of the growing medium within a few months. If the perlite content in a mix is high enough to coat a bed, algae may grow on it. While the algae themselves are harmless, they indicate that the surface of the media is consistently damp enough to encourage the growth of harmful fungi as well.

Dry perlite is extremely abrasive. The first time I used it in quantity, I didn't know how to handle it. I just dumped it into a bed and squinted against the dust. Not only did I cough for a week afterward, but I also ruined a pair of contact lens. To spare yourself this agony, always moisten perlite thoroughly *before* removing it from the bag. Open a corner, stick a hose in, and water the perlite until particles float to the top. Drain the bag by poking holes in the bottom and letting the excess water run out. Perlite is no fun to handle wet, but at least it won't attack you.

Vermiculite

Vermiculite is mica, heated until the thin sheets separate slightly. It has a high exchange capacity, so it retains both moisture and nutrients. Vermiculite also has a tendency to form aggregates, which increases aeration and drainage. As root hairs grow, they probe between the thin sheets where nutrients are held. Small amounts of both potassium and magnesium are released from vermiculite, but not enough to make up for a soil deficit. Although some South African vermiculites are more alkaline, most have a pH of 7.0 to 7.5.

Vermiculite doesn't migrate within the medium the way perlite does, but it breaks down quickly. Try rubbing a wet piece between your fingers—it smears like clay or silt. I replenish it in my growing mixes every year. Fortunately, vermiculite's versatility makes up for the expense, especially when supplies of compost or aged manure are low.

When wet, vermiculite is very difficult to handle or mix. Don't premoisten. Unlike perlite, it won't irritate your eyes or respiratory system.

Sand

Sand for horticultural use is washed to remove salts and is fairly uniform in size. Because sand lacks an exchange capacity, it's able to enhance drainage in a growing mix. But without the presence of perlite, vermiculite or peat moss, sand can compact and reduce aeration.

Work with dry to moderately damp sand and mix it in thoroughly. Unless you're certain of the purity of the sand in your backyard, buy washed sand from greenhouse, garden or building suppliers.

Compost, Leaf Mold and Manure

Organic gardeners, myself included, can be extremely tedious when they talk about compost. But once you're acquainted with it, it's hard not to extol compost's many virtues. A well-made batch of compost can make up for a multitude of other errors. You can count on porosity, balanced nutrient content, a wealth of microorganisms, high exchange capacity, and a pH of 6.5 to 7.0. But it is possible to go overboard—plants don't do well in straight compost. The exchange capacity is too high for good nutrient release and drainage. Although compost is an important addition to soil and other amendments, don't use it exclusively.

People very often make the mistake of thinking that aged manure is interchangeable with compost. That simply isn't so. *Composted* manure is similar, but aged manure, unless very well tended and covered as it decomposes, is usually low in nutrients, particularly nitrogen and potassium. Whenever possible, use compost instead of aged manure. And *never* use manure that is young enough to still look or smell even remotely like the original product. It will continue to decompose in the bed, robbing plants of needed nutrients. This concept is explained in more detail in the next chapter.

I like leaf mold a great deal. It seems to have gone out of vogue, but as far as I'm concerned, it's a great addition to growing mixes. In beds, I use it for part of the peat moss fraction because of its crumbly texture and resistance to decay. But watch the acidity—too much leaf mold can throw the whole mix out of balance. You can't count on leaf mold to add many nutrients, aside from trace elements. But remember that it has a good exchange capacity. Worms love it, too, and will eat great quantities. And making leaf mold is close to effortless. Directions, along with a description of good composting procedures, are given in the next chapter.

Soil

Thanks to ingredients which provide nutrients, aeration and drainage, you can use almost any soil in a greenhouse medium. But the better the soil, the easier it is to make a good mix. Look for a topsoil with crumbly texture, a high percentage of humus (3 to 5 percent) and good nutrient levels. When you start out with good soil, you won't have to amend so drastically.

There are several ways to acquire topsoil—you can dig it up yourself or purchase some. If you choose to dig your own, use a soil that comes from a field or garden rather than the woods. Garden soil is less acid than soil taken from a wooded area. Remember to take only the topsoil, not the lower, more densely packed subsoil. Color tells you where topsoil stops and subsoil starts. Depending upon the minerals it contains, subsoil may be gray, orange or dingy brown. Topsoil is a deeper, richer color.

If you buy, be certain to specify topsoil. And even if you think that the word is self-explanatory, it's best to see and test before buying. Definitions and quality vary; suppliers can sell almost anything they scrape off a building lot as "topsoil." Find out which companies are trusted by local commercial growers.

I've learned this lesson the hard way—soil seems to be an area where Murphy's Law operates particularly well. On one occasion, I should even have ridden with the truck that made the delivery. We were building greenhouses and open containers at a urban community center and had been ordering tons and tons of soil quite routinely. One day the delivery was late; I gave up waiting and went home to supper. No sooner than my fork was raised, the phone rang: 10 tons of dirt were lodged against the back door of the center. No one could get in or out that way. Both the fire marshal and the program director were adamant: the dirt had to be removed immediately. And it was snowing. My son and I donned mittens and mufflers, picked up our shovels, and took a bus downtown. Sure enough, our 10-ton order had been dumped against the back door. We went right to work, but every time we lifted one shovelful, another wet pile descended on us. It took only a minute to realize that we were shoveling *sand*, pure washed sand.

Hours later we had a passable route . . . but through sand. The next morning the company refused to believe me. They had sent soil, so soil it must be. They wouldn't come get it, either. Several weeks later, after every child in the city had taken a slide on it, the mystery was clarified. Growers at the cactus house of the botanical gardens called to inquire if we had their sand. They'd just noticed a pile of topsoil where they should have had sand. We were triumphant—the company had to exchange the two orders. Grudgingly, they did. But nasty as they were, we kept on ordering from them; they had the best soil in the city.

Finding Hidden Pesticides and Salts

It's unlikely that this sort of confusion could happen often, but other foul-ups are common. Try to get a sample of what you're buying and have it tested for pH and nutrients. There are two other tests that will help you determine whether the soil will make a good growing medium for plants. One is a home test for herbicides, and the other is a laboratory test for salinity.

Leftover herbicides are dangerous because they kill many crops. In *Organic Gardening Under Glass* (Rodale Press, 1975), Doc and Katy Abraham describe a practical test to detect herbicides. They advise preparing two similar flats, using *only* the soil in question. Mix 1 tablespoon of activated charcoal, available from garden shops, into the soil for one flat and mark it. Plant tomato seeds in both flats. After the tomatoes have their first or second true leaves, underwater both flats just enough to keep the plants alive but in moisture stress. Measure water and give each flat an equal amount. If herbicides are present, the tomatoes in the flat *without* the charcoal will wilt more quickly and show more leaf distortion and stunting. If there is any difference between the plants' response, don't buy the soil.

There are several causes for excess soil salts. High salt levels may be naturally occurring, as in some desert and coastal soils. They may be the result of irrigation and fertilization practices, or they may be caused by runoff from salted winter roads. As discussed in chapter 5, under Soluble Salts, salt destroys soil texture and inhibits plants' ability to pick up water and nutrients. But damage to plant growth doesn't happen overnight unless salinity is extraordinarily high. The best insurance against high salt levels is a soil salinity test. If that's impractical, buy only from highly respected companies. And once you find good suppliers, stick with them.

A recent law in Quebec prohibits the sale of topsoil. It won't be surprising if other provinces and states follow Quebec's lead in conserving a valuable natural resource. If you have a free corner of your yard, you can "grow your own" soil, as many large greenhouse ranges do. They carefully fertilize, green-manure and covercrop an area for several years before taking the soil. Once it's been removed, they repeat the process to build up a good topsoil layer again. To keep supplies high, they work in rotation. Field A may be taken this year, while field B is taken next year. If you don't have access to any land where you can do this, and you're unable to purchase topsoil, compost can form the base of a mix as long as you add adequate sand, peat moss and perlite to lower the exchange capacity.

Making Your Own Soil Mix

In most cases, soil forms the base of a greenhouse growing medium. No matter what you add, the basic soil with its particular nutrient levels, pH and texture should be your starting point. Begin by getting a good soil test, which will be the best indicator of specific nutrient needs.

You can do your own test with a home test kit, or you can have it done by an independent soil testing laboratory. State and Provincial Departments of Agriculture also have laboratories that do testing. In states or provinces where the greenhouse industry is large or growing, both independent and government laboratories may give you a choice of testing methods. A Bray test is commonly used for greenhouse soils.

In this test, nutrients are extracted with acids. Available levels of nitrogen, phosphorus, potassium, calcium and magnesium are indicated. Many tests also give the soluble salt level.

According to Bart Hall-Beyer, independent soil consultant to many greenhouse growers in eastern Canada, a saturated soil extract test is more appropriate for greenhouse growers. This analysis uses distilled water rather than acids, so it indicates *immediate* nutrient availability.

Soil test values may come back in parts per million (ppm), or high, medium or low. Many laboratories also suggest both fertilizers and rates of application. But if you forget to notify testers that the analysis is for greenhouse beds, you're likely to get recommendations per acre rather than per square foot. Few labs are equipped to recommend organic and natural fertilizers. For my money, it's worth finding a lab or independent consultant accustomed to organic practices. From there, it's relatively easy to ask for recommendations per square foot of growing area.

What do you do if the test results show that your soil is lacking in overall nutrient content? Soils with low nutrient levels require more compost in the initial mix than soils with average to high content. Generally, well-made compost provides each nutrient that a soil lacks. However, if a particular mineral is severely deficient, you may have to add it separately. Natural sources are listed in the next chapter, along with suggestions for their use. Don't forget that soil type and texture determine which amendments you use and in what proportions.

You might be wondering whether you need to pasteurize topsoil for a growing mix. Treat soil with heat only when you're using it in seed-starting mixes. But for growing mixes you'll be using in regular greenhouse beds, pasteurizing soil is just too time-consuming. It can actually do more harm than good, because it can upset the nutrient balance. In the soil mix recipes that follow, any soil that's called for is unpasteurized.

Recipes for Sandy Soils

Very sandy soils with poor texture rarely contain enough nutrients or have adequate exchange capacity. Unadulterated, they won't hold water or added nutrients well, either. You can make a suitable mix for **sandy soil** from:

    2 parts soil

    2 parts compost

    1 part peat moss or leaf mold

    1 part vermiculite

For **moderately sandy soil**, you can use the same mix with a minor adjustment. You might need 1 part perlite rather than peat moss or vermiculite to maintain good drainage.

Recipes for Clay Soils

A clayey topsoil often has good nutrient content but poor texture. It needs the microorganisms in compost to release nutrients and form aggregates, but it also requires a large proportion of drainage materials that don't add an exchange capacity. One mix for a **clay soil** type might be:

2 parts soil

1 part compost

2 parts sand

1 part perlite

If the soil you're starting with is only **moderately clayey**, you could use this mix:

4 parts soil

2 parts compost

1 part vermiculite

3 parts sand

2 parts perlite

Recipes for Loamy Soils

When you have a loamy soil with high nutrient content and good texture, you have your choice of several mixes:

2 parts soil

1 part compost

1 part peat moss or leafy mold

1 part sand

1 part perlite or vermiculite

4 parts soil

2 parts compost

2 parts vermiculite

3 parts sand

1 part perlite

3 parts soil

1 part compost

1 part sand or perlite

1 part peat moss or vermiculite

The choice of peat moss or leaf mold versus vermiculite depends primarily on pH. If the soil is only slightly acid or alkaline, it really doesn't matter which you choose. Use whichever one you prefer or can locate most easily. If you have a really acid soil, however, vermiculite won't increase the acidity, while peat moss and leaf mold will.

These mixes are appropriate for most vegetables and ornamentals. But some plants are finicky and grow best with more drainage or more humus. Special requirements are discussed in chapters 13, 14 and 15, which talk about specific plants.

A Note to the Lazy

Yes, you could just buy a bale of ready-mixed soilless medium. However, if you do, be prepared to spend the next season fussing over fertilizers. Most of the premixed media are composed primarily of peat moss with small fractions of perlite and vermiculite. Chemical nutrients are added, but they don't last for long. In addition, the pH goes acid within a month or so. Used for any length of time, soilless media compact, too. Instead of filling beds and containers, use soilless media as they are intended—as a starting medium for seedlings. If you do add a ready-mixed soilless medium to a soil mix, think of it as part of the peat moss fraction.

The Fine Art of Mixing

After deciding the rough proportions of amendments appropriate for your soil, but before buying a truckload of each, mix a sample batch. (Reputable sources will let you take a topsoil sample.) Mix in a cart or other container that holds 2 to 3 cubic feet. Measure with a consistent and convenient container; I use a big coffee can or a plastic bucket. Fill the container with a load of each material in turn. Mix as you complete each cycle. After you have about 2 cubic feet of mixed media, stir it with your hand. You should be able to move your arm through the mix with very little resistance. If not, add more perlite, sand or vermiculite. As you make changes, *write them down*. Test for drainage by filling a deep container (a pot at least a foot deep does nicely), watering with the water-breaker nozzle and watching how the water drains out. After the medium is thoroughly moistened, water should drain easily from the pot. Let it stand overnight. In the morning look at the surface. If it's smooth rather than rough, add more compost, vermiculite or perlite. Check moisture retention the next day. If the mix is dry below the top inch, more compost, vermiculite or peat moss is needed. If it's still soggy up near the top, add more drainage materials. Test any newly adjusted formula in the same way you tested the first one, and remember to note changes.

Now that you know the proportions of ingredients, you can figure out how much of each to buy to fill all the beds in your greenhouse. Figure the *total* quantity for each bed by multiplying its dimensions (length, width, depth), and then calculate the quantities of each amendment. For example, let's work with a bed that's 6 feet by 6 feet by 2 feet, or 72 cubic feet (ft^3).

Material	Part	Fraction (part/total part)		Volume (ft^3)		Volume of Part (ft^3)
Soil	4	$\frac{1}{3}$	×	72	=	24
Compost	2	$\frac{1}{6}$	×	72	=	12
Peat moss	3	$\frac{1}{4}$	×	72	=	18
Sand	2	$\frac{1}{6}$	×	72	=	12
Perlite	1	$\frac{1}{12}$	×	72	=	6
	12 Total Parts			Total Volume	=	72 (ft^3)

Worksheet for Sample Bed

As shown on the sample worksheet, compute quantities for each bed, add up the totals, and allow for extras—the small amounts of materials that you'll use for pots, flats and bed adjustments through the year. If you work primarily in beds, you'll need to stockpile about 4 to 5 cubic feet of each material. But you should keep larger quantities on hand if you plan to grow lots of seedlings in flats or pots.

Some amendments are sold by the cubic foot while others are sold by the cubic yard. Remember that there are 27 cubic feet in a cubic yard. Please don't think there are only 9. For some reason, almost everyone makes this mistake the first time through. The great day of delivery arrives, the shovels and carts come out—and there isn't enough vermiculite. Talk about frustrating—especially if you live in a remote area where deliveries come only once a month!

You can mix growing media for large beds in a wheelbarrow, or preferably, right in the beds themselves. You'll already know approximately how much material will fill a bed, but because the ingredients have to be completely mixed, add small quantities of each in the correct proportion. Mix thoroughly after each cycle. I don't add more than 2 cubic feet of any material at a time. And because I am easily and often distracted, I keep count by ticking off a list as ingredients are added. Fill the bed to about an inch of the top, water it very well and watch it drain. If you need to make adjustments, you'll want to do it before you plant.

Adjusting pH

Test pH after mixing the medium and again in several weeks. For most crops, you want a reading of 6.5, but there's some latitude, of course. Anything between 6.2 and 6.8 is acceptable as long as you remember to keep checking throughout the season. Above or below those figures, however, the mix needs adjustment.

Adjusting Acid Soils

Lime makes soil more alkaline. The calcium carbonate in lime causes hydrogen ions to be displaced from colloidal surfaces. If you send the test out to a lab, you'll get suggested application rates back with the results. But even so, you should understand that lime's effectiveness varies with soil type. Twice as much lime is needed to produce a desired change in an extremely clayey soil as in a sandy one because of the difference in exchange capacity between the two soil types.

Greenhouse media and moderately clayey soils react the same way to lime; they both have a high content of colloidal surfaces. They also lose alkalizing minerals—potassium, calcium and magnesium—rapidly through leaching. But still, add lime carefully. Too much ties up boron, resulting in unhealthy cabbage family crops and tomatoes that ripen unevenly.

Several kinds of lime are commonly available. Ground calcitic limestone and ground dolomitic limestone are the slowest to act and the longest-lasting. Dolomitic lime adds magnesium along with calcium. Because greenhouse tomatoes are prone to magnesium deficiencies,

Application Rates of Ground Limestone*

When pH is:	Add:
5.4	$3\frac{1}{2}$ – 4 cups
5.6	3 – $3\frac{1}{2}$ cups
5.8	2 – $2\frac{1}{2}$ cups
6.0	1 – $1\frac{1}{2}$ cups

*Rates are suggested for a moderately clayey soil and are given for 50 square feet of growing area. Limestone may be calcitic or dolomitic.

this is the best choice unless your soil has a high magnesium content. Use hydrated lime cautiously, if at all. Use only *half* the recommended amount at a time because it reacts so quickly that it may burn plant roots.

It's easiest to add lime to media that are already in the bed. Sprinkle a measured amount on the surface and mix it into the top 6 to 8 inches. When the bed is watered, it will leach downward. To determine how much lime you need to add, refer to the chart Application Rates of Ground Limestone.

It would be nice if you could retest for pH immediately after adjusting. However, lime takes several weeks to react with peat moss; any test you do will register low until the reaction is complete. Be careful—if you're impatient, you may overdo it. Don't try to get a reading of 6.5 right away. Have faith that the lime will work, and wait to test and adjust again in a couple of weeks. If you do have to add more lime later, sprinkle it between plants and water it in.

Adjusting Alkaline Soils

Acetic acid solutions are often used to make greenhouse media more acid. Acetic acid, available from any pharmacy, is a concentrated form of the acid in vinegar. It, too, is applied after the medium is in place. If the soil pH is 8 or higher, pour about a gallon of 10 percent solution over every square yard of well-moistened medium. (One part acid to 9 parts water makes a 10 percent solution.) In place of this solution, you could use 2 gallons of cider vinegar, which is 5 percent acetic acid. If the soil pH is 7.0 to 7.9, use a gallon of 10 percent acetic acid or a half-gallon of cider vinegar for each 4 or 5 square feet. In a week test the growing mix about 3 to 4 inches below the surface. If it's still too alkaline, repeat the procedure with straight vinegar or a 5 percent acetic acid solution.

Adjusting the Soil Mix

I'm always amazed at how much a soil mix can change during a growing season. The first noticeable change is a drop in the level, usually due to compaction. But some changes are invisible; nutrients are absorbed and leached and the medium often becomes more acid or alkaline.

Nutrient adjustment can be somewhat complicated. I rely on a fertilization schedule that is outlined in the next chapter. Because I make certain to include general fertilizers such as compost as well as foliar sprays for trace elements, I've been able to avoid having to add specific nutrients during the growing season. Tomatoes can be an exception to this rule, however. They may need more magnesium as the fruit is filling out. Directions for fertilizing tomatoes are given in chapter 13.

I like to check pH every 8 to 12 weeks. If there's been a radical change, I lessen the interval between tests. In most cases this schedule is adequate. If the medium has become too acid, sprinkle lime between plants and water it in. If it has become more alkaline, use an *extremely* dilute (approximately 2 to 3 percent) acetic acid solution in place of pure water for a couple of waterings. Continue testing the soil during this period, and stop using the acidic water when pH returns to 6.3 or so. To continue adding some acidity, use leaf mold as a mulch and side-dressing.

Drainage may also deteriorate over a growing season, especially if the soil is compacted by rough watering or if microbial action is diminished. If water puddles even slightly before sinking in, reevaluate your watering technique. The stream of water may be too rough, and you may need to switch to a gentler nozzle such as a water breaker. It's also a good idea to dig some compost or vermiculite into the top few inches of the growing mix. Be careful not to injure any roots in the process. You could also add worms to the mix if they are not already present. More extensive modifications have to wait until the crop has been harvested.

At the End of a Season

I like to plant in succession so that new plants are being seeded or transplanted as mature ones are harvested. But at least once a year, it's necessary to clear each bed of plants and refurbish the soil mix. Summer crops require the highest nutrient levels and the most watering, so I generally work on the soil mix at the end of the spring season. And I rework it again in September or October, before seeding and transplanting fall crops.

Clearing a bed gives you an opportunity to check on the condition of the soil mix at the lower depths. In each bed or large container, dig down to the bottom in several locations. I prefer to use my hands because they can tell me much more about the texture than my eyes alone. Smell the medium, too. It shouldn't smell sour or moldy. If the growing mix seems quite compacted, soggy, or smells bad, dig in more drainage materials before adding new soil or amendments.

If the medium was made well in the first place, it will be only slightly compacted at the bottom. Loosen it by sticking a spading fork into the bed at close intervals and wiggling it around to let air into the mix. Try not to turn over the layers of media, since many of the micro-organisms that have built up in your "topsoil" die when moved to a lower depth where oxygen is not as available. When you move these microbes around, it takes some time for them to reestablish effective populations.

If you haven't been testing for nutrients or pH during the season, do it while the bed is clear of plants. Test when the soil mix is uniformly moist but not soggy wet. With a wooden or stainless steel spoon take several samples, about 4 inches below the surface, from each growing area. Put all of the samples from one bed in a labeled bag, mix them and toss back all but half a cup. Depending upon the results, you may want to change the recipe by adding a larger fraction of compost or by reversing the percentages of vermiculite and peat moss or leaf mold. But if the mix has been working well, stick to it and adjust pH and nutrients as you did when you originally made the mix.

Whenever you add new materials, incorporate them into the top 6 to 8 inches only, so that microbial populations aren't greatly disturbed. Some disruption is inevitable, but a seed population will survive if you don't completely bury the original surface. You'll be adding some new populations along with the compost in the new mix.

Some people change the entire soil mix every few years. What a laborious task! Don't embark upon it unless you are certain that it's necessary. In my opinion, the only good reason for emptying a bed is to get rid of a soilborne pest or disease. Otherwise, you can revive a mix by loosening it and adding new material to the lower depths. If you're concerned that salts have built up, just leach the bed thoroughly after it is clear of plants. Several good leachings should wash the salts away. Nutrient deficiencies are easily remedied with the addition of more compost and attention to fertilizing during the growing season.

CHAPTER 7
FERTILIZERS FOR THE GREENHOUSE

Crops in some greenhouses are so healthy that they seem to sparkle. Leaves are large and firm; all the colors are bright; and both flowers and fruit are plentiful. Of the many factors that combine to create good plant health, environment and nutrition are the most important.

"Feed the soil, not the plant" is a basic tenet of organic horticulture. It assumes that microbes "eat from the plate first." Consequently, good plant nutrition arises from good microbial nutrition. And it's as true in the greenhouse as in the outdoor garden, especially when organic and natural fertilizers are used.

Think of greenhouse soils as particularly "hungry." While this description is amusing, it's also useful because it carries a necessary sense of immediacy. This large appetite is caused by the constantly warm temperatures, close spacing between plants, a three- to four-season year and frequent leaching. If nutrients aren't replenished, plant deficiencies will certainly develop. Nutrient-deficient plants don't look very healthy, nor are they as nutritious. When plants are undernourished, yields fall and pests and diseases are attracted.

Outside, gardeners can provide nutrients that feed soil organisms by turning under a crop for green manure. But greenhouse bed space is too dear for green manuring. Instead, growers increase microbial action by adding compost or aged manure. Besides soil life, compost and manure also contain large concentrations of nutrients. A fraction of these are immediately available; the rest of the nutrients are released as the material decomposes further. This characteristic, called slow-release fertilization, means that nutrients are gradually, but steadily, supplied over a long period of time. They are there during all the phases of a plant's growth. Plants aren't endangered by a sudden excess availability of one mineral or another. Slow-release fertilizers also ensure that microorganisms in the soil have a continuing food supply and will be populous enough to break down other fertilizers added throughout the season.

Compost

Compost is the mainstay of most home-scale fertilizer programs. It adds humus, forms aggregates easily so that both moisture retention and aeration are improved, contains microorganisms, and provides a slow-release and balanced nutrient supply.

Composting has acquired an unfortunate mystique. People treat it as if it's difficult or impossibly laborious. But this just isn't so. You can make the job unnecessarily tedious, moderately time-consuming or almost no trouble at all. When I was growing up, my mother composted everything she could lay her hands on with a very simple system. She collected quantities of dry refuse throughout the year, such as brush, weeds and spent flower stalks. When she had enough green weeds or lawn clippings to make up the balance of a pile, she'd heap them with an appropriate measure of dry stuff, water, cover and walk away. Kitchen wastes were always dumped on the top of the newest compost pile. She didn't adhere to a turning schedule, although she'd sometimes turn the pile when she dumped a bucket of kitchen garbage. This system didn't make a fast compost, but weed seeds and pathogens didn't come through in the finished product. Over the course of a summer, she stockpiled enough compost for a large family garden and a small bedding plant/perennial business. I'm very glad of the example; it taught me that composting can be a painless part of the daily domestic routine.

Composting relies entirely upon using ingredients in the right proportions and maintaining a good environment for microorganisms and soil animals. The smaller the materials and the more they're turned, the faster it goes. If you shred everything first and turn it every three or four days, it's possible to make a finished compost in about two to three weeks. With a slower system like my mother's, it may take two or three months, depending on the weather. And for those people who take the path of absolute least resistance—in other words, just toss stuff on a pile when they have it—finished compost will certainly take a good three to five months of warm weather.

Housing the Compost Pile

A well-designed composting bin must have air spaces. Provide drainage with holes near and directly in the bottom. Elevate the bin slightly above the ground, or even better, leave it bottomless and set it directly on well-drained soil or sand. Bins should be at least 3 feet wide by 3 feet long by 4 feet high to allow enough area for composting. If you plan to make enough compost to fully supply a greenhouse, build two or three enclosures, side by side. Start piles in sequence. I work with two bins. I wait about two weeks after filling one bin before starting

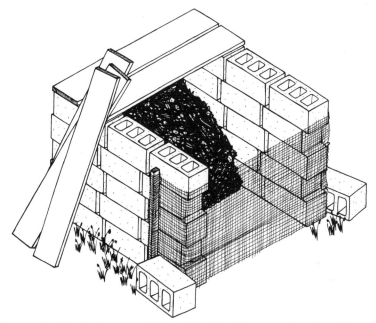

Concrete Block Compost Bin: *A bin like this won't cost a thing if you scavenge the materials. The pieces of lumber protect the pile from rain. The spaces between the blocks allow good air movement. The hardware cloth front can be removed when you need to turn the pile or remove the finished compost. Two spare blocks can hold the hardware cloth in place.*

to fill the next. When compost in the first bin is finished and removed, I move material over from the adjacent bin as part of the turning process. Then I build a new pile in the emptied bin.

If you're not keen on carpentry or other do-it-yourself construction, you may prefer to buy a ready-made bin. The most common are suspended metal drums, fitted with a crank for easy turning, and metal or plastic enclosures that slide apart in sections. Don't stint on price here. In my experience, the least expensive bins fall apart too quickly.

Carbon-to-Nitrogen Ratio

Like all other living things, microorganisms require a certain ratio of carbon to nitrogen. If nitrogen supplies in the pile are too high, microorganisms reduce the amount of nitrogen by converting some into ammonia, a gas that just floats away. Not only does this waste nitrogen, but it also smells nasty.

Some carbon from decomposing materials is always converted and thrown off as carbon dioxide. If the carbon content in the pile is too high, more carbon dioxide than usual is released. But more important, decomposition slows and finally stops until a balanced amount of nitrogen is added.

Compost piles should be built with a combination of materials that, taken together, contain about 20 to 25 times as much carbon as nitrogen (the C:N ratio). A tended compost beginning with a C:N of 25:1 ends up with a ratio of 10:1 to 15:1, the ideal range for fertile soils.

Few people memorize the carbon and nitrogen content of each compost material. Thank goodness this sort of tediousness is entirely unnecessary. Instead, use a simple rule of thumb: Green, wet material contains a high percentage of nitrogen, while dry material contains relatively more carbon. Layers of about 6 inches of dry material to 2 inches of green material usually give a good C:N ratio.

Dry ingredients include old hay, dried weeds, autumn leaves and wood chips or sawdust. Green materials include grass clippings, green weeds and green garden residues. Kitchen wastes have an average C:N of 25:1, but are used as part of the green layer. (A word of caution: Avoid adding greasy scraps or bones from the kitchen, since they'll attract dogs, wildlife and undesirable rodents.) Manures, even those containing dry bedding materials, are high in nitrogen, in part because the bedding materials soak up nitrogen-rich urine. Manures can be used in the green layer or on top of it.

Finding Compost Materials

Weeds without developed seeds, garden and greenhouse residues, kitchen scraps and grass clippings are the easiest materials to find. Rural growers can rely on animal manures and spoiled hay, but as I discovered while working on city garden projects, urban growers need creativity and persuasiveness to acquire enough compost material. But don't give up, it can be done.

I've cajoled friendly neighbors, day-care centers and vegetarian restaurants into separating and saving compostable garbage for me. Generally these people are well aware of the need to recycle nutrients, so they are willing to go to a bit of extra trouble. In each case I provided a covered pail and adhered to a pickup schedule. I asked only vegetarian restaurants for garbage because meat scraps draw dogs and cats.

It's not too hard to find a good supply of grass clippings. Scout for clippings from lawns *with* dandelions; their presence tells you that no weed killers have been used. Clippings from treated lawns may carry harmful residues that don't belong in a compost pile. Landscaping services sometimes cooperate by informing you of their lawn mowing work for the week. If you arrive on the scene as they are working and supply your own bags, they're usually happy to see you. Be prepared to take some good-natured teasing along with the clippings. I've found that eccentrics get more cooperation than people with a mission, so I don't even bother talking about recycling. If forced to explain myself, I prattle on about the way my flowers respond to a good compost.

If the police in your area keep horses, they'll usually give away manure, providing you bag and transport it yourself. Some cities prohibit carrying manure in an open truck; investigate the laws before approaching a stable. Zoos might seem to be ideal sources. However, I haven't always found this to be true. In many cities, manures from any animal susceptible to hoof-and-mouth disease can't be taken off the premises for six months. Consequently, many zoos are canny enough to have a good composting program of their own; they use the finished material to keep their lawns and park areas in good shape. But it never hurts to ask. Perhaps your zoo does have some extra manure.

I once collected hair from beauty shops—but only once. As soon as I dumped it on the pile, I realized that the proportion of dye and other strange chemicals was extraordinarily high. That was enough to make me give up that source.

Whatever your neighborhood, you'll soon develop a good eye for garbage. Don't be surprised to find yourself regularly cruising dumpsters behind grocery stores. They dispose of huge quantities of fruits and vegetables, especially at the end of their workweek. If you visit during working hours, it's best to explain your scrounging activities to the manager. Some stores don't want to attract attention to the barely spoiled produce in the bin. Again, the persona of a mildly dotty gardener has served me well.

Dry material is a bit harder to find in the city. Few people have piles of spoiled hay or waste straw. Carpentry shops have sawdust, but you don't want too high a proportion of this carbon-rich material in a single pile. Autumn leaves work, if they are a year old and already crumbly. If you use newly fallen leaves, they'll mat, reducing aeration in the pile. I get around this dilemma by packing leaves in plastic garbage bags for use the following year. Meanwhile, they make good insulating material to set around the bottom of a greenhouse or cold frame. As a last resort, I once made my own dry material by beating the municipal mowing crews to weeds on a vacant lot. I harvested them and then let the weeds dry for a week or so.

Building a Compost Pile

Use 6 inches of dry materials for the bottom of the pile. Water and mix them until all surfaces look wet, or until they're as moist as a damp sponge. Then add a 2-inch layer of green material. Over this, sprinkle a scant inch of good topsoil, finished compost or manure to introduce microorganisms.

Next, you can add a dusting of mineral fertilizers such as rock powders, bone meal or wood ashes. Some composting directions recommend adding lime to reduce acidity. Don't do it! It's pure lunacy since lime reacts with nitrogen to form ammonia. The last thing you need is ammonia wafting through the evening air. Besides, even if the original ingredients are very acid, the finished compost will have a pH of 6.7 to 7.5.

Some people add compost activators, which are commercially available mixtures of bacteria. In reality, you're gaining only a slight advantage by importing special bacterial strains, especially if you've used manure. After all, microorganisms make up almost half the volume of manure from grass-eating animals. In addition, compost materials and soil on roots also contain all the microorganisms necessary for decomposition. In the right environment, microorganisms reproduce quickly. If conditions aren't conducive to their growth, premixed strains die or form inactive spores as fast as any others.

Now it's time to begin again. Add another layer of dry ingredients. Water them and continue as before until the pile is about 3 feet wide by 3 feet long by 3 to 4 feet high. If more material is available, add it to the sides rather than the top. Too great a height compacts the pile, leaving less space for oxygen. Make a final check to see that the pile is adequately moist. Surfaces should glitter in the sunlight, and when you squeeze a handful, it shouldn't drip. Cover the pile to protect against rain, walk away and let it work for a few days.

Rapid microbial activity heats materials in the center of the pile to 160 to 180°F within three or four days. Toward the outside, it's cooler. This variation is fine—different decomposing organisms prefer different temperatures. When a pile is turned, material on the outside is moved to the center and vice versa. In this way each material is exposed to every different temperature range. Interior temperature is important because it indicates whether the pile is working well. Weed seeds, pest eggs and many pathogens survive all but the hottest conditions. Use a soil thermometer to check the temperature.

After three or four days at the correct temperature, mix the pile so that the outside materials are moved to the interior, where they'll get a chance to heat up. Leave the pile for another few days before turning and checking temperature and moisture again. After this, turning frequency depends upon your schedule and the demand for finished compost. You can turn it every four or five days, every couple of weeks or leave it in place and fluff it up with a spading fork every month or so. Depending upon the size of the original materials, the season and the frequency of turning, the compost should be ready within three weeks to three months.

If the interior temperature remains between 160 and 180°F for the first two to three weeks, compost can be considered finished when the

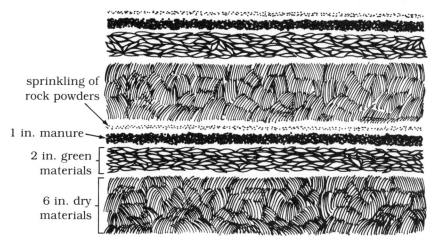

sprinkling of
rock powders

1 in. manure

2 in. green
materials

6 in. dry
materials

Layering a Compost Pile: From the bottom up, layer dry materials, green materials, manure and rock powders. Repeat until the pile is about 3 feet tall.

temperature drops to about 70°F, or about the time that earthworms move into it. If you rely only on visual and tactile inspection, a compost with a good deal of small carbonaceous material, such as sawdust, can trick you. It can cool and look finished before all of the carbonaceous material has broken down. If you apply it to the soil in this unfinished form, microorganisms will "steal" soil nitrogen to fuel their activities while they finish the job. Plants growing in this environment will become nitrogen-deficient until the carbonaceous material has been decomposed and the nitrogen contained in the bodies of the microorganisms is returned to the soil.

You can use compost in the soil mix, in seed-starting mixes and as a nourishing top-dressing for established plants. When compost supplies are low, use it judiciously. Save it for starting mixes and add it to the top few inches of the soil mix rather than work it into the entire bed. Nutrients leach down to root level as the bed is watered. If compost runs out, you can substitute peat moss, vermiculite or aged manure in the growing medium.

Spring and summer are the best composting seasons because of their warm temperatures. Try to make a full year's supply while the sun shines. Use some in fall beds, and store enough to use in next spring's beds and starting mixes. Store both compost and aged manure in a dark, cool, dry spot. It's best not to let it dry out. I use doubled plastic bags or covered containers to store my precious compost reserves.

Leaf Mold

I don't really like leaves in my compost piles. For one thing, their carbon-to-nitrogen ratio is anywhere between 60:1 and 110:1. And they turn slimy and mat down when they're wet, thoroughly ruining the aeration of a pile. Finally, they contain so much lignin that they take forever to decay. But much as I don't like composting leaves, I do love leaf mold.

Making leaf mold is my favorite sort of job—there's hardly any work involved. Start by piling leaves in an unobtrusive spot. Windrows about 3 feet high and 3 feet wide are the right size. If there's a prevailing wind in your area, erect a snow fence or chicken-wire barrier on the downwind side. I fence on both sides because the wind shifts with the season in my area. Let the leaves decay for at least one, but preferably two years. Some people water them periodically with diluted urine or manure tea. This hastens decay, but it certainly isn't mandatory. Extend the windrow each year and remove finished leaf mold from the bottom of the old pile where it has decayed the most. It should smell sweet and have a crumbly texture. Within another few months, the top layers on the old pile should be finished as well.

Leaf mold is a wonderful addition to soil and potting mixes, but can also be used as a combination mulch and side-dressing in any large container or bed.

Using Fertilizers

Fertilizers can be confusing. There's a wealth of them, and each has its own set of characteristics. Those termed "chemical" are either synthetic compounds or natural substances treated with acids to make them more soluble. In a chemical fertilizer, a greater than normal amount of the nutrient in question is immediately available for absorption. "Organic" fertilizers are derived from organic substances such as fish, blood or seaweed. "Natural" fertilizers are natural products that haven't been changed in any way other than grinding. Rock phosphate, limestone and langbeinite fit this category. Both natural and organic fertilizers contain only small amounts of immediately available nutrients. Microbial action, natural weathering and acids in the soil solution make the balance available over a longer period of time.

Practitioners of organic agriculture use organic or natural fertilizers in part out of respect to soil life. When a large quantity of immediately available nutrients is added, balances within the soil ecosystem are disturbed. Some chemical fertilizers are too acid or carry too many salts for good soil health. By using only slow-release, natural and organic products, organic growers hope to create a good soil environment. Because of the high proportion of available nutrients, it's easier to make mistakes with chemical fertilizers. But don't be lulled into a false security; mistakes happen with organic fertilizers, too. No matter what fertilizers you choose, pay attention to application rates and methods.

When it comes to applying fertilizers, you have your choice of several methods. You can add them to a compost pile; spread them on the surface of the growing medium (top- or side-dressing); sprinkle on the medium and mix them into the top few inches (incorporated); water them into the soil mix (liquid application); or spray them on leaves (foliar feeding). The method you choose depends on the characteristics of the fertilizer and of the nutrient, crop maturity and growth habits, the season, and the desired result.

Rock powders, bone meal, wood ash, bloodmeal and leatherdust are commonly added to compost. The high proportion of microorganisms and organic acids in a compost pile changes a large fraction of these fertilizers into a form plants can use. When you apply the finished compost, nutrients are readily available to plants. This is particularly important for rock powders, which are slow to break down into usable form. Another bonus of adding fertilizers to the compost pile is that leaching losses are significantly decreased. The high humus content of the pile provides plenty of exchange sites, which means that normally easily leached nutrients such as calcium, magnesium and potassium are better retained.

Compost and aged manure are the most common side-dressings, but other solid fertilizers can be sprinkled on the top of the medium as well. Once on the soil surface, they continue to break down, leaching nutrients into the soil with each watering. Before decomposing to become part of the soil mix, compost and manure form a protective mulch, keeping roots moist and cool. In the early spring this often makes the soil too cool for warm-weather plants, but during hot weather a top- or side-dressing can help to save a crop in an overheated greenhouse.

Solid organic fertilizers such as bloodmeal, seaweed, feathermeal and leatherdust contain a high proportion of compounds that must be decomposed to be useful. You can add these to compost, of course, but if you wish to use them directly, they're most effective when incorporated into the top few inches of the growing medium. There microorganisms can begin their attack, making nutrients gradually available.

Liquid application puts soluble nutrients directly into the root zone. Fish emulsion, liquid seaweed and manure or compost tea are often watered in to get fast results. Liquid application is also used in preference to side-dressing or incorporation during seasons when the soil temperature falls below 55°F (below this temperature, soil microbes start to slow their activities and aren't as efficient at breaking down solid organic fertilizers). Practices vary, but I prefer to make frequent applications of highly dilute solutions. The supply is steadier and there's less danger of overdoing it.

Foliar feeding gives fast results. Liquid seaweed and fish emulsion are the primary foliar fertilizers. Again, weak solutions applied frequently work best for me.

General Fertilizers

A general fertilizer is one that contains all necessary nutrients in good balance. As you might expect, compost and aged manure head this list. Fish emulsion (usually 4 to 5 percent nitrogen, 4 percent phosphorus, 1 percent potassium and trace elements) is also classified this way by some growers. It more truly fits the description when combined with liquid seaweed (usually 2 percent potassium).

When side-dressing with compost or manure, apply a 1- to 2-inch layer between all plants in the bed. Don't draw it closer than 2 inches to plant stems for fear that the moisture it holds will encourage fungal diseases. It shouldn't touch bottom leaves for the same reason. This makes it an excellent fertilizer for tomatoes and cucumbers, but a poor choice for nearly mature lettuce or other leafy crops. With low-growing plants like these, liquid fertilizers won't cause the kinds of problems side-dressings will.

Both compost and manure can be made into liquid "teas." Suspend a burlap or muslin sack filled with $2\frac{1}{2}$ quarts of compost or manure in a 5-gallon bucket of water. Let it soak for a day or two. As soluble nutrients leach out, the water gradually turns the color of weak tea. Not only is the tea a fertilizer, but the leftover compost or manure still holds nutrients. Add it to a compost pile or side-dress with it. Because most of the immediately soluble nutrients have been leached out, it makes a very slow-acting side-dressing. Meanwhile it serves as a good protective mulch and long-term fertilizer.

Most producers of fish emulsion recommend diluting it at the rate of 10 parts water to 1 part emulsion for application to soil. Some growers use this application rate with no difficulty, while others report an increase of fungal diseases. My preference is to use it at about half the strength recommended on the bottle. Assume this dilution rate for all the fish emulsion recommendations I make. The only time I swerve from this practice is when I occasionally add fish emulsion to compost—then I tend to use the standard dilution rate.

When both seaweed and fish emulsion are used, the general practice is to add 6 parts fish emulsion to 4 parts liquid seaweed. Again, dilute to only half the recommended strength. Besides the nutrients it supplies, liquid seaweed has other valuable attributes. It gives plants more resistance to fungal diseases and whitefly attack. It also hastens tomato ripening, a real boon for impatient gardeners.

Specific Fertilizers

Fertilizers containing only a few nutrients are called specific fertilizers. These are used less frequently because compost and other general fertilizers usually make them unnecessary. However, there are times when the best cure for deficiency is a specific fertilizer. For example, if all other elements aside from magnesium are in good balance, a general fertilizer will help to make up the magnesium deficiency, but the balance between it and potassium and calcium may still be off. Better to add the magnesium separately in that case. A soil test is the best indicator of specific nutrient needs. Follow the directions given in the section At the End of a Season in chapter 6 for sampling techniques.

Home soil test kits can give good results, but to be safe, compare your results on a sample with those of a laboratory on the same sample. If the results are the same, continue to test your own soil with confidence. However, if the results differ, assume that the laboratory is correct.

In the following discussion of nutrient sources, you'll find optimal nutrient ranges given, based on a saturated soil extract analysis (SSE). I've included the recommendations that soil consultant Bart Hall-Beyer generously gave me, because you might be able to find a laboratory that can do the SSE test, and Bart's experience with greenhouse media is invaluable.

Nitrogen

Chemical analysis of nitrogen is chancy at best. Consequently, many laboratories estimate its content as 5 percent of the carbon content. This system works as well as most, so don't be appalled if your laboratory does it.

Soil nitrogen should be 80 to 140 ppm (SSE). At lower concentrations, you must add nitrogen or plants will suffer from a deficiency. Nitrogen deficiency symptoms include generally poor growth, especially on young shoots, yellowing leaves and bud drop. However, I've seen many more cases of *excess* nitrogen availability in home greenhouses than I've seen deficiencies. Very green leaves, succulent leaves and stems, unusually rapid growth and susceptibility to aphids and fungal diseases all signal too much nitrogen. In most cases the problem was generated by liberal nitrogen applications during the winter. When the soil temperature is lower than 50°F, nitrifying bacteria aren't active enough to convert organic nitrogen sources into available forms. But some people are just plain obstinate; they fertilize the same way, no matter what the season. Problems don't show until spring, when the soil warms and microbial action picks up. Suddenly there's far too much available nitrogen and plants suffer from an excess. Remember—it's better to exercise restraint during cool months.

Compost, manure, fish emulsion, bloodmeal and leatherdust are all good nitrogen fertilizers. Both bloodmeal and leatherdust contain about 12 percent nitrogen, but leatherdust costs about half as much as bloodmeal. It does have a drawback, though; it may contain chemical dyes and noxious tanning residues. Check with the source before buying. Cottonseed meal and cotton gin wastes used to be widely recommended as nitrogen sources. Unfortunately, cotton is treated with more pesticides than any other crop in the United States and carries dangerously high residue levels. Organic growers should be aware of this and find substitutes for cotton by-products.

Both bloodmeal and leatherdust can be used in compost. But you can also mix bloodmeal for liquid application. A liquid feeding releases nutrients to plants more quickly, so it's good to use when you see signs of a deficiency, such as yellowing leaves. Add 1 tablespoon per gallon of *hot* water. It doesn't hurt to dissolve it first in a quart of boiling water, making up the balance with hot tap water. Don't be casual about applying dissolved bloodmeal; even at this dilution it's a very high nitrogen fertilizer. Too much can easily burn plant leaves. Apply it to premoistened soil, working fairly quickly to avoid overapplication. Then water it in with clear water, making certain to wash bottom leaves.

When you're trying to overcome a serious deficiency in the midst of the growing season, you need the fast release of a liquid application. At other times, when a slower rate of release is preferred, use dry bloodmeal or leatherdust. Sprinkle the material very sparingly between rows and scratch it into the top couple of inches of medium. This method of application guarantees a slower nutrient release.

Ideally, winter soil mixes should have enough nitrogen from the fall replenishment to see crops through until spring. In reality, the last planting of leafy greens sometimes looks slightly nitrogen-deficient in late January or February. Use a very dilute solution of liquid seaweed and fish emulsion for foliar feeding or water with a weak manure or compost tea. Don't make another move without checking soil temperature. It's likely to be too cold for good nitrogen release and pickup.

Phosphorus

For healthy plant growth, an optimal range for phosphorus is 8 to 16 ppm (SSE). When there's a dificiency, plants can't absorb other nutrients and photosynthesis is slowed. You'll notice phosphorous deficiencies by retarded growth and maturation and red- or purple-colored leaves and stems. On tomatoes, the color shows first on the undersides of the leaves and then spreads.

In acid soil, phosphorus combines with aluminum, iron and manganese to make insoluble compounds. Even when soil phosphorous levels are high, little is available to growing plants. Decomposing organic matter in the soil offers a partial solution; its by-products combine with both iron and aluminum, leaving more phosphorus available. Apply phosphorus-containing fertilizers only to soil mixes with good humus content and a pH that isn't too acid. Otherwise, it's like throwing good money after bad.

Rock phosphate, colloidal phosphate, bone meal and fish emulsion are reliable sources of phosphorus. Both rock and colloidal phosphate are normally added to compost. Use about half a pound to every 3-cubic-foot pile. This amounts to only a light sprinkling on each green or activator layer. This may seem pitifully minuscule, but remember that other compost ingredients contain phosphorus. At this rate, you'll never see a phosphorous deficiency if you add compost to the medium or use it as a side-dressing.

Added directly to a greenhouse bed, rock phosphate can't produce immediate dazzling results. It takes too long to break down. But if soil in a bed is to stand for several years, you can certainly add it to form a reserve bank. Sprinkle 1 pound over every 10 square feet of growing area, mixing it into the top few inches. The medium should contain at least 2 pounds of manure or compost for every 1 pound of rock phosphate to ensure break down.

My favorite phosphorous source is steamed bone meal. It smells horrible but it works wonderfully. Some phosphorus is immediately available while the rest is released slowly. Apply 1 cup to every 10 square feet of bed area or compost pile.

Fish emulsion provides the fastest phosphorous supply. Routinely use it as a starter solution in combination with liquid seaweed when you transplant. Spring seedlings are particularly responsive to this treatment.

Potassium

Potassium is in good supply when a soil test measures 110 to 180 ppm (SSE). If the test shows much more than this, plants may take up too much and suffer a magnesium deficiency. Without enough potassium, deficiencies show on both old and young leaves. Old leaves become mottled and scorched along the margins, while young leaves look more wrinkled than usual. Tomatoes show both scorched leaf margins and uneven ripening of fruit, usually around the shoulders. Lettuce becomes more susceptible to fungal diseases. Potassium deficiencies are often caused by excesses of nitrogen or phosphorus.

Potassium leaches out of any soil quickly, but leaching losses are even more pronounced in greenhouse beds. Composting potassium sources conteracts leaching; colloidal particles in the humus hold the mineral making it more resistant to leaching, and thus available over a longer period of time.

Sul-Po-Mag, wood ashes, seaweed meal and wilted but still green comfrey and alfalfa contain high levels of potassium. Sul-Po-Mag (sometimes called K-Mag) is ground langbeinite, a rock containing 22 percent potassium, 11 percent magnesium and 22 percent sulfur. You can get it from garden suppliers and some mail-order firms. No more than 2 pounds of Sul-Po-Mag or wood ashes should be used in a compost pile. A half pound of seaweed meal is sufficient. These quantities get plants off to a good start. If leaching is severe during the growing season, side-dressings or liquid applications of compost and manure teas will compensate for the lost potassium.

Because wood ashes are alkaline and repel slugs, many people use them as a mulch or side-dressing in the garden. This practice also adds potassium, but, particularly in a greenhouse bed, can lead to a buildup of excessive salts. The sodium chloride content in wood ashes is quite high. If an ordinary soil test indicates that total salts are 120 ppm, or if an SSE soil test gives a reading of 1,500 or higher, don't side-dress with wood ashes. You'll aggravate the situation. If there's no danger of creating an alkaline condition, use wood ashes sparingly.

Both comfrey and alfalfa must be grown outside. It would simply take too much bed area to grow appreciable quantities in the greenhouse. Bees love comfrey, so plant it around fruit trees or berries to attract their attention. But think carefully before setting it out. Once established, comfrey is as hard to eradicate as Jerusalem artichokes.

Alfalfa is one of the best cover crops. It adds nitrogen and aerates soil with its long, sturdy roots. But seed is expensive, and you won't realize alfalfa's full benefit until you have left it in place for about three years. It's very picky about pH; if the soil is more acid than 6.5, the seedlings don't establish themselves well and they're not as likely to overwinter without attrition. When used as a fertilizer, alfalfa should be mowed just before blooming. Use the clippings as mulch. They can also give strength to a newly transplanted crop because, like seaweed, alfalfa contains high levels of growth-promoting hormones. Dig about ¼ cup of wilted clippings into the top few inches of the soil around each transplant.

Both comfrey and alfalfa can be used as a nutrient tea or mulch. You must "brew" the tea well in advance. Soak a quart of leaves in a gallon of water for two or three weeks. Cover the pail or the water will evaporate. Strain the resulting concoction and dilute it by one-third before watering with it. Plants respond to these teas toward midseason, or in the case of tomatoes, just as the first fruit is beginning to swell. Don't use it more than once a month if you're also using a general fertilizer.

To side-dress with alfalfa or comfrey, place it on the bed surface without bringing it into contact with bottom leaves. Potassium leaches out with every watering. Leave the mulch in place and dig it in after you've harvested the crop.

If growing comfrey and alfalfa and then making teas and mulching seem too laborious, remember that compost, manure, fish emulsion and liquid seaweed all supply adequate potassium if they are used regularly. Tomatoes are the only crop that I feed with alfalfa or comfrey tea.

Calcium

Calcium supplies in a soil should be 250 ppm (SSE). Deficiencies show on terminal buds and new leaves, but the symptoms look different from crop to crop. Lettuce leaves are malformed and scorched on the margins. Tomatoes may develop blossom-end rot, a soft brown spot on the blossom end of the fruit. Leaves of cabbage family crops have yellowish spots and may curl and brown on the margins and tips. But in greenhouse situations, this family is more likely to suffer from too much calcium, rather than too little.

Calcium leaches easily, but greenhouse deficiencies are easy to correct because several commonly used soil amendments contain calcium. Every time you add lime to correct pH, you're also adding calcium to the soil. Steamed bone meal and rock and colloidal phosphate all contain high calcium levels, too.

Gypsum also contains calcium and is less alkalizing than lime or bone meal. Use it in the compost pile or growing beds as you would bone meal. I sometimes crumble a bit of scrap gypsum rock into potting mixes for calcium lovers such as cacti or bulbs.

Magnesium

Magnesium supplies are adequate when a soil test indicates 60 ppm (SSE). Magnesium leaches quickly under indoor growing conditions so greenhouse crops, especially tomatoes, suffer from magnesium deficiencies more often than those in the open. Deficiencies can mimic tobacco mosaic virus, so it's sometimes tricky to make the correct diagnosis. In both cases, old leaves develop yellow spots and streaks between the still-green veins. A common greenhouse pest can be the tip-off that it's a deficiency. Whiteflies are attracted to magnesium-deficient tomatoes and are often the first indicator of a problem.

When a magnesium deficiency is great enough to show up on a soil test, the best remedies are Sul-Po-Mag or Epsom salts. Use Sul-Po-Mag in compost as described earlier under Potassium, or, like Epsom salts, dilute at the rate of 1 ounce per gallon of boiling water. Use this solution in place of regular water once a week for two weeks. If the crop won't be harvested for a while, repeat in a month or as soon as symptoms reappear. This deficiency is more common when humus content is low, or when too much potassium is available. To prevent a possible magnesium deficiency, use compost in the soil mix and add potassium-rich fertilizers gradually throughout the season.

Sulfur

Most soils near industrial areas contain adequate sulfur because it's thrown off as fossil fuels are burned. In some regions, however, "flowers of sulfur" must be added to compost to make up for a widespread soil deficiency. Your local extension agent will know whether soils in your area are sulfur deficient and, if so, where to find a source to amend them.

An easy way to see that there's enough sulfur for greenhouse crops is to compost plants that are sulfur accumulators, such as cabbage family crops. When these are grown in soils that contain sulfur, they absorb the mineral, then "donate" it to the compost as they decompose.

Sulfur deficiency symptoms include delayed maturation, stunted growth and light green leaves with even lighter veins.

Micronutrients

Compost, manure, fish emulsion and liquid seaweed all contain a variety of micronutrients. Liquid seaweed is the most reliable and fastest-acting source. However, if you're using general fertilizers, the soil mix is likely to contain an adequate supply of micronutrients. Deficiencies in good soils occur in response to either acid or alkaline conditions or nutrient imbalances.

In *The Nature and Properties of Soils* (Macmillan, 1974), Nyle C. Brady lists nutrient antagonisms. In small greenhouses, the most common of these are:

- Iron deficiency as a result of too much manganese (manganese is made more available by soil pasteurization)
- Boron deficiency as a result of too much lime
- Copper deficiency as a result of too much nitrogen
- Manganese deficiency as a result of too much sodium

An iron deficiency can look like a nitrogen or magnesium deficiency since yellow leaves are symptoms of all three. With a shortage of iron, the yellowing continues until the leaves are so pale that they're almost white. Iron deficiencies are less frequent than nitrogen or magnesium deficiencies, so don't assume that iron is the problem when you see yellowing leaves. Bloodmeal is an excellent source of iron; use a weak liquid solution if you're certain that the nutrient is deficient.

A boron deficiency affects cabbage crops by making their stems hollow and stunting heads of cauliflower and broccoli. Leafy cabbage crops may show small, scorched leaves. On lettuce receiving too little boron, growing leaves are malformed, leaf tips are burned or spotted and, in severe cases, growing tips shrivel and die. Contrary to most micronutrients, boron deficiencies are common in some areas. Many soils in the Northeast are boron-deficient, for example. In the field, growers often spray soluble boron at the rate of 2 pounds an acre. A recipe for greenhouse beds is given in chapter 14 under Cabbage Family Crops. Liquid seaweed sprays keep boron levels high.

A copper deficiency is likely to show on tomatoes first, dwarfing them. The leaves also look a little too blue and are not as firm in texture as they should be. Lettuce looks bleached on the stems and leaf margins. Other crops are less susceptible but eventually discolor and suffer from slow growth.

Manganese is associated with iron utilization in plants. The deficiencies look so similar that only a soil test or tissue analysis can say for certain which deficiency is causing the problem.

Preventing micronutrient deficiencies is much easier than correcting them. Maintain good soil moisture and pH levels and use general fertilizers as often as necessary to keep the macronutrients in balance. To supply a good balance of micronutrients, foliar spray with a half-strength liquid seaweed solution.

Fertilizing Schedules

Blanket fertilizing schedules are dubious, at best, because growing mixes, composts and environmental conditions are always so different. I often get phone calls from people requesting a fertilizer schedule for a crop I've never seen. People are disappointed to learn that I won't give an ironclad prescription over the phone. I refuse because I don't have enough information to be reliable. Besides, I depend as much on visual cues as on soil tests. Healthy plants are unmistakable. If they look bedraggled, I check for pests, diseases or environmentally caused damage first. Pests and diseases are good indicators because they often erupt in response to nutritional problems. You learn to look for an excess of nitrogen when aphids have taken over a crop, a magnesium deficiency when whiteflies are rampant or a disturbance in the calcium-magnesium balance when lettuce shows tip burn. Similarly, environmental mismanagement can disturb growth and set the stage for pests, diseases or even nutritional difficulties. Both nitrogen and phosphorus pickup are altered by soil temperature, for example. It may be necessary to improve environmental conditions before beginning to add supplementary fertilizers. It's always a mistake to narrow your vision to only one symptom and only one solution; plants live in a world of interdependencies.

My best advice is to see that the initial mix has good fertility, drainage and pH. Take care that the appropriate environmental requirements for each plant are met and begin supplemental feeding gradually, usually with foliar sprays. Liquid seaweed is the safest and most reliable emergency tactic. If plants begin to look slightly under the weather, use a half-strength dilution for foliar feeding.

Compost or manure tea is next on my list of preferred fertilizers. I water it in several days after giving a foliar feeding to a distressed crop. Otherwise, I wait a couple of weeks. Timing is important. Plants respond best to a slow, steady supply of nutrients rather than to a couple of huge blasts. And it's easier to guard against creating an imbalance or excess if you add nutrients gradually.

In general, fertilizer schedules depend upon the crops being grown, the season of the year and the initial fertility of the soil mix. Summer crops grow more quickly and require more nutrients than those grown in cool weather. This means that warm-season crops are fertilized more frequently. If the soil mix is rich in compost or manure, an appropriate maintenance routine for deep-bed summer crops might include:

Months 1–3: Foliar feeding with liquid seaweed once a month.

Month 3: Side-dressing with compost or aged manure at beginning of month.

Months 4–6: Foliar feedings with liquid seaweed every two weeks through the season and applications of compost or manure tea every two weeks through the season. Or, foliar feedings with liquid seaweed every two weeks through the season and a side-dressing of compost or aged manure once a month.

A soil mix without much initial fertility may need augmentation earlier. It might be necessary to begin biweekly foliar feedings in the beginning of the second month, and six weeks into the season, to begin the schedule given above for months four through six. Watch your plants; once they begin to lose the sparkle of good health, begin with foliar feeding and proceed from there.

Fertilizing during the winter is a trickier business by far. Unless the greenhouse is quite warm, you can't rely on fast microbial action to break down materials. My solution to the problem is simplistic but reliable. I'm careful about refurbishing the soil mix as soon as summer crops are removed. At the very least, I add a good portion of compost or aged manure. Soil temperatures are still high enough to promote good soil activity, and both transplants and direct-seeded crops get a good start on the season.

Once the soil cools, I rely on foliar feedings with liquid seaweed or a seaweed–fish emulsion blend. The crops grow slowly during this time of year anyway, and harvesting patterns take account of slow growth. Initially, alternate plants are pulled, but after the bed is thinned, only outer leaves are taken from each plant. By February the sun is bright enough, even in northern Vermont, so that microbial action is picking up. Depending upon the age of the crop, I move to a regular schedule of twice-monthly nutrient teas at this point.

You can also use weak nutrient teas in the dead of winter. Aside from foliar sprays, they are the most effective fertilizers when the soil is cool. Because I go into the season with good fertility, I very rarely need to supplement during this time. I recommend my system for its low maintenance.

Always remember that fertilizer schedules are not inflexible. Soils, leaching practices and environments differ so much that each grower must experiment with fertilizers and schedules to find an appropriate combination. In addition, some crops benefit from nutrient application at specific times in their growth. Tomatoes, for instance, respond well to a feeding of potassium and magnesium when their first fruits are just beginning to swell.

To adjust fertilizer routines, you must watch the plants carefully. Look for anything unusual: scorched or yellowing leaves, stunted or distorted growth or delayed maturation. Remember that a poor environment can cause many symptoms, too. However, if nothing in the environment seems amiss, increase fertilization when you see signs of ill health. Unless you know for certain that a particular nutrient is low, it's best to use a general rather than a specific fertilizer. Even trained plant pathologists can't always identify a particular deficiency just by looking. If the general fertilizer doesn't work and everything in the environment is in order, consider sending leaf samples to the nearest state or provincial laboratory for tissue analysis. Call them first for directions about gathering and handling the samples. Sampling techniques vary between plants and usually involve picking a specific leaf, in order of growth, from a random sampling of the crop. I like tissue analyses because they indicate nutrient levels within the plant, not in the soil. With both a soil test and a tissue analysis, a vegetable specialist can identify almost any nutrient problem for you.

CHAPTER 8
PLANTING IN THE GREENHOUSE

Starting plants from seed is an art. Almost everyone can get good germination and healthy growth from vegetable seeds planted in the spring garden, but in less favorable conditions or with difficult seeds, good techniques are essential to success. Attention is the other key to good seedling care. If you forget to remove a cover on time or overwater a flat, the seedlings suffer. They can look "saved," but their subsequent vigor and yields may not match those of unstressed seedlings.

I don't like extra work. Given a choice between an unessential task and a shortcut, I'll opt for the fast, easy way every time, especially in the midst of a busy spring. My seedling production has varied with the years, but it's on a definite increase. While I once grew several hundred seedlings a spring, my current output is many thousands. I love seedlings, but by late July when the last summer crop is ready for final transplanting, I am heartily tired of filling flats, draining soaking water, squinting over teensy little seeds, mixing seaweed solutions for fertilizing, and misting baby plants and hardening them off. At that point it's difficult for me to imagine the excitement I'll have in January when the seedling year starts again. My excitement is partially derived from the pleasure of coddling all those babies, but I also love the challenge of finding new and better ways to organize the operation.

My seedlings have taught me a very good lesson: Save time with good organization, advance planning and mass production, but don't cut corners when it comes to caring for seedlings. If you do, you'll have trouble later in the season. Increase the number of seedlings you raise over the years as you develop good systems. If you realize that you've got more plants than you can care for comfortably, be ruthless: Give some away or throw them out. Seedling culture shouldn't be sloppy. Well-established plants can take a bit of negligence—seedlings can't.

The art of raising seedlings is dependent on the combination of good technique and strong intuition. Experience doesn't hurt, either. As seasons go by, you "see" plants more clearly. Routine tasks don't seem quite so routine as you learn when and how much to water and fertilize, when and how to transplant without causing stress and where to place seedlings through their different stages of growth.

Seeds

When a seed is planted, it absorbs moisture from the surrounding soil. If the moisture content, soil temperature and light intensity are correct, enzymes within the seed break its dormancy. The primary root pushes out of the softened seed coat and into the soil, where it can begin to absorb water and nutrients. The primary stem pushes the cotyledons and first true leaves through the soil and out into the light. Once the first true leaves begin photosynthesis, the plant is on its own as a new individual.

Appropriate germinating conditions vary among plant species. For example, seeds of frost-tender plants won't germinate well at low soil temperatures, while those of cool-loving plants are more difficult to start in warm soil. Some seeds require light to begin their activities, and others require darkness. (These needs are covered for common greenhouse crops later in the chart Light Preferences and Soil Temperatures for Germination.)

Starting vegetable seeds is pretty straightforward. If you pay attention to the basics, the seeds germinate and the plants grow. But few greenhouse growers confine themselves to vegetables. Eventually the lure of fancy ornamentals must be answered. In general, ornamentals such as impatiens and snapdragons require greater care during germination and the first stages of growth.

Some seeds go into dormancy before all of the primary structures have been formed. The completion of embryo development is stimulated by periods of moist, cool conditions. Sometimes, cool periods must alternate with warm conditions before growth resumes. This pattern happens naturally in the field while the spring is settling. But germination percentages outdoors aren't particularly high; you get better results by controlling the environment.

Other seeds are fully formed but need a simulated winter to break dormancy. Some seed companies indicate whether special treatment is necessary. Read the catalog description and all codes on the packet with care. If they call for **stratification**, you're usually safe in assuming that the seed should be planted in a moist flat, covered with plastic, and stored at about 40°F for three weeks before being moved to progressively warmer and brighter areas. The crisper compartment in the refrigerator is a great stratification chamber if your basement is inappropriate. Should the seed require a longer cool period, the packet will specify the duration. Similarly, if the seed must be frozen, many companies have the courtesy to say so. However, if you buy from houses that do a high volume of inexpensive seed or those catering to professional growers, stratification directions may be sketchy to nonexistent. If you don't get good germination on a particular seed, check a good reference book.

Scarification is another term you'll run into. It means that the seed coat must be slightly injured to promote germination. In nature most of these seeds pass through the intestinal tract of a bird or other animal, where intestinal acids partially erode their rough coats. When they're dropped on the soil, water can penetrate the presoftened seed coat.

The fastest way to scarify seeds is to rub them along a piece of fairly coarse sandpaper. Don't *remove* the seed coat; scratching is sufficient. Some companies scarify seed before they send it out, others indicate the requirement and some don't do it or mention it. Suspect the need to scarify when you're working with a big, tough seed that doesn't germinate well under normal conditions.

It's easy to get the terms stratification and scarification confused. Imagine that a seed is "scared" to be scarified and you'll never confuse the two again.

Buying Seeds

If you are already a gardener, you know about the fascination of seed catalogs. If not, you can look forward to your initiation into the annual rite of ordering seeds. It normally begins in early January when you write for catalogs from various seed houses. Once you've ordered from them, most companies send next year's catalog automatically.

It's difficult to choose only a few varieties from the hundreds offered. Outside gardeners are wise to buy only from companies located in a similar climate because their varieties will have the same temperature and photoperiod preferences. A greenhouse brings greater latitude; northern growers can grow long-season hot peppers, while those in the South can grow cool-weather plants during the winter. But don't go out of your region for every variety. Both photoperiod and light intensity can affect plant performance in the greenhouse. In areas with low light intensity and short photoperiods during the early spring, for example, Vendor tomatoes perform better than Michigan-Ohio tomatoes. With higher light and a relatively long photoperiod, the situation is reversed. This difference is subtle enough so that growers in northern Vermont should use Vendor while growers in southern Ontario can get away with Michigan-Ohio. I recommend varieties in chapters 13 and 14, which deal with warm- and cool-weather crops, but because I haven't grown in every region of the country, take my suggestions only as guidelines. Experiment and compare notes with other growers in your area.

Whenever you are choosing seed, go through the catalog noting these key characteristics: days to maturity, disease resistance, size of the mature plant, distinguishing characteristics and whether the seed is hybrid or open-pollinated.

Days to maturity is only an approximation and assumes normal spring weather. Depending upon environmental conditions, the estimate can be inaccurate by several weeks. Spring-planted tomatoes, for example, can easily be two weeks "late" in a cloudy year. Because of the waning light intensity and photoperiod, fall greens take two to three weeks longer than the same variety planted in the spring. Use the listed days as an indicator of the *relative* speed of one variety versus another. Whenever practical, choose short-season varieties; they occupy growing area for less time, ultimately making your greenhouse more productive.

For most vegetables the days to maturity are counted from the day the seed is planted. However, for tomatoes, peppers, eggplants and, in some catalogs, broccoli and cauliflower, this figure is counted from the transplanting date. To determine the time between sowing and harvesting, add six weeks to the number given for tomatoes, broccoli and cauliflower and eight weeks for peppers and eggplants.

Plant size is an important consideration because greenhouse space is limited. Good crop placement is determined, in part, by plant size and shape. When choosing varieties think about where you will plant the crop as well as how much it will yield. Bush cucumbers, for example, give a good return on space occupied when they're planted in tubs. In beds, however, the higher-yielding vining varieties are a better choice because they can be trained vertically. Most seed catalogs give a fairly accurate indication of the size and relative yields of dwarf varieties when planted outside. However, even dwarfs grow larger in a good greenhouse environment, so give them extra space above and beyond what the catalog calls for.

Variety differences can be enormous. Distinguishing characteristics include color, flavor, and climate and soil preference. Some things, such as color in chard, are relatively unimportant, but others determine success or failure. Keep the greenhouse environment in mind when choosing varieties. For example, spring lettuces should be bolt-resistant, while fall greens must grow well in low-light conditions. Some discussion of important characteristics is included in the sections on individual varieties in chapters 13 and 14.

Starting Seeds

Most home greenhouse crops are started in small flats or pots and then transplanted into beds 4 to 12 weeks after germination. Transplanting saves space; one crop can mature in the bed while the replacement grows to transplant size in a small container. But some plants grow so quickly or are so resistant to being moved that they're seeded directly into the bed. To help you determine which crops prefer

Seed-Starting Practices

Usually Transplanted	Not Usually Transplanted
Broccoli	Beet
Cabbage	Carrot
Cauliflower	Chard*
Celery	Chinese cabbage*
Cucumber	Kale*
Eggplant	New Zealand spinach
Herbs	Onion sets
Lettuce	Pea
Melon	Radish
Pepper	Spinach
Tomato	

*These crops can be transplanted if care is taken not to disturb their sensitive roots.

which treatment, refer to the chart Seed-Starting Practices. You can use flats to start all vegetables that are usually transplanted, except for tender-rooted melons and cucumbers.

Over the years, more and more of my best plants have been started not communally in flats, but individually in pots. This is not a space-conserving system. Nor is it inexpensive in medium, time or containers. But it's worth it. I start melons, cucumbers, early tomatoes, peppers, eggplants and many herbs and ornamentals in pots. I find that each of these crops yields more when started with a good initial root ball.

Preferences for starting media vary from grower to grower and from crop to crop. I normally use two or three types through the spring, depending upon my schedule and the crops I'm growing. You can choose from sterile, soilless media without nutrients; sterile, soilless media with nutrients; nonsterile, lightened soil mixes; or pasteurized, lightened soil mixes.

Planting depth is determined by both seed size and light requirements. Small-seeded plants generally produce short primary stems and roots. If they're planted deeply, the primary stem can't push the cotyledons or first leaves above the soil. The seedling dies before you even see it.

Many small-seeded plants need light to germinate well. If you can't find a light recommendation, cover tiny seed lightly. The light preferences of various vegetables are listed in the chart on page 128.

Large seeds should be covered to twice their size. If the seeds are long and pointed, like those of marigolds and cucumbers, push the

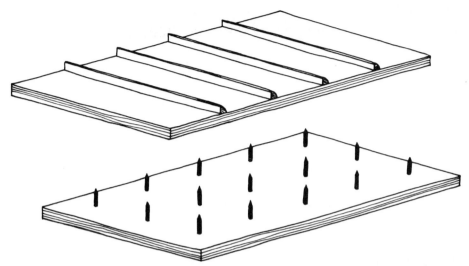

Seed-Sowing Accessories: *A row marker, top, and a dibble-board make it quick and easy to mark seed spacings in a prepared flat.*

most sharply pointed end into the soil first. The root emerges from the pointed end.

If the medium is premoistened, flats and containers don't need to be watered right away. Small seeds make an exception to this rule; it's best to mist planted seeds so that they lodge between wet bits of vermiculite and peat moss. This is also your opportunity to give them a dose of liquid seaweed. Covered flats and containers may not need watering until the seeds germinate. Check them twice a day. During germination the medium shouldn't change color or dry on the surface. But don't keep it soggy, either.

Remove covers as soon as the first seed in the flat has sprouted. Occasionally fungus shows on the first germinating seeds. Remove the cover immediately if you see a gray or white fibrous growth around the seed. If you're lucky, you're just looking at roots, but sometimes it's a fungus. Move the flat into bright light and hold back on watering. After making certain that the growth is a fungus, pick out affected seedlings and throw them away. With quick action, disaster can usually be forestalled.

Soil Temperature

Most seeds prefer higher soil temperatures during germination than during growth. Place those with the highest temperature preferences in the warmest areas or on a heating cable; those that like cool

Light Preferences and Soil Temperatures for Germination

Plant	Light Needs	Temperature Range (°F)	Optimum Temperature (°F)
Beet	Darkness	40–85	80
Broccoli	Darkness	40–85	75
Cabbage	Darkness	40–85	75
Carrot	Darkness	45–85	80
Cauliflower	Darkness	40–85	75
Celery	Darkness	60–70	70
Chard	Darkness	40–80	75
Cucumber, European	Darkness	65–95	90
Cucumber, standard	Darkness	65–90	85
Eggplant	Light	60–90	85
Lettuce	Light	35–80	75
Melon	Darkness	60–95	90
Onion	Darkness	35–85	75
Oriental greens	Darkness	35–85	70
Parsley	Darkness	45–85	75
Pea	Darkness	40–75	70
Pepper	Light	60–95	85
Radish	Darkness	40–85	75
Spinach	Darkness	35–75	70
Tomato	Light	50–85	85

temperatures, place in the lower, cooler areas. Save shady areas for seeds that need darkness for germination.

Soil temperatures in the spring and fall greenhouse will probably be high enough for starting most cool-weather crops. But in the early spring, temperatures may be too low for warm-weather seedlings. Check the soil temperature in a representative flat during both the early afternoon and before sunrise when the flat reflects its night temperature. Night soil temperatures are just as important as daytime temperatures. If they dip below the recommended range, germination is inhibited. The seed may lie dormant or rot. Heating cables and propagating mats solve the temperature problem. As discussed in chapter 4, these cables act to warm the flats from below. Propagating chambers, also discussed in chapter 4, hold heat even better. To help you give your newly planted seeds the best environment for germination, refer to the chart Light Preferences and Soil Temperatures for Germination.

Air Temperature

Air temperature isn't crucial to germination as long as the soil temperature is high enough. But, for most seeds, germination is a relatively fast process. The greenhouse air must be warm enough to promote good growth once seeds have sprouted.

Fortunately for those of us who dread the utility bill, seedlings are stronger if grown in a slightly cool environment during their first few weeks. Seedlings of warm-weather crops thrive in temperatures of 65°F during the day, 50°F at night. Cool-weather crops prefer a 55 to 60°F day and a 45 to 50°F night. In fact, some plants bolt prematurely when exposed to extremely high temperatures during the seedling life. Cauliflower seedlings are particularly sensitive; they head prematurely if grown either too cold or too hot during their first weeks.

If the greenhouse is too warm for some crops during their seedling growth, move them to cold frames when they are forming their second true leaves. They are most sensitive from this point on.

Direct Seeding in Beds

Planting a greenhouse bed is very similar to planting an intensive bed in the garden. Prepare a plan in advance so that you know how many of each seed to plant and where to put them. (Seasonal plans are included in the next chapter as examples.) Prepare and water beds at least a day in advance of planting. Assemble all of the necessary seeds, labels, soilless mix for covering seeds and a measuring stick before you start.

Measure off the rows before planting. The Spacing Guide in the next chapter gives planting distances of the most common greenhouse vegetables. As you measure, mark the row and turn the stick on its side to make small furrows.

Plant the seed at the correct depth. Beds sometimes encourage deep planting, so pay attention. If the seed needs light to germinate, or if you've had trouble with fungus diseases in the past, use a soilless mix in the furrow or as a light cover. After planting, mist the entire bed thoroughly. It's rare to cover a bed with glass or plastic. The depth of the bed helps to protect the seed from drying out. If you reduce air circulation, there's more danger of damping-off. Watering can't follow a formula. If the weather is hot and bright, seeds may need misting twice a day, but in cooler, humid periods they may go for a couple of days without watering.

The World of the Seedling

Beginning gardeners are sometimes shocked to discover that keeping seedlings alive and healthy is more difficult than getting seeds to germinate. Young plants need precise care. Once again, balance is important. They must be adequately, but not excessively, watered; they must have enough, but not excessive amounts of, soil nutrients; and they like a great deal of light. Air circulation is crucial; seedlings use more carbon dioxide (CO_2) relative to their size than at any other time in their lives. And because they are so succulent and tender, seedlings are especially attractive to pests and fungi.

Watering is one of the most exacting duties of a greenhouse grower. With seedlings, the soil should be moist at all times at the lower depths, but it shouldn't be saturated for long. Young roots respire very quickly and require good quantities of both air and water. Overwatering is the most common error. Water each flat and pot individually, according to its particular needs. Use warm water to keep soil temperatures high enough. And remember, only a misting nozzle is gentle enough for young seedlings.

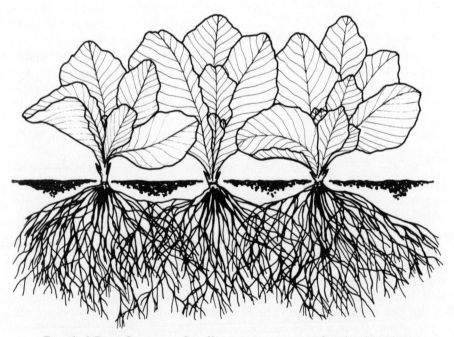

Tangled Root Systems: *Seedling roots are out of sight, but they shouldn't be out of mind. To minimize root damage to neighbors during thinning, hold the surrounding soil in place as you remove a tiny plant.*

Occasionally I forget to water on time. Few things produce such immediate and intense anxiety as a wilted greenhouse. But don't despair too much, for most plants can make a good comeback if they're rescued properly. Begin by misting leaves with the Fogg-It nozzle. Then water all edges of flats and beds, move to the centers and saturate the soil. After you've been through the whole greenhouse, start again, this time watering more quickly. Watch the plants carefully for the next few days. Their water resources have been depleted and they'll tend to dry out more quickly.

Air movement increases the availability of CO_2, decreases the incidence of fungal disease and also makes plants sturdier. Pretend that you are a soft wind and gently shake or blow on the plants each day. Ideally, this should be done to every plant in the greenhouse, even mature ones, at least once a day. Blowing doesn't dispense with the need for consistently good air circulation, but will produce thicker, stronger stems. If you don't have the time to minister to your plants this way, an interior blower or circulating fan provides enough air movement to keep seedlings growing well.

Thinning isn't necessary when you've seeded plants at the correct spacing. But mistakes are easy to make—we all have to thin sometimes. Remember that the root system is much more extensive than the aboveground portion of the plant. A row of seedlings may look like a group of individuals, but underground the roots intertwine to form a dense community. When you pull one plant, all of the other plants in the area are affected, too. Root hairs are pulled away from soil particles and broken off. To minimize damage, thin when the first true leaves are enlarging. It's helpful to place your fingers on the soil surface on both sides of the young plant. Gently hold the soil in place as you pull with the other hand. For tender early salads leave double the required number of leafy crops and pull alternate plants when their leaves touch.

As the time for transplanting approaches, plants may be a bit in advance of the season. If they are becoming crowded, transplant them into larger quarters. If they look as if they may bloom before final transplanting, try to slow them down. Do this by underwatering slightly and by keeping them a bit cooler than usual. Don't let them get so dry that they begin to wilt, but hold back full water rations. You don't want to give this treatment to newly transplanted seedlings, however, because underwatering is injurious to their health. Decreasing water and lowering temperature are the only safe ways to retard a plant. Withholding light and/or nutrients can cause irreparable damage.

Transplanting

Transplanting is an exacting operation. With a little practice, it becomes easy. Practice good techniques until they're automatic—

transplanting affects the plant's whole life.

Plants in a nutrient-based mix or those being fertilized need transplanting at the first sign of crowding. Root crowding is indicated by very fast drying of the soil medium. For some plants—lettuce and celery, for example—this may happen long before the leaves of adjacent plants touch each other.

Leaves of tomatoes, peppers, eggplants, broccoli and cauliflower begin to touch just as their roots are running out of room. Don't delay transplanting; a setback in growth at this stage of a plant's life influences its later health and yields for the worse.

When it's impossible to transplant crowded seedlings from a soilless mix at the correct time, feed with a weak liquid fertilizer solution. Liquid seaweed, fish emulsion and compost or manure tea are all appropriate. Fertilizing will sustain the seedlings for a few days, but don't put transplanting off for too long, otherwise there may be severe damage.

Before transplanting, thoroughly drench the roots. Roots in wet soil separate more easily so this step is especially important for seedlings in flats. I use a seaweed–fish emulsion blend for most crops.

Prepare new flats and pots before you remove the seedlings from their former homes. When moving very small plants, fill the new container almost to the top. Older plants have a larger root ball; be sure to leave enough room for it.

Pencils, dibbles and fingers all poke nice holes in flats. I like to make the holes before I begin to transplant because the work goes faster. Usually I can set the root ball into the hole with one hand while the other gently firms the soil around it. No doubt you'll develop some ambidextrous tricks during transplanting time.

To move a small seedling into a peat or plastic pot, hold it in the center of the pot, between the fingers of one hand, while you add and gently firm the soil around the roots. Fill the pot to half an inch below the rim to leave room for watering.

My favorite tool for removing plants from flats is an old table fork. It loosens the soil nicely without cutting roots too badly. Wiggle the fork down into the medium around each plant. Then very gently slide it between the soil and the bottom of the flat, just under the seedlings. Two or three may come up at once. Lift them out, working slowly enough so that their roots have time to separate. A slight push-pull movement, something akin to rocking a car out of a snowbank, works better than a steady pull.

Never hold plants by the stem. Tiny vascular bundles lie close to the stem surface and may be damaged if they're pinched. Try to handle only the soil, but if you must touch a plant, hold it by the leaves, preferably the seed leaves. After each "forkful" of seedlings has been lifted out, separate them from each other by slowly pulling the root balls apart with your fingers.

Keep roots moist through the whole process. It's best to remove only a few plants at a time so that they stay wet. If they're coming out in groups, sandwich them between layers of a wet towel until you're ready to separate and transplant. When you have to leave a flat unfinished, cover any exposed roots with moist soil mix.

Moving seedlings from containers or peat pots into larger pots or beds is easier than moving them from flats. For one thing, they are so much bigger that you don't have to be so finicky. If you are removing plants from plastic pots, place two fingers across the pot, enclosing the stem, turn it upside down and tap on the bottom until the root ball falls out.

Before you do anything to plants in peat pots, thoroughly soak them. If the peat pots still look tough and solid, peel them off or cut slits down the sides to make an easy exit for roots. At the very least, tear off the rims of the pots to the soil line before planting.

When transplanting into permanent beds, mark plant positions and scoop out some soil from each planting hole. If the bed mix is nutritionally weak, add a handful of compost and a sprinkling of bone meal to every hole for tomatoes, cucumbers and melons. Once you've done the preparation, hold each plant upright in its planting hole. I gently enclose the stem between my first two fingers so that it doesn't get squeezed. Fill in the soil, pressing hard enough so that roots make good contact. After all the plants are in place, water the bed well.

If some of your seedlings are going into large pots as permanent homes, place drainage material in the bottom of each pot and add your standard growing mix.

Newly transplanted seedlings need time to reestablish their root systems before they can withstand bright light or high temperatures. If seedlings have been moved into flats or pots, place them in shady areas of the greenhouse for a few days. I usually stick them under benches. But without shady areas or when seedlings have been transplanted into beds, you have to make some shade. Screen the young plants with bamboo window shades, cheesecloth or greenhouse shading net until they take hold. Keep the seedlings well watered. If temperatures are too high, keep a circulating fan on and mist in the afternoon. It generally takes two to three days before root systems are actively growing into the new medium. You'll know when this happens by looking—they perk up and begin rapid growth again.

Hardening Off

Some of your seedlings may be destined for the garden rather than the greenhouse. You must harden these plants before transplanting them outside. Hardening off helps plants make the transition from the greenhouse to the garden by encouraging them to store carbohydrates.

Hardening also acclimates plants to outside conditions.

Hardening off is a progressive process, not something you do in a day. Begin hardening seedlings by moving them to a cold frame on a sunny day for a couple of hours. Leave the glazing propped open so that they feel the air temperature and wind. If you don't have a cold frame, move the seedlings to a somewhat shaded and protected spot during the day. Don't take them directly into the sun their first few days out; start them off in partial shade or behind something that filters the light like bamboo curtains and cheesecloth-covered frames. Increase their light exposure and time outdoors each day.

Plants that are underwatered during their hardening off process make an easier transition to the garden. When water supplies are low and temperatures are cool, plants respond by storing carbohydrates. This gives them a reserve to draw upon during their period of adjustment following transplanting into the garden.

Try to time hardening off so that, by the second week, nights will be warm enough to leave the plants out. Particularly hardy plants—such as cabbage family crops, pansies and carnations—can withstand a light frost with no damage. Lettuce and other greens perform best if nights are 35°F or above. Healthy tomato plants can survive temperatures as low as 26°F, but their growth and subsequent fruiting is severely retarded. It's best to wait until night lows average 45°F before leaving them out. Eggplants and cucurbits are the most sensitive to low night temperatures. If possible, don't expose them to temperatures below 50°F.

A week is the minimum time for hardening off. Tender crops seem to perform better if the process is slower, usually about two weeks. This extra time can save the crop from a sudden cold snap. You can bring tender plants inside for the night. Don't bother to transplant crops before the soil is warm. You won't be gaining any advantage since cool soil slows their growth.

It's easy to protect outside crops with season-extending structures. Plastic tunnels, cold frames and other structures increase temperatures so much that plants are able to withstand transplanting about two weeks earlier than normal. But if you use these structures, make certain not to harden the plants first—you don't want to slow their growth.

❧ CHAPTER 9 ❧
CROP SCHEDULES AND PLANTING SCHEMES

Crop placement and timing are important in a greenhouse. Space is at a premium, microclimates shift and seasons flow into each other. As you gain experience with a particular environment, crop schedules and planting schemes become second nature. But still, writing a detailed plan for each season helps with organization. As the year progresses, keep records on the growth, yields and general performance of each crop. It's surprising how much you can forget from one year to the next; good notes jog your memory. Use the charts and suggestions in this chapter only as a starting point and change them in response to your own experience.

Spring Crop Scheduling

Spring comes to the greenhouse when the days begin to lengthen, about mid-February in most regions. If the greenhouse has been running all winter, beds are probably full of the last of the fall- or winter-planted greens. Pots of herbs and winter-flowering ornamentals may be scattered here and there, and if artificial lights are installed, new seedlings may be almost ready to transplant into bed positions.

Artificial lights give greater flexibility during both winter and early spring. But for now we'll focus on a greenhouse with natural light and save discussion of artificial lighting schedules for the winter crop section.

Plants that will grow to maturity in the greenhouse are the first to be started. They all need the highest light levels possible at this time of year, so I clear a section of the brightest bed in the house for them. I'm also careful to start everything in pots or flats to make the most of well-lit areas. Lettuce and other greens start my season, followed by tomatoes, peppers and eggplants. Melons and cucumbers are the final plants to be started.

The chart Spring Crop Scheduling gives a rough approximation of the crop timing I use during spring. But timing varies according to regional differences and particular climatic conditions. A cloudy spring holds crops back while a sunny one pushes them ahead.

Spring Crop Scheduling

Crop	Seed	Transplant	Harvest
Lettuce	mid-February	late March	early May
Tomato	late February	early April	late June
Pepper	late February	mid- to late April	late June
Eggplant	late February	mid- to late April	early July
Cucumber	early March	early April	late June
Melon	early March	early April	early July

Scheduling Garden Seedlings

Next come seedlings for the outside garden. Scheduling these plants is a matter of counting backward from the time they'll be set outside. That date is determined by the last frost date in your area and by the plants' hardiness. The chart How to Figure Seed-Starting Dates gives a good schedule for starting common garden plants, no matter what your climate.

If you're accustomed to starting plants on a windowsill, the dates given in the chart may seem late to you. But plants grow much more quickly in a greenhouse and don't need as long a lead time. In my cold spot of northern Vermont, for example, frost-free dates range from June 1 to June 10. Traditionally, gardeners start tomatoes on Town Meeting Day, the first Tuesday in March, giving them 12 weeks before transplanting. "Windowsill" tomatoes are just ready to bloom in early June. But each year, new greenhouse owners discover that the old schedule is disastrous. In a greenhouse, twelve-week-old plants set fruit long before the frost-free date. And though it might seem gratifying to set out fruiting plants, their final yields never match those of plants transplanted before blossoms open.

Starting schedules can be confusing, especially if you're growing a wide variety of plants. For example, even though broccoli and tomatoes both require six to seven weeks' growth before setting out, their schedules differ as their hardiness differs. To make it easy to remember starting dates, translate the general schedule given in the chart into calendar dates. For an idea of how this works, see the sample from my Vermont starting schedule for first outside plantings without protection. If I'm using some sort of season-extending structures, the schedule is moved ahead by several weeks to take account of early transplanting.

Write your starting schedule on a big calendar in waterproof ink and hang it near the potting area. Sad experience has also taught me

How to Figure Seed-Starting Dates

To determine when you need to start seeds for plants for the outdoor garden, first figure out their safe transplanting dates, taking into account last frosts and plant hardiness. Then count back the given number of weeks from that date to find the seed-starting date.

Weeks from Seed Sowing to Transplant Size	Plant
18–20	Perennials and biennials (including most herbs), geranium (both cuttings and seeds), tuberous begonia, thunbergia, pansy
14–15	Ageratum, carnation, lobelia, snapdragon, verbena, browallia, petunia
9–10	Annual phlox, coleus, schizanthus, salpiglossis, annual poppy, standard marigold, impatiens, petunia, scabiosa, salvia, gazania, celery, eggplant, pepper, leeks
8–9	Annual delphinium, annual dianthus, dwarf marigold, nicotina, portulaca, sweet alyssum, asparagus seed
6–7	Tomato, cabbage family crops, larkspur, celosia, annual baby's breath, nasturtium, chives, annual herbs
5–6	Melon, cabbage family crops, lettuce, squash
4	Melon (a second planting in case first is lost to late snow or frost), cucumber, lettuce, squash (see comment after melon)

to note quantities on the calendar; otherwise, I get absentminded and plant more flats than the greenhouse can hold at once. I also find that by planting the same varieties in series, I can juggle space on the heating cable and guarantee a backup crop if something horrible happens to the first.

Spring is the most hectic period of the year. Early greenhouse crops need care just when you're also seeding and transplanting for the outside garden. But it does pass. Before long, most of your work is summer maintenance.

Author's Outdoor Seedling Schedule		
Plant	Transplant Date	Starting Date
Basil	June 1–10	April 22–29
Broccoli	May 15–20	March 27–April 8
Cauliflower	May 15–20	March 27–April 8
Cucumber	June 10–15	May 4–11
Eggplant	June 10–15	March 20–April 6
Impatiens	June 1–10	March 25–April 1
Lettuce	May 15–20	April 10–17
Pansy	May 10–15	December 27–January 2
Parsley	May 15–20	March 27–April 8
Pepper	June 1–10	March 21–April 1
Petunia	May 15–20	February 27–March 12
Primula	May 10–15	December 27–January 2
Snapdragon	May 10–15	January 30–February 6
Tomato	June 1–10	April 22–29

Summer Crop Scheduling

The summer greenhouse is used for warm-weather crops such as cucumbers, melons, peppers, eggplants and tomatoes. Many herbs also perform well, and if temperatures stay below 80°F, lettuce can be a good summer crop.

Most people start their summer plants in spring. But still, some new plantings are always being made. Fall greenhouse tomatoes are normally started in flats or pots during the first or second week of June. They must be transplanted to bed positions in mid- to late July, so it's important to plan to have a clear bed in a warm, well-lit position available by this time. I often interplant heat-resistant lettuce between tomatoes to take advantage of their shade. The tomato harvest begins in September or early October. Depending upon the environment, late plants can give you vine-ripened fruit through November or even beyond.

In the North, peppers, eggplants and melons don't produce well beyond the beginning of October. After several frustrating years of babying them along for only a halfhearted yield, I've given up. In a greenhouse with consistently high temperatures and artificial light, or in a more moderate climate, a fall crop could be practical. If you want to give them a try, start these crops in early June for a harvest beginning in October.

You can start fall greens as early as August. The beds are likely to be full of heavily bearing crops at this time, so start all of your greens, even those that resent transplanting, in small containers. Peat pots are a good choice for oriental greens because the plants sometimes bolt prematurely when their roots are disturbed. You can hold greens in starting pots for four to six weeks, but don't let them get rootbound.

Winter-blooming ornamentals cheer my spirits. I prefer fresh cut flowers to lettuce any December day, so I'm careful to plant them on time. A few ornamentals need summer planting to come into good winter bloom. Starting schedules for winter flowers are given in chapter 15.

Some growers prefer not to use the greenhouse at all during the summer. In warm climates this certainly makes sense, especially if you're paying good money to keep it cool. But don't dismiss it entirely, because a greenhouse makes a luxurious drying chamber.

Herbs, vegetables and fruits all dry well given the proper conditions. Directions for drying specific crops, including optimum temperature ranges, are included in most recent books dealing with food preservation.

The greenhouse has to be prepared before it becomes a good drying area. If it's attached, you may want to close it off from the main house

---

Housekeeping Chores in the Greenhouse

Early spring or late summer are good times to clean the greenhouse. In summer, let the bright sun help you clean. Remove all the plants, cover beds with an organic mulch or polyethylene, close the vents and let the greenhouse bake for a few days. Temperatures will rise high enough to kill many pests and diseases. After baking, open the vents and let the greenhouse cool before rolling up your sleeves for some good old-fashioned scrubbing.

Wash wooden, masonry and metal surfaces, including bench mesh and screens, with a 10 percent laundry bleach solution. I use a big scrub brush for large areas and a smaller vegetable brush to get into the crannies around vent areas. After scrubbing, rinse everything with a pure water spray. The glazing, both inside and out, should be hosed off. If you've got very dirty glass, use the manually compressed air sprayer to get a cleanser onto high areas. You can use a commercial glass cleanser, but since most of these products contain ammonia, be sure to air the greenhouse well before bringing plants back in. A less troublesome cleaning solution for glass is an old-fashioned mix of vinegar and water (use 8 teaspoons vinegar to 1 gallon of water).

Don't forget basic maintenance chores. Recaulk around loose glazing; scrape and repaint peeling areas; and fix all the little things that you've put off. Don't bring plants back into the greenhouse until you're sure that all fumes are gone.

so that it remains as dry as possible. And you'll need a good oscillating fan to drive off moisture released within the greenhouse. For good drying, relative humidity should be as low as possible.

To keep microbial populations high during this process, don't let the soil mix in beds dry out completely. Put several inches of straw or rotted hay over all bed areas to retain moisture. Cheesecloth- or nylon-screened frames can be hung from the cable system. If held at least 8 inches above the mulch, air can circulate under the food. Amazing amounts of water come off during drying: a tomato is 99 percent water and a zucchini isn't that much less. You must keep air circulation high to prevent rot and to speed drying. If insects are present, drape a layer of cheesecloth over all the drying frames. A couple of inverted drinking glasses will hold the cloth off the food.

Fall Crop Scheduling

The early fall greenhouse holds the last of the spring-planted tomatoes, peppers, eggplants, melons and cucumbers as well as some summer greens, herbs and ornamentals. Tomato plants started in mid-February will be finishing their peak production in early September. Since the June-planted tomatoes may not be fruiting until late in the month or early in October, you may wish to keep spring tomatoes in place until the end of September. But if the vines aren't vigorous, pull them. Old plants attract pests and diseases. Fall is the worst time to let problems get out of control, in part because the environment is conducive to the proliferation of both pests and diseases. It's also a bad time to do a major cleaning because you'll lose valuable days when the photoperiod is just long enough to support good growth.

Peppers and eggplants produce farther into the fall season than tomatoes started at the same time. If they're healthy, leave them in place until production slows. By the time the average daytime temperature falls below 60°F and nights average below 50°F, fruit set and ripening slow to a dead halt. In a climate like Vermont, bed space is more productive holding young leafy crops after October.

Melons and cucumbers may have to come out as early as September. Again, make your own judgment based on the health of the plants and their yields if left in place for a couple more weeks.

Many people move fruiting crops from the garden into the greenhouse. In my opinion, the prolonged harvest is rarely worth the risk. I realize that I'm in the minority, but I'll stick to my approach. Even if you inspect carefully, pests are almost certain to come in with the plants. And too, garden crops are old and more problem-prone than they were in their youth. I prefer to sidestep potential hassles by leaving them outside. But if you do bring crops in, choose only the healthiest, inspect them carefully and segregate them in an area that can be curtained with polyethylene. As soon as the first aphid, fungus or virus shows, open the door and chuck the whole plant. Don't think twice about discarding the plant. You can't think as quickly as pests and diseases can spread.

You can plant fall vegetables anytime during August, September and October. In the North the photoperiod shortens quickly toward the middle of October. Without artificial lights, fall crops should be planted before the middle of the month to give them enough time to grow to a good size before winter. The farther south you are, the more your leeway increases.

Broccoli is a good fall crop, provided you start it early enough. For a fall harvest, add two weeks to the catalog dates to maturity. In Vermont a crop seeded in August is ready for harvest in November and produces sideshoots until December. Celery is another good fall crop. Planted in early August, it matures in November and holds well through the winter.

Kale, beet greens, lettuce, parsley, chard, turnip greens, collards and spinach are more choices for fall planting. But oriental greens are the most spectacular of all the fall crops. You'll find cultural directions and variety recommendations in chapter 14.

Try to time the starting schedule so that fall and winter greens are transplanted into beds soon after the fruiting crops are pulled. Succession planting saves having to clear and refurbish all the beds on the same day.

Winter Crop Scheduling

Winter is probably the most pleasant season in a home greenhouse. Just when it seems as if all growing things have come to a halt outdoors, indoors your fall-planted greens yield heavily through the coldest, darkest months. With a good selection of fresh herbs, the winter diet becomes even more varied.

Natural light levels aren't high enough in the winter to give seedlings a vigorous start. You can start some ornamentals in January without supplementary light, but their growth is slow. Vegetables aren't only slow, they're weak. If you make fall plantings of greens in succession and harvest only outer leaves, you may never feel the need for artificial lights. But if you hanker after really early tomatoes, bedding plants and well-established perennial herbs and ornamentals, a set of fluorescent lights is invaluable.

Under lights, you can start tomatoes right after Christmas if minimum temperatures average 65°F during the day and 50°F at night. Use a heating cable to guarantee good germination, and provide the plants with a 12-hour day.

If ambient air temperatures are still nippy, a propagating chamber may be appropriate until you're able to move the tomatoes to their permanent positions. Transplant late December sowings into high-light, warm areas in the greenhouse in mid-February. Depending upon the variety and the natural light intensity, your tomato harvest will begin in late April or early May.

Peppers and eggplants are the next crops to start, but since I've had better luck with crops transplanted in March, I wait until January. Melons and cucumbers respond best to a 16-hour day during both their seedling and adult life. Consequently, I wait to start them in the spring.

You can also use lights to replenish the midwinter supply of greens and other cold-tolerant vegetables. In a cool environment and under lights, these crops grow as if it's spring. If temperatures are too low for early tomatoes, plant fresh greens, broccoli, cauliflower and even short-season edible-podded peas to brighten the last days of winter. Use 3- to 4-inch peat pots to start the peas, and let them grow for four weeks under lights before transplanting to beds. Incidentally, flowering sweet peas like the same treatment.

Lights are almost indispensable for those who want early spring flowers or perennials for spring sales. Photoperiod requirements vary between crops, but you can't go too far wrong with a 12- to 14-hour artificial day during their first six weeks of growth. Early scheduling is tricky and may take a couple of years to develop. Like all other plants, ornamentals are healthiest when transplanted before their buds have opened. But sometimes they begin to bud before the weather has settled. It's possible to slow them down by moving the flats into a cool area and reducing water slightly. As soon as the danger of heavy frosts has passed, you can shift hardy plants such as snapdragons and carnations to a cold frame. Move them in stages, initially taking them out only for the day. After a week or so, they'll be ready to stay out all night. The cool temperatures retard both their growth and bloom.

If you're growing bedding plants for sale, you'll want to have some in bloom for eager customers. Despite advice to the contrary, many people like to set out blooming flats for "instant" gardens. For your own plants, follow the guidelines given earlier in the chart How to Figure Seed-Starting Dates. Start plants for sale about a week earlier, and never hold them back by reducing temperatures or water. A blend of liquid seaweed and fish emulsion or a dusting of bone meal are good fertilizers for bedding plants. A high phosphorous content promotes blooming.

In the coldest areas of the country, running a freestanding traditional greenhouse during December, January and early February is expensive. I certainly won't pay that kind of utility bill. But the time isn't really wasted. In the same way that southern growers use summer heat for cleaning and maintenance, northern growers can use the icy temperatures of winter.

Begin by removing all plants and turning off the auxiliary heat. Sudden freezing doesn't hurt the soil but does kill many pests and diseases. As a matter of fact, it's the best recourse when problems get out of hand. The more sudden the freeze, the better it works. Close off attached greenhouses from the main house and open the vents to the outdoors. Leave freestanding units completely open.

If your greenhouse features water barrel heat storage, be forewarned that water barrels burst when allowed to freeze. Check water temperatures with a soil probe *every day*. As soon as the water measures 36 to 34°F, close the vents and add supplementary heat. Be cautious: broken barrels are more than most of us can handle.

A few years ago, friends of mine took a winter holiday, leaving their attached greenhouse unheated. Predictably, it froze. When they returned in January, everything looked fine. But then came the February thaw. Water leaked from every barrel and froze over the floor. The place could have doubled as an ice rink. My friends vacillated between joking about laying down sawdust paths and wondering why they were crazy enough to install barrel storage. But finally, spring asserted itself. The time came to bite the bullet and clean up. Their first job was getting the electric heater unstuck. Successive layers of road salt melted enough ice so that it could be lifted out. After that, supplementary heaters turned the floor into slush that could be shoveled into carts and dumped outside. A few days of high temperatures, artificially induced, finished drying the floor. And then began the great barrel migration. Broken ones were removed, and once again new barrels had to be located, purchased, transported, set in place and filled. It wasn't their favorite spring. Since then, they've used the auxiliary heater.

Incidentally, if you've had visions of building a solar greenhouse with water barrel storage but without auxiliary heating, take note. You may face a similar problem one cold winter. Avoid it at any cost—it's hard to love a greenhouse that causes that much aggravation.

Crop Layouts

Crop placement satisfies everyone's urge for creating order out of chaos. Where you place particular plants depends on their temperature and light requirements, root dimensions, aboveground size and form and their best companions.

Layouts can be complex or simple, depending upon your preference. Sometimes I monocrop one bed and stick 15 different crops in the next. But there are a few guidelines you should keep in mind:

- Never leave bed areas empty. As soon as one crop is harvested, transplant another into the space.

- Plant tall crops to the north and/or west of small crops and train them vertically.

- Whenever practical, diversify beds; that is, make sure they hold a variety of crops.

- Arrange diversified beds so that good companions are next to each other.

- Use microclimates within the bed appropriately.

The best way to approach bed layout is to think of it in patterns. Straight rows, zigzag rows and blocks are all suitable planting designs. Straight rows are self-descriptive. Plants are spaced closely within the row, but adjacent rows, either single or double, are widely separated. This layout makes the most sense in an outdoor garden with mechanized cultivation, but wastes space in a greenhouse. Due to their growth habits and trellis systems, peas, cucumbers and melons are the only crops to even consider planting this way. Set their rows directly under overhead cables and train the vines to grow up attached strings. When you use trellises or fencing, set plants several inches from the support.

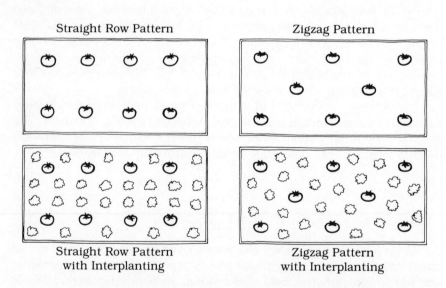

Straight Row Pattern Zigzag Pattern

Straight Row Pattern
with Interplanting

Zigzag Pattern
with Interplanting

Planting Patterns: Straight rows are best suited to climbing crops grown on trellises. A zigzag pattern gives plants more space, light and better air circulation. With both of these arrangements, you can practice interplanting.

In a zigzag pattern, individual plants give higher yields as a consequence of more root space, higher light levels and better air circulation. Again, place vining crops directly under cables. You'll find that with both straight and zigzag arrangements, there's extra space for intercropping.

Many small plants grow well in blocks rather than rows. In a block planting you allow the same distance between plants in all directions. Use the in-row spacings generally recommended for a crop to determine the planting distance in a block arrangement. Because plants are equidistant on all sides, no space is wasted.

Spacing

Spacing within each pattern depends upon crop requirements. Generous spacing wastes valuable space, but stingy arrangements create a junglelike atmosphere where fungus diseases thrive. Use the Spacing Guide on the next page as a reference for greenhouse spacing distances and patterns. For the sake of people without outside growing area, I've included some crops, such as beans and onions, that are rarely found in greenhouses but can be grown there.

Interplanting and Companion Planting

Interplanting refers to layouts where two or more crops are planted side by side. When well planned, interplanting makes good use of space. Neighboring crops with different nutrient demands and different rooting depths are chosen so they don't compete directly with each other. Some plants also make good companions because they influence each other favorably.

Companion planting is often dismissed as an old gardener's tale because few combinations have been systematically investigated. But verified or not, some very good growers swear by certain groupings. My experience has borne out information about unhappy companions. I've also had good luck with some of the favorable plant pairings. Experiment for yourself and, at the very least, interplant to save space.

Space constraints prevent you from interplanting exactly as you do in the garden. Rather than tucking insect repellent and trap plants into the beds, I achieve the same effect by hanging pots above the plants. Marigolds drive off some insects because of their odor, while nasturtiums and parsley trap aphids. Scented geraniums, flowering parsley and other small-flowered plants provide food and a habitat for tiny beneficial wasps, while pots of sage, hyssop and chives may discourage stray cabbage moths from laying eggs.

Some companions, such as basil and oregano with tomatoes, aid each other through root exudates (substances released by roots). These

Spacing Guide

Plant	Seeding Distance (inches)	Trans- planting Distance (inches)	Recommended Pattern
Bean, bush	3–4	—	Row or zigzag
Beet	3–4*	—	Block or interplant
Broccoli	1–4†	18–30‡	Zigzag
Brussels sprouts	1–4†	18–30‡	Zigzag
Cabbage	1–4†	12–24‡	Zigzag
Carrot	1	—	Block
Cauliflower	1–4†	18–30‡	Zigzag
Chard	3–4*	8–12	Block, zigzag or interplant
Chinese cabbage	4–6*	8–10	Zigzag or block
Chives	½	6	Block or one plant to a pot
Cucumber, European	3–4	18–30	Zigzag, row or one plant to a pot
Cucumber, standard	3–4	18–20	Zigzag, row or one plant to a pot
Eggplant	3–4	12–30‡	Zigzag or one plant to a pot
Garlic	2	—	Block or grow in pot
Kale	4*	6–8	Block or interplant

kinds of companions are most effective when they're planted next to each other, in the same soil. Even so, I interplant them only if I've got lots of extra room. Herbs grow so well in hanging pots that the slight increase in tomato vigor doesn't seem worth the space.

Under certain environmental conditions, lettuce and tomatoes make good greenhouse companions. The lettuce will tolerate the slight shade created by the tomatoes, and the greens will be ready for harvest by the time the tomatoes need more growing room. For best lettuce flavor and texture, day temperatures shouldn't exceed 75°F. Buttercrunch, Kagran and Grand Rapids are good interplanting varieties. Lettuce

Spacing Guide

Plant	Seeding Distance (inches)	Trans- planting Distance (inches)	Recommended Pattern
Lettuce, head	4*	8–12	Block, zigzag or interplant
Lettuce, leaf	3–4*	6–10	Block, zigzag or interplant
Onion, seeds	½*	—	Interplant or grow in pot
Onion, sets	2*	—	Interplant or grow in pot
Oriental greens	4–6*	8–10	Block, zigzag or interplant
Parsley	1–3†	4	Interplant, block or grow in pot
Pea	3–4	—	Row
Pepper	1–3	12–24‡	Zigzag
Radish	1½	—	Block or interplant
Spinach	3–4*	—	Block
Tomato	1–4†	16–30‡	Zigzag

*These crops are thinned as they grow. By maturity at least every other plant will have been thinned and eaten.

†This distance depends upon the medium into which they are seeded and whether they are to be transplanted before being moved into permanent bed positions.

‡The smaller spacing refers to crops that are planted in groups without other crops. The larger spacing allows interplanting between the crop.

grows best when transplanted at only four weeks of age, so start it two weeks after seeding the tomato crop. Transplant both crops into beds on the same day.

Cucumbers and melons grow too quickly to be nice companions. Outside, trellised plants are often used to shade midsummer lettuce, but in the greenhouse they deserve a bed to themselves. If you want to interplant among cucurbits, radishes are the only crop with time to mature before being shaded out. Peas, even dwarf varieties, grow to amazing heights in a greenhouse. Interplanting between their rows is only a waste of good seed.

Companion Plants for the Greenhouse

Plant	Companions Recommended	Companions Not Recommended
Bean, bush	Beet, cabbage family crops, carrot, eggplant, lettuce, marigold, summer savory, celery	Onion, fennel
Beet	Bush bean, onion, cabbage family crops, lettuce	None
Cabbage family	Onion, sage, marigold, nasturtium, dill, beet, mint, chamomile	Tomato
Carrot	Lettuce, onion, pea, tomato, sage	Dill
Chard	See Beet	
Chives	Cabbage family crops, beet, carrot, lettuce, pepper, tomato, sage, savory	Pea, bean
Cucumber	Radish	None
Eggplant	Basil, oregano, parsley	Cabbage family crops, cucurbits
Garlic	Cabbage family crops, tomato, lettuce	Pea, bean
Lettuce	Tomato, carrot, onion, radish	None
Onion	See Chives	
Parsley	Tomato, eggplant, pepper, carrot	None
Pea	Carrot, radish, cabbage family crops	Onion, chives
Pepper	See Tomato	
Radish	Bean, carrot, cucumber, lettuce, pea, squash, melon	None
Tomato	Basil, oregano, parsley, carrot, onion, mint, marigold, nasturtium	Cabbage family crops, cucurbits

Due to variations in root depth, nutrient requirements and pest preferences, diversified blocks of greens perform better than mono-crops. Aphids don't like Chinese cabbage, for example. They hesitate before walking across its prickly leaves to get to the next lettuce plant. Shading is the only danger of this system; a group of tall plants toward the south will shade smaller ones in the interior. Get to know the growth habits of each variety before using it in a diversified block.

Use the chart Companion Plants for the Greenhouse only as a general guide. Over the course of several seasons, you'll probably find good companion pairings not listed here, or you may find that some of the listed companions don't seem to help each other at all. For example, I plant spinach with almost any crop that requires a high nitrogen supply. Even though it isn't mentioned as a companion to them I use it with lettuce and other greens. These crops make good neighbors because of their similar nutrient needs; when you plant them together, they all benefit from extra nitrogen applied to the bed.

Planning the Crop Scheme

A crop scheme is a plan for the greenhouse. It includes the number of plants of each variety that you will grow; the positions that each will occupy; and dates for seed starting, transplanting, setting into permanent position and end of harvest. Some people may be so organized that they can dispense with this step, but I don't fall into that category. Without a plan, I'm likely to plant too early or too late, or sow entirely too much of one thing. I use my crop scheme as a framework; though I usually deviate from it a little as the season progresses, the basic plan stays the same.

To come up with a crop scheme of your own, begin by listing all of the plants for the season, the desired quantitites of each, their size and environmental requirements and any companioning ideas inspired by the earlier chart Companion Plants for the Greenhouse. The charts Cool-Weather Crops and Warm-Weather Crops will be useful guides in planning your crop schemes.

I use a drawing of the interior to sketch crop placement. This step helps me allow enough space for each plant, both horizontally and vertically. It's important to keep light and temperature zones in mind. As you go, list planned dates to start, transplant and pull each crop, making certain that there's enough time for peak production before the next crop is moved into the space. Write relevant dates on the greenhouse calendar.

For an example of year-round planning, I've included the following crop schemes. These are based on Layout 2 for the traditional freestanding greenhouse shown in chapter 3. Don't be dismayed if your plan is entirely different. These schedules and crop choices are appropriate for the North and reflect my taste and growing style. I've also tried to minimize confusion by simplifying them a bit.

Cool-Weather Crops

Crop	Height (inches)	Temperature (°F) Night–Day	Light	Days to Yield from Seed
Beet greens	10–14	45–65	Moderate–low	40–65
Broccoli	24–36	45–65	Bright	75–90
Brussels sprouts	24–36	45–65	Bright	100–120
Cabbage	12	45–65	Moderate	60–120
Cabbage, Chinese	12–18	45–65	Moderate	45–90
Carrot	12	50–75	Bright	60–90
Cauliflower	18–36	50–65	Bright	50–85
Chard	12–18	50–75	Moderate	50–60
Chives	10–16	45–75	Moderate	60–90
Lettuce, head	6–8	50–70	Bright	50–75
Lettuce, leaf	6–8	45–65	Moderate–low	45–60
Onion sets	12–16	50–65	Moderate–bright	75–95
Oriental greens	12–18	40–65	Moderate–low	45–70
Parsley	12–16	45–65	Moderate	70–100
Pea	5–6	45–65	Moderate–bright	55–70
Radish	6–8	45–75	Moderate–bright	21–30
Spinach	8–10	40–60	Moderate–bright	40–60

Warm-Weather Crops

Crop	Height (inches)	Temperature (°F) Night–Day	Light	Days to Yield from Seed
Bean, bush	24–36	60–80	Bright	50–70
Cucumber	5–6	65–85	Bright	50–75
Eggplant	24–36	60–80	Bright	110–130
Melon	48–72	60–85	Bright	70–90
Pepper	24–36	60–80	Bright	110–130
Tomato, cherry	12–72	60–80	Bright	95–139
Tomato, standard	60–72	60–80	Bright	100–140

Spring Crop Scheme

Bed 1 West Side

Fall and winter greens—harvest as space is needed for flats

Bed 1 East Side

Start first seedling flats, following seedling schedule

Bench

Under lights—tomatoes, peppers, eggplants, melons, cucumbers, potted herbs and ornamentals

Bed 3

Broccoli—start Jan. 7, transplant Feb. 22, last harvest Apr. 15–25
Beet greens—direct-seed Feb. 22, last harvest Apr. 15–25
Spinach—same as beet greens
Lettuce—start Feb. 1, transplant Feb. 22, last harvest Apr. 15–25

Bed 4

Tomatoes—start Jan. 7, transplant Feb. 22, last harvest July 1–15
Chard—start Jan. 7, transplant Feb. 22, last harvest Apr. 1
Lettuce—start Jan. 21, transplant Feb. 22, last harvest Apr. 1
Pac choi—same as lettuce, start in peat pods
Osaka—same as lettuce, start in peat pots
Chinese cabbage—same as lettuce, start in peat pots

Bed 5

Tomatoes—start Jan. 7, transplant Feb. 22, last harvest July 15
Lettuce—start Jan. 21, transplant Feb. 22, last harvest Apr. 1

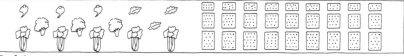

Bed 1

Spring Planting Layout

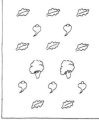

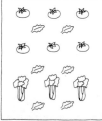

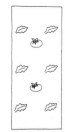

Bench   Bed 3   Bed 4   Bed 5

Summer Crop Scheme

Bed 1 West Side

Eggplants—start Mar. 30, transplant June 1, last harvest
   Oct. 15–30
Peppers—same as eggplants
Cherry tomatoes—start Apr. 20, transplant June 1, last harvest
   Oct. 15–30
Lettuce—start May 1, transplant June 1, last harvest July 10–15
Herbs—same as eggplants

Bed 1 East Side

Peppers—start Feb. 11, transplant Apr. 15, last harvest
   Sept. 15–30
Eggplants—same as peppers
Cherry tomatoes—start Mar. 1, transplant Apr. 15, last harvest
   Sept. 15–30
Lettuce—start Mar. 11, transplant Apr. 15, last harvest
   May 15–June 1
   Herbs—same as peppers

Bench

Potted herbs
Starting flats
Potted ornamentals

Bed 3

Melons—start Mar. 28, transplant Apr. 25, last harvest Oct. 15
Radishes—direct-seed Apr. 25, last harvest May 25–30

Bed 4

Tomatoes—start Jan. 7, transplant Feb. 22, last harvest
   July 1–15

Standard cucumbers—start May 11, transplant June 15, last
  harvest Oct. 15

Bed 5

Tomatoes—start Jan. 7, transplant Feb. 22, last harvest
  July 1–15
Tomatoes—start June 1, transplant July 15, last harvest Nov. 25
Basil and oregano—start May 15, transplant July 15, last harvest
  or move to pots Nov. 25
Lettuce—start June 15, transplant July 15, last harvest
  Aug. 1–15

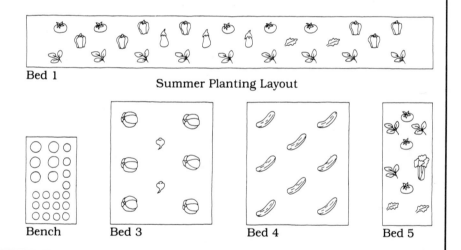

Bed 1

Summer Planting Layout

Bench   Bed 3   Bed 4   Bed 5

Fall Crop Scheme

Bed 1 West Side

Broccoli—start Sept. 18, transplant Oct. 30, last harvest Dec. 18
Cauliflower—start Sept. 18, transplant Oct. 30, last harvest
   Dec. 10
Chinese cabbage—same as broccoli
Pac choi—same as broccoli
Potted herbs—established

Bed 1 East Side

Broccoli—start Aug. 18, transplant Sept. 30, last harvest Nov. 18
Cauliflower—same as broccoli
Chinese cabbage—same as broccoli
Beet greens—direct-seed Sept. 30, last harvest Dec. 30
Spinach—same as beet greens

Bench

Starting flats under lights
Potted herbs and ornamentals

Bed 3

Mixed greens—start Sept. 3, transplant Oct. 15, last harvest
   Dec. 15

Winter Crop Scheme

Bed 1 West Side

Lettuce—start Nov. 6, transplant Dec. 18, last harvest Feb. 15
Starting flats

Bed 1 East Side

Lettuce—start Oct. 7, transplant Nov. 18, last harvest Jan. 15
Lettuce—start Sept. 29, transplant Nov. 10, last harvest Jan. 1
Mixed greens—start Oct. 7, transplant Nov. 18, last harvest Feb. 15

Bench

Potted ornamentals
Starting flats
(Remove to house for Feb. 15 spring cleaning week.)

Bed 3

Mixed greens—start Nov. 1, transplant Dec. 15, last harvest Feb. 15

Bed 4

Mixed greens—start Nov. 1, transplant Dec. 15, last harvest Feb. 15

Bed 4

Mixed greens—start Sept. 3, transplant Oct. 15, last harvest Dec. 15

Bed 5

Mixed greens—start Oct. 15, transplant Nov. 25, last harvest Feb. 15

Bed 1   Fall Planting Layout

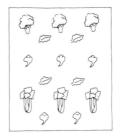

Bench   Bed 3   Bed 4   Bed 5

Bed 5

Mixed greens from fall planting—last harvest Feb. 15

Spring Cleaning—week of Feb. 15–22

Bed 1   Winter Planting Layout

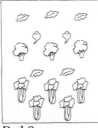

Bench   Bed 3   Bed 4   Bed 5

ᐤᣫᣫ CHAPTER 10 ᣫᣫᐤ
CARING FOR GREENHOUSE PLANTS

Greenhouses require daily attention. Big jobs can be put off until the weekend, but environmental control, watering, pollinating, record keeping and general observation won't wait for a break in your schedule.

A daily morning routine is invaluable. Depending upon the size of your greenhouse, the season and the degree of automation, it won't take more than 15 to 30 minutes to make a daily check.

You'll develop your own work system, of course, but just to get you started, I'll describe mine. I generally stagger into the greenhouse, coffee cup in hand, and grab the record book. With a water-resistant pen I note minimum and maximum temperatures. Then I reset min-max thermometers. If there's a night curtain, I remove it. Depending upon the season, I open vents, activate fans or reset thermostats. Next comes the general tour. I mosey around looking for insects, diseases, harvestable crops and jobs that need doing. When appropriate, I jot notes in the record book. If I'm off to work, I do the crucial jobs before leaving and save the rest until evening or the weekend.

Watering

Morning is the best watering time. During the day the resulting increase in humidity is easier to control and leaves have a chance to dry before dark. Watering looks deceptively easy; in fact, it's one of the most difficult jobs to do correctly. In a well-run commercial operation, only the most experienced staff members are given this job. It's a well-acknowledged fact: "The person who waters makes the profits." Poor watering practices devastate a crop faster than a swarm of aphids.

Overwatering is the most common mistake. In soggy soil, roots can't get enough oxygen. Metabolism slows and roots may even rot. But for good plant growth, the soil must be kept evenly moist, all the way to the bottom of the container. To achieve the right balance between too much and too little, it's important to understand how water moves in soil. When you apply water from above, each successive layer absorbs as much as possible before letting the water drain to lower depths. It's fine to water lightly only when the bed is fairly moist and drainage is rapid. But when a bed is dry, light watering moistens only the top layer. If this pattern becomes habitual, roots will grow laterally instead of probing deep into the soil. Shallow roots can't support heavy topgrowth or reach nutrients below the surface layer.

Both the soil mix and the environment determine watering frequency and quantity. Light soil mixes with good aggregate formation retain moisture without being soggy. With too much drainage material, soils dry quickly. At the other extreme, wet soils contain too high a percentage of water-retentive ingredients without accompanying aggregate formation.

Under cool, humid and cloudy conditions, both plant transpiration and moisture evaporation slow. In the Northeast, for example, beds holding established crops may go for as long as a week between waterings in midwinter. In the summer when it's warm and bright, you may have to water every other day. Small pots and flats may need water twice each day. When it's humid, prevent fungus diseases by watering only when absolutely necessary.

Growers use different methods to determine soil moisture levels. You can tell when a pot is dry just by lifting—dry pots are light. Some people rap a knuckle against containers; a high-pitched ping indicates that the soil is dry. I don't do anything fancy; I just look at the soil surface and stick my finger in if I have any question.

In beds, let the surface layer dry between waterings. Fingers are the best moisture sensors. Stick your finger 3 to 4 inches into the soil. If it's dry below the top couple of inches, water. Remember that edges dry more quickly than the interior. I often water only the sides of a bed or the outermost rows of a group of pots.

Seedlings don't have long roots. It's important to keep their media moist from top to bottom. Keeping the lower depths moist encourages them to develop a deep root system. As they grow, encourage deep rooting even more by gradually increasing intervals between waterings.

Watering should be gentle. Always use a misting nozzle for seedlings, whether they're in pots, flats or even a bed. In a mixed greenhouse containing both seedlings and mature plants, I attach a Y shutoff valve to the end of the hose. With this attachment I can carry a Fogg-It and a water-breaker nozzle simultaneously. I can switch nozzles as needed, so I'm not tempted to use the wrong one.

Warm water, lukewarm to the touch, is always the best choice. As discussed in chapter 4 under Watering Systems, you can build a warming system if you don't have piped hot water. In addition to temperature, be concerned about chlorine in the water. Chlorine damages plants, especially seedlings. In areas where chlorine content is high, draw seedling water a day in advance. Let it sit uncovered so that the chemical can volatize.

Water close to the soil surface. Some ornamentals—African violets, for example—are so fussy about water on their leaves that they develop burned spots under droplets. Big drops act like magnifying glasses, intensifying light and heat. In addition, fungi attack moist leaves. If you're misting to control temperatures, do it early enough in the day so that leaves dry before dark. I use fans instead of misting when there's fungus anywhere in the greenhouse.

Leaching must be done periodically. Unfortunately, I can't give you ironclad rules about frequency. How often you do it depends on the soil mix. In my experience, mixes with lots of aged manure require more leaching than those with compost.

Small whitish incrustations on soil particles are a warning sign that it's time to leach. You'll see these salt buildups only when the soil surface is dry. As soon as you spot them, leach immediately, weather permitting. Like watering, leaching causes problems when the environment is already too humid.

Fertilizing

The fertilizer schedules given in chapter 7 are only guidelines. As we discussed there, if you see nutrient stress, it's time to fertilize, no matter what the schedule says.

I like to take some care with it so I save this job for the weekend. Foliar fertilizers are best sprayed early in the morning, before the sun is strong. The stomates in leaves are open then because photosynthesis is rapid and transpiration is moderate.

Apply liquid fertilizers after watering. When the soil is already moist, they're able to penetrate to root depth. Also, the chances of burning roots with too strong a concentration are reduced. I usually use liquid fertilizers in the morning so that I can mist any drops off the leaves. Obviously, you don't want to leach beds for several weeks after fertilizing with a liquid.

Side-dressings are most effective when you add them to moist soil and then water. The time of day doesn't matter; I've done side-dressings in the middle of the night upon occasion. I usually wait until morning to water them.

Pollinating

Outside, flying insects pollinate fruiting crops. But without a nice bee population, you'll have to take on this job yourself. Midmorning is the best pollinating time because bright light, dry air and moderately warm temperatures stimulate pollen grains to drop from the anthers.

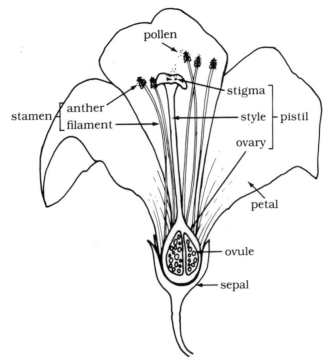

Interior of a Flower: This single flower contains both male pollen and female ovaries. Tomatoes, eggplants, peppers, beans and peas have flowers like this.

In cloudy conditions, pollen isn't very motile. Commercial growers pollinate between 10:00 A.M. and 2:00 P.M. on bright days. If possible, follow their example. Otherwise, do it earlier in the day rather than later, and always before watering.

Flowers of tomatoes, peppers, eggplants, beans and peas contain both male pollen and female ovaries. When stems are jostled, pollen falls from the stamen onto the pistil and travels down the style to the ovule(s). In favorable greenhouse conditions, tapping overhead cables every few feet down the row does the trick. But in cloudy periods or very early in the morning, you may find it necessary to use a finger to jiggle each flower on tomatoes, peppers and eggplants. Peas and beans don't require this special attention, but like every other plant, they're healthier if their stems are jostled every day.

Cucurbits have separate male and female flowers. It's easy to tell them apart: female flowers have a miniature fruit at the base, while males arise directly from the petiole. Collect pollen from the male an-

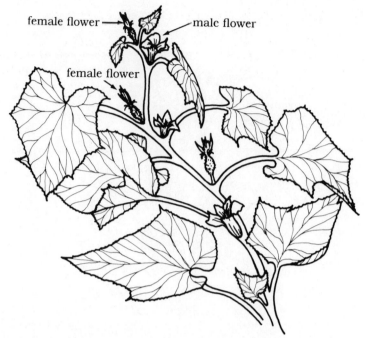

female flower ——→ ——male flower

female flower

Cucurbit Flowers: *As seen on this cucumber plant, cucurbits have separate male and female flowers.*

thers with a small, soft paintbrush and transfer it to the stigmas of the female flowers. Or pick a couple of male flowers, peel off the petals and move them from female flower to female flower, brushing the anthers against the styles.

There is one exception to this general rule about pollinating cucurbits. One of my most awkward moments as a consultant was occasioned by European seedless cucumbers, which produce mostly female flowers and are self-pollinating. A distressed grower called to ask if I could visit her diseased cucumbers. So I set off, fully expecting to see a bad case of *Botrytis* disease. But one look at the bizarrely twisted fruit told me the story—they had been pollinated. "Flies," I said authoritatively. "Flies are the problem; you must have a loose screen." So we searched for a loose screen, and then we looked for cracks in the building. But there weren't any. Almost as an afterthought, I wondered aloud how the flowers had gotten pollinated. The grower looked stricken; she'd worked so hard to find the few male flowers and had been so careful with her paintbrush. She'd never been told that pollinating European seedless varieties transformed them into eerie gargoyles.

Checking for Pests and Diseases

Being a good observer is important in all aspects of gardening, from choosing the healthiest seedlings to knowing when to harvest. But good eyes are essential for pest and disease control. Pests and diseases reproduce quickly; if you don't spot them right away, they can achieve epidemic proportions. "Just looking" is a real part of every morning's work.

Begin by looking at the plants in each growing area as a whole. Is their color good? Are plants erect? Are leaves turgid? Then, choosing random plants, look more closely. Each pest congregates at a specific site. Aphids like growing tips, mealybugs snuggle up between stems and petioles, and whiteflies hide on the undersides of leaves.

Diseases have observable symptoms, too. For example, late blight creates small, water-soaked areas near leaf margins, while fusarium wilt makes petioles droop. You'll find more specific information on identification and control of pests and diseases in chapters 11 and 12.

General Sanitation

Clean greenhouses are pleasing to the senses. But even if aesthetics don't work as a motivator for you and housework isn't your forte, try to keep the greenhouse clean. Cleanliness is the best protection against pests and diseases.

The following is a list of unavoidable jobs. It's by no means exhaustive because housecleaning is *not* my strong point. Add to this basic list as the thought strikes you; there's no such thing as "too clean" in a greenhouse.

- Wash your hands after touching a plant affected by a pest or disease. If you use tobacco, wash in hot, soapy water before going into the greenhouse. This reduces the possibility of transmitting tobacco mosaic virus to your plants. Skim milk is an even more effective rinse.

- Wash all greenhouse surfaces frequently with a 10 percent solution of laundry bleach. Keep a bottle of mixed solution handy so that you can wipe knives and other tools each time they're used.

- Wash pots and flats with the bleach solution as soon as they're empty. If you don't get around to it on time, move them out of the greenhouse until they're washed. Stack them upside down for storage.

- Hose the glazing, both inside and out, once a month during warm weather. If you're feeling stalwart, you can also wash the glazing during the winter thaw.

- Keep the area around the greenhouse free of weeds. Grass, ground covers and beds of pest-resistant ornamentals work well as foundation plantings. Some people mulch the area. If vents are screened, this system is certainly the least labor-intensive. But slugs and mice love mulch, and without screens, they'll soon make their way into the greenhouse.

Harvesting

Proper harvesting is as poorly understood as watering. Harvesting procedures determine both the flavor and nutritional quality of your food. Most fruits and vegetables contain their highest levels of nutrients, particularly vitamin C, at the end of a sunny day. Afternoon harvesting isn't just a matter of convenience—it's a matter of the best possible nutrition.

To know when your greenhouse vegetables are at their peak and ready to pick, consult chapters 13 and 14, where specific harvesting guidelines can be found.

Record Keeping

Over the years, I've kept all sorts of records. In the beginning I never wrote anything down, but as soon as I was employed as a "professional," I was forced to keep records as a part of the job or research project. I resented it at first, but I learned enough from each of these endeavors to appreciate the value of good notes. If record keeping doesn't fill your heart with joy, learn to do it automatically. Don't give yourself a choice about it. My style, early-morning somnambulant jotting, is fairly painless.

In Appendix B, Monitoring the Greenhouse, you'll find samples of worksheets that I use to keep track of what's going on in my greenhouse. There's a daily record to note the weather, inside environmental conditions and completed daily tasks. There's a planting record to help you organize the seed-sowing and transplanting schedule, plus a harvest record to let you see how much your greenhouse is producing.

The pleasure of running a greenhouse is nothing more than the pleasure of doing small but necessary daily tasks. It's nice to have vegetables and flowers year-round, but the final yield is rarely an effective motivator. Enjoyment of the mundane work is what's behind most good growers.

ᮣᖴ CHAPTER 11 ᖵᮣ

CONTROLLING GREENHOUSE PESTS

Pests are almost unavoidable in greenhouses. I wish I could pretend otherwise, but it wouldn't be fair. We all have small skirmishes, larger battles, and occasionally, a drawn-out campaign against them. Good management skills minimize infestations, but even healthy, well-managed plant environments aren't immune. Just as some plants produce more prolifically in an artificial environment, some pests are also favored.

Outside, pests fall prey to a number of different insect predators, parasites and even diseases. But a greenhouse doesn't support the rich diversity of a natural environment. Because there are fewer natural controls, pest populations can quickly build to damaging levels.

The stability of the environment also creates problems. In the garden a rainy spell reduces mite populations, while a hot and dry period limits whitefly reproduction. Climatic changes in a greenhouse are minor in comparison to these natural extremes, so pests aren't subjected to this natural control.

Most growers encounter few pests during their first year. And if they practice good control techniques from the beginning, serious problems may never develop. But when pests are allowed to build up, the second or third year may be difficult enough to tempt normally cautious people to use pesticides.

In the long run, pesticides don't work. Insects reproduce and evolve so quickly that they become increasingly resistant; each generation has more immune individuals than the last. Changing or strengthening a poison increases its effective time span, but as these changes are made, the grower and his or her family are exposed to more lethal chemicals.

With the exception of a few botanical pesticides, chemical substances injurious to pest or disease organisms are also injurious to people. It's only a matter of degree. It takes stronger concentrations and/or a longer period of exposure to damage our much larger bodies. But the partially closed environment of a greenhouse prevents rapid disbursement of the pesticide, so the grower is exposed to higher than usual concentrations. Owners of attached greenhouses must be especially careful because air passes from one place to the other.

It's fortunate that harmful chemicals are entirely unnecessary. Preventive measures, environmental manipulation, mechanical means and biological control with beneficial insects are more reliable. And they're more interesting. But to use them well, you must know something first about the pest in question.

This knowledge is not innate. Some people are graced with a curious, respectful attitude toward "bugs," which helps them to learn quickly. But even when this approach doesn't come naturally, almost anyone who watches pests closely becomes fascinated by their complex lives.

The goal of a pest-control program is to prevent pest populations from increasing to damaging levels. But the definition of "damaging" changes with the crop. For example, tomatoes aren't injured by a moderate number of aphids on the leaves, but the same population may make salad crops unappetizing and can ruin the appearance of a foliage plant. To some extent, appropriate control methods vary with the crop.

Prevention is the first line of defense. Sanitation practices, crop diversity and crop rotation decrease the chances of pest infestations. Other control methods vary according to the pest. In the sections that follow, you'll find a discussion of major greenhouse pests and effective controls to use against them.

Biological Controls

Biological control of pests is rapidly being adopted by greenhouse growers. Biological controls include predators, parasites and diseases that attack pests. When used well, they're the most effective means of pest control. The discussion in this chapter is only an introduction to the subject. *Windowsill Ecology* (Rodale Press, 1977) by William H. Jordan, Jr., is an excellent reference on indoor biological control. It discusses control programs in a comprehensive, accurate and straightforward manner. Most organic growers consider it an indispensable tool.

The use of biological control species is accepted in England, Europe and the Soviet Union. Growers in these countries have developed refined techniques that allow them to forgo the use of pesticides. This exciting work has encouraged the development of insectaries (laboratories devoted exclusively to the rearing of parasites and predators) in this country, too. As techniques and species are identified, predators and parasites are reared commercially and put on the market. At present, most are sold through the mail. Keep up with new species and suppliers through gardening and greenhouse magazines.

Ordering Biological Controls

In most cases you notice a pest infestation about the time when a control species should be introduced. Panic generally strikes; you decide that you need lady beetles, lacewings or whatever without a day's delay. Fortunately, insectaries are organized to respond to frantic calls. As a bonus, they all seem to hire exceptionally warm, knowledgeable people. When you call—and do call if the situation is serious—be ready to describe the pest, its density and current environmental conditions. Density is figured by counting numbers of pests on at least ten randomly chosen leaves and then taking the average. The insectary will tell you how many parasites or predators to order, how to release them and, depending upon the environment, how soon to expect results. They'll also ship them with the next mail, trusting you to pay immediately. If you have questions after the biological control arrives, call back for instructions.

Aphids

Aphids are my favorite pests. They're fascinating and, in my opinion, very pretty. I'm lucky to like them because they have the distinction of being the most common greenhouse pest. I'm always surprised to meet someone who claims they've never seen one. Naturally occurring controls keep populations low in well-managed fields and gardens, but they don't kill them off entirely.

Aphids are small, soft-bodied insects. They come in a variety of colors: green, black, yellow, peach or rose. All aphids sport from their hind ends a pair of projections called cornicles, visible with a ten-power lens. They have a succulent appearance and tend to cluster together. You'll find them most often on growing tips, but they also appear on the crown or on old leaves.

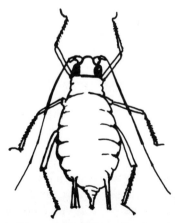

Aphid Adult: This insect has the distinction of being the most common pest in the greenhouse.

Aphids feed unobtrusively by sucking fluids from phloem cells. You won't see holes, although you may notice a telltale puckering on leaves because the aphids sometimes inject a mild toxin as they feed. Aphids also carry diseases, particularly viruses, from one plant to the next.

Despite their small size, these pests have voracious appetites. Since they can't use all the sugar they eat, it's excreted. This excretion, called honeydew, provides food for ants, aphid predators, and a fungus called sooty mold. Ants are so dependent upon honeydew that they herd aphids from one plant to another. In heavy rains they scurry around, moving aphids under leaves. Ants will also attack and kill aphid predators and parasites. The other insects that feed on honeydew don't protect the aphids, they just take advantage of the free meal.

To control aphids, banish ants from the greenhouse. A sugar or honey solution spread on brown wrapping paper attracts ants. I developed this method by remembering the fallen Popsicles of my youth; within a few hours the asphalt looked like moving coffee grounds. Dump trapped ants into a bucket of water with a drop of gasoline or kerosene. Scoop out their hills and empty the eggs and larvae into the bucket, too. Pots of tansy, placed close to doors and vents, may repel newcomers.

Sooty mold doesn't harm plants directly, but it blocks sunlight and clogs stomates, which in turn interferes with normal photosynthesis, respiration and transpiration. You may never see it. Only a large infestation of aphids can produce enough honeydew to support a thriving sooty mold growth. Nonetheless, wipe foliage with a warm, damp cloth every few days when aphids are in the greenhouse. (The only time you might not want to do this is when you have an indoor population of beneficial gall midges. This is explained later in this section.)

Life Cycle

Both the life cycle and reproductive capabilities of aphids make them formidable adversaries. Outside, they greet spring by hatching from eggs laid the previous fall. The first generation is composed almost entirely of wingless females. These "stem-mothers" feed where they hatch, generally on trees, shrubs and hardy weeds. Their winter host plants vary with the species of aphid and the ecosystem. Incidentally, over 5,000 aphid species have been identified.

Stem-mothers give birth to another generation of wingless females. They don't lay eggs; these babies are born as fully formed, small aphids. Even as they are born, a new generation is growing inside them, and inside these unborn mothers, yet another generation is forming. With a good microscope, you can see aphid within aphid. At moderately warm temperatures, only a week elapses from the birth of one generation to the birth of the next. All of this frantic reproduction is parthenogenetic, meaning that it takes place without male fertilization.

As the spring warms, a generation is born that includes males and winged females. They mate and the females fly to summer host plants, some of which are probably in your garden or greenhouse. Stem-mothers dominate each succeeding generation until fall, when both male and winged females are born again. This generation moves back to winter host plants, lays eggs that survive winter and the cycle begins again.

In a greenhouse, even though males and winged females appear toward the end of the summer, few eggs are laid. Usually, fall and winter temperatures are high enough to stimulate consistent parthenogenetic reproduction through most of the year. But sad to say, even though aphid populations decrease during the coldest, darkest months, they're rarely eliminated.

In greenhouses where winter temperatures are consistently cool, eggs may be laid and winter populations may shrink drastically. But the greenhouse is a season extender for aphids, too; their spring hatching occurs several months before aphids hatch outdoors.

Aphid Control

Aside from screening all vents, the most effective preventive measure is close inspection of all plants and pots you bring into the greenhouse. It's wise to enclose any new plant, pot and all, in a cover made of tightly woven cloth. (Organdy works well and greenhouse suppliers sell material made for this purpose.) Push small stakes into the pot to prevent the material from touching the leaves, and attach elastic to enclose the bottom. Keep the plant shrouded for a minimum of a week. Look closely when you uncover it. If aphids are apparent, remove the plant from the greenhouse and consign it to either the house or the garden.

Aphids tolerate a wide range of environments, but sudden temperature extremes sometimes kill them. Try freezing or baking, as described in chapter 9. Eggs survive freezing, of course, but if it's sudden, reproduction may still be parthenogenetic. Baking, at soil temperatures over 100°F, reduces populations significantly enough so that other control programs can take effect after the greenhouse goes back into operation.

Mechanical control includes hand squashing and hard water sprays. Although these methods are appropriate when the first aphids appear, they leave many survivors. No one has the patience to squash every aphid on every leaf and hard sprays just slow them down. Hardy individuals pick themselves up and, like the itsy-bitsy spider, "crawl up the stem again."

Botanical Repellents and Pesticides

Botanical repellents and pesticides are made from poisons or irritants produced by plants or, in the case of soap, by animals. Used judiciously, they can be just as effective as chemical sprays.

Many gardeners claim that garlic, onion and red pepper sprays repel sucking insects. But frankly, I've seen too many aphids fight down the nausea and continue eating to place much stock in such sprays. Out of deference to those people who may have good luck with spraying, I've included a recipe.

The most common repellent spray used against sucking insects, including aphids, is made by combining:

- 3 cloves garlic, chopped
- 1 onion, chopped
- 1 tablespoon cayenne powder
- 1 teaspoon soap flakes (optional, helps spray adhere to leaves)
- 1 quart warm water

Pulverize the solid ingredients in a blender or with a mortar and pestle and then add the water. Let the solution sit overnight in a covered container and strain it through several layers of cheesecloth before putting the spray in a hand mister. Mist both sides of leaves. If you've used soap, rinse with warm water the next day. Soap clogs stomates.

Fermented stinging nettles make a spray that many people swear by. Place about a pound of nettles in a gallon of water, cover the bucket and let it sit in a warm spot for a week. Hold your nose when you uncover the bucket—it smells terrible! Dilute the solution with 5 parts of water to 1 part of nettle concentrate and spray it on the plants. In addition to repelling aphids, it suppresses some fungus diseases. Plants also respond beautifully to the tea as a foliar feed.

Because I live in an area where nettles are not indigenous, I plant them outside in out-of-the-way corners. Once established, they live through the harshest conditions. Pick them with heavy gloves, for they deserve their name.

Soapy sprays kill aphids on contact. I use a concentrated insecticidal soap that is available through growers' associations, suppliers to organic growers and some health food stores. Dilute as directed on the label. I've found that this commercial soap is more effective than homemade soap solutions. But if you can't find the insecticidal soap in stores, make your own solution by dissolving a heaping tablespoon of soap flakes or liquid soap in a quart of hot water. Be sure you're using soap and not detergent. Remember that soapy sprays must be washed off plants within a couple of hours after spraying.

Used frequently, soapy sprays do more harm than a battalion of insects. Not only do they clog stomates, but they can damage the leaf cuticle if applied in too strong a concentration. Save soap sprays for emergencies. I tend to use them when a "controlled" population suddenly expands. Wait at least a week after spraying before introducing beneficial insects into the greenhouse.

Nicotine is a natural poison found in milkweed, tobacco and horsetails. It's strong stuff and, like many synthetic poisons, penetrates plant tissues. If you eat something that's been sprayed within the past month, you'll be eating it, too. Some people use nicotine in preference to chemical poisons, but the difference is negligible. Treat nicotine with the same caution that you reserve for those substances.

Rotenone was originally made from the roots of derris, a South American plant. Now most is synthetically compounded. Like nicotine, rotenone is extremely lethal, killing most insects and soil animals that come in contact with it. It also kills birds and fish. In its favor, rotenone degrades to natural, harmless substances within a week to ten days.

Wettable rotenone is particularly effective against aphids. If an infestation gets away from you, rotenone can save the day. But use it only as a last resort; I try to save it for ornamentals going to other people. If possible, remove plants from the greenhouse before treating them. Don't use it in conjunction with biological controls; after you've applied rotenone, wait a week to ten days before introducing insect predators or parasites.

Ryania, made from the bark of a shrubby plant that grows in Trinidad, has been off the American market for some years, but has recently been reintroduced. I haven't had a chance to try it on greenhouse pests, so I can't report the effectiveness on aphids or other pests. Ryania is quite specific and leaves many insects unharmed. Look for research reports and magazine articles within the next few years describing the best uses for ryania.

Aphid Predators

Lady beetles and lacewings are both effective predators of aphids and are currently available from most biological-control suppliers.

Lady Beetles

The lady beetle species sold most often is called the convergent lady beetle. In both its larval and adult forms, the lady beetle feeds on aphids, although the adult also requires pollen or honeydew.

A convergent lady beetle's life cycle is simple. The female lays clusters of yellow to orange, upright, cylindrical eggs on plant leaves, benches or pots. Depending upon temperature, eggs hatch in a few days to a week. Peculiar-looking larvae emerge. Most people describe them as alligator-shaped because they have an elongated body, tapering at both ends. But it's just as easy to identify them by their wonderful coloring of orange and red spots on a blue or black background. Tufts of hair eggs (3–5 days)

adult

larva (14–21 days)

pupa (7–10 days)

Life Cycle of the Lady Beetle: The days indicated for developmental stages assume an adequate food supply and daytime temperatures of 70 to 80°F. (After Linda Gilkeson, A Guide to the Biological Control of Greenhouse Aphids.*)*

protrude from the ridges running across their long abdomens. After they hatch, the larvae are quite small. But as they eat, they outgrow and finally shed their skins.

The period between each molting is called an **instar**. At warm temperatures, lady beetle larvae go through four instars in three weeks, and at each instar the larvae have a larger appetite than at the last. Their development slows in cool conditions. At the end of the fourth instar, larvae settle down to pupate on a leaf, in a pot or in a crevice. Unlike caterpillars, they don't spin cocoons. Under a transparent shell, the transformation from blue-black larva to orange-red lady beetle is visible. This stage takes anywhere from a week to ten days.

Lady beetles are sold as adults. Because adults need large numbers of aphids to sustain them, many will starve if you release them all at once. Instead, release them in batches. The reserves will stay in a semidormant state for several weeks in the refrigerator. Please warn guests. I've had people react poorly when confronted with a bag of sluggish lady beetles. Rerelease them periodically. If you can't use them all in the greenhouse, let them go outside.

Release lady beetles at twilight by setting them on infested plants or directly on the bed surface. You want them to find aphids before morning. While eating, they're less likely to become agitated and crash against the glazing. But be prepared for a few fatalities.

Lady beetles must eat pollen or a suitable substitute before laying eggs. It's helpful to have a number of plants in bloom at all times. You can also supplement their diet with a mixture of 1 part water, 1 part granulated sugar and $\frac{1}{2}$ part brewer's yeast. Some suppliers sell a special formula called Weast, which contains brewer's yeast and whey. The added whey makes it more nutritious.

Dribble beads of the feeding mixture on waxed paper taped to leaves or petioles in each infested bed. Place the papers close enough to stems so that lady beetles can crawl onto them easily and securely.

Lady beetles are most useful on smooth-leaved plants in spring and summer. They don't like prickles, and aphid populations may be too small to support them during late fall and winter. Under these conditions use other biological controls. Incidentally, I don't know anyone who's been clever enough to keep a year-round, unmutated population. To my knowledge, no one knows just what causes the problem, but most second-year greenhouse lady beetles are weak when they emerge from winter dormancy.

Lacewings

The green lacewing is the only species being marketed in North America. You've probably seen the delicate adults clinging to screens on summer evenings. Like moths, they're attracted to light. Because my children demand the security of a lit bathroom at night, I often find lacewings on the sink in the early morning. The characteristic features of the adult are its large, intensely green, diaphanous wings and long antennae.

Adult lacewings do not eat insects; provide them with the mixture described earlier for lady beetles. But the larval form is another matter entirely; lacewing larvae eat most small insects. Both lady beetle and lacewing larvae are reputed to eat their siblings. I haven't witnessed this behavior in lady beetles, but like everyone who's worked with lacewings, I've frequently seen brother eat hatching brother. As a matter of fact, I've learned not to let uninitiated staff release lacewings because observant people are appalled by the cannibalistic display.

Lacewing larvae are shaped something like lady beetle larvae, but have a more mundane grayish-green to brown coloration. Under a hand lens, a lighter stripe from thorax to hind end is visible. They also sport tufts of bristles on their backs.

Most suppliers ship lacewing eggs packed in rice hulls. Directions suggest releasing them as they hatch. However, this method increases

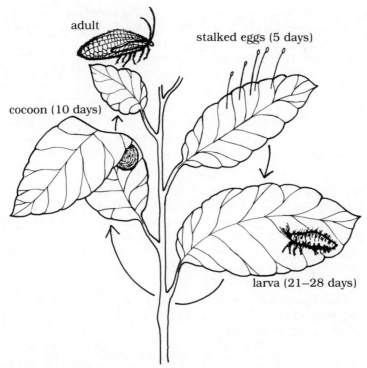

adult

stalked eggs (5 days)

cocoon (10 days)

larva (21–28 days)

Life Cycle of the Lacewing: *The days indicated for the developmental stages of this aphid predator assume an adequate food supply and daytime temperatures of 70 to 80°F.*

their opportunities for cannibalism. If day temperatures average 70°F, and nights don't go below 50°F, it's safer to pick out the eggs with a tiny, moistened paintbrush and place them, widely separated, on infested plants. Distribute the hulls with their hidden eggs very sparsely on the bed surface. Hatching larvae are too small to notice. But within two weeks, you will see larvae lifting aphids off the leaf surface to suck their fluids. You might also see a weird, irregularly shaped creature crawling along; some lacewing larvae decorate themselves by hanging empty aphid skins from the tufts on their backs.

Lacewings complete three instars within two to three weeks and then spin a white cocoon, most often in an axil of an infested plant. It takes ten days to two weeks for the adult to emerge.

If well fed, the adult lives for a month or so before laying her eggs on the leaves of infested plants. The eggs, which are light-colored cylinders on tall stalks, are easy to recognize. The lacewing obviously understands her children because she keeps eggs widely separated. At average temperatures of 70°F, larvae hatch in about a week.

Predatory Gall Midges

Linda Gilkeson and her co-workers at the now defunct Ark greenhouse project on Prince Edward Island, Canada, noticed that a small orange maggot was preying on aphids. After identifying it and conducting an extensive literature search, Gilkeson discovered it to be the larval form of *Aphidoletes aphidimyza*, a gall midge that had recently been introduced to biological control programs in the Soviet Union, Finland and England. Luckily, *Aphidoletes* is indigenous to all regions of North America.

Gilkeson has worked with *Aphidoletes aphidimyza* since 1978 and is currently breeding strains that resist winter dormancy until the daylength is only eight hours. This strain of gall midge will probably be commercially available during the next decade. But even now, indigenous *Aphidoletes* open exciting possibilities for aphid control because they survive over the winter and tolerate lower temperatures than other aphid predators.

In the summer of 1980, Gilkeson, Miriam Klein and Maureen Sirois conducted a field study to determine practical ways to trap aphid predators and parasites. In *A Guide to the Biological Control of Greenhouse Aphids*, they describe these methods. (See the Bibliography for information on how to order this booklet.)

Briefly, they advise that you collect *Aphidoletes* larvae by picking aphid-infested branches from outdoor plants and placing them in a 1-pint plastic bag. Blow up the bag and to keep it inflated, close it with a twistie tie. Keep the bag shaded for a few days, making certain that it's inflated at all times, and wait for orange, segmented maggots to crawl onto the sides. Pick up the maggots with a tiny, moistened paintbrush and transfer them to shaded areas on aphid-infested greenhouse plants. You can't see this without a magnifying lens, but the gall midge larvae grab aphids and inject a strong paralyzing toxin into the aphids' knee joints before sucking their fluids. After several weeks of feeding, they drop to the soil to pupate. A tiny flying adult emerges in about two weeks.

Although gall midge adults feed on pollen from the blossoms of dill, parsley and other small-flowered plants, feed them as described earlier for lady beetles. Like lacewings, they're attracted to lights and burn themselves up if night lights aren't screened. They also fly into spider webs. Daytime finds them clinging to the undersides of leaves.

Aphidoletes reproduce sexually, laying eggs near aphid colonies. The eggs are tiny orange specks that hatch in only a few days. If you've imported them into the greenhouse, don't wipe honeydew from leaves unless absolutely necessary. The eggs are too small to avoid.

Many insects go through a period of hibernation, called **diapause**, during the winter. *Aphidoletes* hibernate as pupae buried only an inch

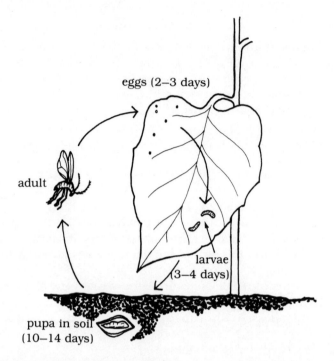

eggs (2–3 days)

adult

larvae
(3–4 days)

pupa in soil
(10–14 days)

Life Cycle of Aphidoletes aphidimyza: *The days indicated for developmental stages assume adequate food supplies and daytime temperatures of 70 to 80°F. (After Linda Gilkeson,* A Guide to the Biological Control of Greenhouse Aphids.*)*

in the soil. With artificial lights and warm temperatures, they may stay active as long as aphids and food for the adults are available. But even if they don't remain active over the winter, adults emerge just about the time that aphids hatch in the spring.

Syrphid Flies

Syrphid flies—or hover flies, as they're sometimes called—are also excellent aphid predators. With yellow and black stripes across the abdomen, the adult fly looks like a small bee or wasp. Adults feed on nectar, hovering near a flower like a hummingbird before darting in to eat.

Syrphid flies lay single, white, cylindrical eggs close to aphids. The maggots that hatch within a few days have transparent skin. With a hand lens or very good eyesight, you can watch the throbbing of their various colored internal organs. Feeding habits easily identify syrphid fly larvae. They tap their narrowed heads in a semicircle much as a blind person taps a cane; like lacewing larvae, they lift aphids into the air while sucking fluids.

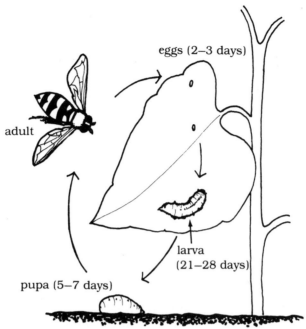

eggs (2–3 days)

adult

larva
(21–28 days)

pupa (5–7 days)

Life Cycle of the Syrphid Fly: *The days indicated for developmental stages assume an adequate food supply and daytime temperatures of 70 to 80°F.* (After Linda Gilkeson, A Guide to the Biological Control of Greenhouse Aphids.)

Syrphid fly larvae are not commercially available. But you can find them in the field on aphid-infested plants. You may even trap some in an *Aphidoletes* collecting bag. Transfer them as you do *Aphidoletes*. To my knowledge, no one has established a year-round colony of syrphid flies in a greenhouse.

Aphid Parasites

Parasites spend part of their life cycle inside another insect, using their host's body as a food source. At present, no aphid parasites are sold in North America, although they are available in England and Europe. Fortunately, indigenous aphid parasites often migrate into greenhouses, even those with screens, so it's wise to know what they look like and how they interact with aphids.

Both braconid and chalcid wasps parasitize aphids. You may never see the tiny, quarter-inch adult wasp lay an egg inside an aphid; however, you'll notice the resulting aphid "mummies." Mummies are bronze, pearly or black and show an unusual luster. They seem hard-shelled,

Braconid Wasp at Work: *Here you see this parasitic wasp attacking an aphid. (After Linda Gilkeson,* A Guide to the Biological Control of Greenhouse Aphids.*)*

lacking the normal wet look of aphids. They're perfectly preserved, and it takes careful observation to identify them in the midst of a crowded aphid colony where all ages congregate and none are especially mobile. When you look for mummies, look for a difference in texture.

Aphid colonies are visually complicated. Among the aphids are bits of white or gray material that seem glued to leaves. This fluff is simply old aphid skins shed during molting. The skins stick to hairs on leaves and honeydew. Don't confuse them with aphid mummies; mummies still look like aphids.

After a parasitic wasp egg hatches, the larva feeds for several days and then glues the dead aphid to a leaf. The larva pupates inside the aphid skin for several more days before cutting a hole in the back of the mummy and emerging as an adult. Even without a hand lens, you can see the hole.

When you spot unpunctured aphid mummies on a leaf, don't remove them from the greenhouse. Instead, kill living aphids and leave the mummies intact. To help the next generation of wasps do their work, tape leaves with mummies to supports or cables near aphid colonies.

Whiteflies

Greenhouse environments are particularly favorable to whiteflies. They're present outdoors in most climates, but their populations are usually too low to be noticed. But once they enter a greenhouse, watch for a population boom.

Like aphids, whiteflies feed by piercing the leaf and tapping the phloem stream. But whiteflies are much sneakier; they congregate and feed exclusively on the undersides of leaves. The only way to detect the first invaders is by jostling plant stems; adults flutter briefly before settling down again. Whiteflies are particularly attracted to cucumbers, tomatoes, fuchsias, salvias and geraniums. But in a pinch, they'll eat just about anything.

The adults are tiny (about one-sixteenth of an inch), strikingly white flies covered with a waxy powder scarcely visible to the naked eye. Adults feed on leaves toward the top of the plant. Here they reproduce sexually and lay small eggs on stalks, placing them in irregular circles. The hatching nymphs look like nothing more than specks. They're mobile for a few days and usually migrate to lower leaves, where they attach themselves to feed through four instars.

The nymphs are called scales because they look like the insect of that name—small oval or circular flattened domes. They're a translucent green and completely featureless until the last instar. At that stage, waxy material grows from their undersides, elevating them slightly

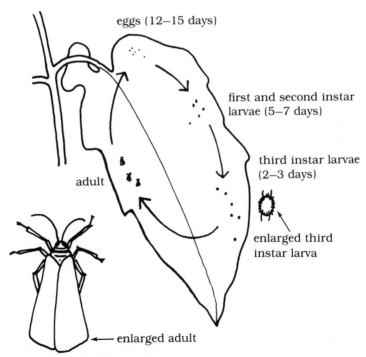

eggs (12–15 days)

first and second instar larvae (5–7 days)

third instar larvae (2–3 days)

adult

enlarged third instar larva

enlarged adult

Life Cycle of the Whitefly: The days indicated for the developmental stages of this pest assume an adequate food supply and daytime temperatures of 70 to 80°F.

from the leaf surface. They also grow small filaments, radiating from all sides. Within a few days of this development, the adult emerges.

Like most insects, their life span and developmental rate are dependent upon temperature. They develop more quickly at temperatures averaging 80°F, but live longer and lay more eggs when days average 65°F. Consequently, they adapt very well to artificial environments.

Whitefly-control programs should begin at first sighting. Two mechanical controls are somewhat effective. One of these controls is based on whiteflies' fatal attraction to the color yellow. Sticks or stiff paper painted yellow and coated with Tanglefoot or Ced-O-Flora trap adults, sometimes before you know they're around. Tanglefoot is just gooey, but Ced-O-Flora contains an extremely poisonous hemlock extract. Most garden supply shops sell these materials. Several suppliers to organic growers sell trapping papers treated with Tanglefoot, along with metal stakes to support the traps. Place one or two yellow traps in each bed in early spring long before you've seen any whiteflies. Replace the traps when they lose their stickiness.

A vacuum cleaner, believe it or not, is one of the best whitefly controls. Remove the nozzle and hold the tube a few inches from the top of the plant. As you shake the stem, fluttering whiteflies are sucked up.

Used together, these controls are effective against adults, but they don't affect scales. To attack scales, you need to enlist the aid of a parasitic wasp.

Whitefly Scale Parasite

Encarsia formosa is a chalcid wasp that parasitizes whitefly scales. The adult wasp is quick and tiny. Under a hand lens, a yellow abdomen under rainbow wings shows up, but you're more likely to notice the flitting motion of these wasps. They almost jump from one spot to another, feeding and laying eggs in the third and early fourth instar scales. Within a week or two, depending upon temperature, parasitized scales turn a shiny black color. Check pruned leaves for blackened scales before relegating them to the compost. When you do find evidence of developing Encarsia, scrape off any unparasitized scales and tape the leaves to overhead wires or stakes in a bed. Adult wasps will emerge to parasitize other scales.

Adult Encarsia feed on honeydew, and occasionally on first and second instar whiteflies. Because whiteflies produce copious amounts of honeydew, supplies are plentiful as long as you don't wipe the leaves. But I'd rather keep the leaves clean and feed the wasps a half-and-half mixture of water and honey, streaked on waxed paper.

Encarsia reproduce most prolifically and develop most quickly in temperatures averaging 75 to 80°F, with bright light and long photoperiods. But as you recall, whiteflies lay more eggs at lower temperatures. For the most effective whitefly control in a cool greenhouse, release the wasps every week or so until the whitefly population seems to be under control. Some commercial growers time Encarsia release to coincide with the whitefly's third instar development. Don't feel your timing has to be this precise. Once there are whiteflies in your greenhouse, instars of all ages are continuously present.

Parasites are used at higher rates than predators because each larva kills only one pest. It also takes them longer. William Jordan suggests a rate of 20 parasites for each infested plant when the whitefly population is high. It may take six weeks to two months to completely control the pest, but during this time damage decreases steadily.

Encarsia are shipped as pupae, inside blackened whitefly scales, on tobacco or tomato leaves. Hang the leaves around infested plants. The emerging adults will locate the whitefly scales.

Though most of the literature is pessimistic about retaining Encarsia populations over the winter, several growers have done so. When the Wintergreen Community Greenhouse in Orange, Massachusetts, was operating, horticulturist Karen Idione was delighted to discover that Encarsia had survived many weeks of below-freezing interior temperatures. In the spring, emerging adults controlled the first whiteflies. At the Ark greenhouse on Prince Edward Island, Canada, Linda Gilkeson ordered Encarsia only once during her three years of management. Each winter, low populations of both Encarsia and whiteflies continued to be active on geraniums and salvia in warm, bright areas.

Despite these two growers' successes, overwintering populations aren't guaranteed. Chances improve if artificial lights run from 12 to 14 hours each day in a warm area. If Encarsia manage to wipe out the whiteflies, the wasps will die, too. Watch the percentage of blackened scales; when 80 percent are parasitized, it's time to protect the whiteflies. Remove some leaves with blackened scales to let whiteflies build up a small population. Don't be afraid to support a few pests in a food-producing greenhouse—in the long run you're improving the natural balance of the enclosed ecosystem.

An Alternative to Encarsia

When you're unable to get Encarsia, pyrethrum is the best last-resort remedy. But it's not as much fun to use. Pyrethrum is a botanical pesticide that kills indiscriminately. It's hard to find real pyrethrum these days, but the synthetic kind degrades just as quickly and, like the original, doesn't bring long-term environmental damage. Nevertheless, use it with care. Even in minute quantities, it affects some people with a rash or hay fever-like symptoms. Like rotenone and soap, allow pyrethrum to degrade for a week to ten days before introducing beneficial insects into the greenhouse.

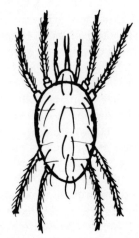

Spider Mite: *This greenhouse pest prefers to dine upon cucumber, melon and various ornamental plants.*

Mites

Two-spotted spider mites and false spider mites prey on many plants, their favorites being cucumbers, melons and selected ornamentals.

Mites are too small to see without a hand lens, but their damage isn't. Two-spotted mites leave webs on tips and buds. The false spider mite isn't quite so cooperative; look for tiny pinprick spots by holding random leaves against the light. When you see spots or puckering with no evidence of aphids, get out the hand lens and start looking for mites.

Contrary to popular belief, mites aren't insects. They're members of the spider family. They hatch with only six legs but grow the last two very quickly. The life cycle is fast; mites usually go unnoticed until populations, and damage, are high.

As soon as you suspect that mites are present, spray both sides of each leaf and all buds and axils with a hard water spray. If that doesn't kill them, it will at least dislodge them. Reproduction is slowed when relative humidity is 80 percent or so, a dubious control measure that can lead to fungus diseases. Rotenone, pyrethrum and soap sprays all reduce populations. (These are discussed earlier under Aphids and Whiteflies.)

Predatory Mites

You can also enlist the aid of predatory mites in your battle against spider mites.

Both *Phytoseiulus persimilis* and *Amblyseium californicus* are sold commercially. For greenhouses *A. californicus* is recommended.

It prefers high temperatures near those that favor destructive mites. *P. persimilis* functions better at lower temperatures. Predatory mites look a great deal like their victims except that their legs are evenly placed around their small bodies. Destructive mites have two pairs of legs pointing forward and two pointing to the rear. But even with a hand lens, it's hard to distinguish between the good and the bad mites.

Order more predatory mites than you need since they don't travel well. They will arrive in small glass vials or plastic straws. Keep the containers cool and shaded until twilight; then, using a hand lens, pick them out with a tiny, moistened paintbrush. Mites aren't very mobile, so place them on the undersides of leaves, close to the top of the plant. In bright light, temporarily place cheesecloth shading frames around the plants to shade the predators. Keep the shading in place for at least a week to ten days, and do everything possible to keep daytime temperatures under 75°F. Even *Amblyseium californicus* functions better than the pests at lower temperatures. The shading may slow plant growth a bit, but not as much as mites do.

The only reliable way to determine the effectiveness of predatory mites is by keeping track of spider mite damage. If new leaves show fewer and fewer pinpricks and if webbing decreases drastically, predators have pests under control. Wait two to three weeks after release for signs of improvement. If damage persists, order new mites and rerelease them. The environment may have changed enough to enable them to become better established.

Mites overwinter in a diapause state, resting on benches, pots or even permanent plants. Some predatory mites survive along with the destructive ones, but watch for mite damage in mid-January to early February. You can't count on a huge controlling population to make it through the winter, and you may have to buy a new batch.

Other Mite Predators

From time to time both lacewing larvae and lady beetles eat mites. If any of these beneficial insects is in your greenhouse, mite populations may be checked. Unfortunately, neither lacewings nor lady beetles discriminate between mite species; predatory mites taste just as good as pests. In the best of all possible worlds, aphids and spider mites won't appear simultaneously. But life isn't always convenient. If faced with this problem, use a soap spray on the mite-infested plants and hope that the aphid predators stay clear.

Mealybugs

Mealybugs are a kind of scale insect. Elliptical, ridged creatures, covered with a waxy substance, they're likely to be found in the axils of ornamentals, especially avocados and false aralias. The first clue may

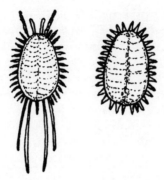

Mealybugs: *Shown here are two different species. These pests tend to bother ornamentals and leave vegetables alone.*

be a drop of honeydew. I've never seen a mealybug on a vegetable plant, but assume that this is only by chance.

Mealybugs rarely build high populations in home greenhouses. They reproduce and develop slowly, even in the best of environments. If you examine plants with any regularity, you'll notice when two or three move in on an ornamental from outside the greenhouse. Kill them by squashing or dabbing with a cotton swab dipped in alcohol. If, by some peculiar twist of fate, a large infestation occurs, use lacewings as controls.

Scales

Scales are also infrequent in home greenhouses because it's relatively easy to spot the first arrivals. They look like flattened disks with or without a small "nipple." Sometimes they look like a bump on the stem. If you suspect that you are looking at a scale rather than a bump, confirm your suspicions by lifting it off with a thin knife or nail file. Scales come off easily; soft scales are intact when scraped loose, but armored ones may lose only their shell. If the "scale" is part of the plant, you'll injure the stem by removing it. Insect scales leave no mark.

When populations are low, the best control is removal with a knife as described above. If this is impractical, buy a predator or parasite. Prune off an infested branch and take it to your local extension agent for species identification. Predators and parasites for scale insects are specific. You'll have to tell the insectary the full Latin name of the particular scale in your greenhouse. With a heavy infestation, the best recourse is often plant disposal.

The two most general control species for soft scales are lacewings and *Metaphycus helvolus. Aphtis melinus* and *Comperiella bifasciata*

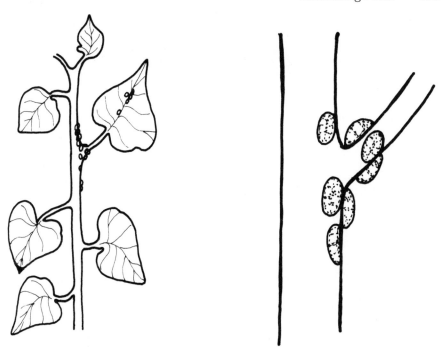

Soft Scales: *These plant pests look like flattened bumps on plant stems and leaves.*

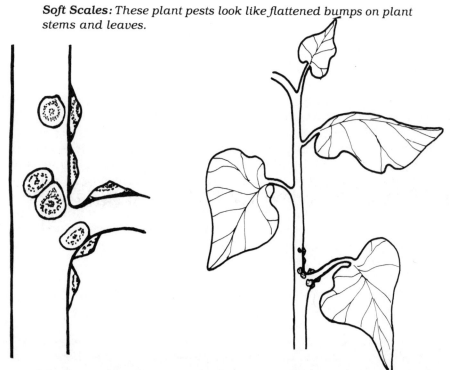

Armored Scales: *The way to distinguish these from soft scales is the presence of a raised area, or nipple, in the middle.*

are both parasites of armored scales. The insectary will tell you how many to order and how to care for them.

Nematodes

Nematodes, also called eelworms, are microscopically small worms. While most species are harmless to plants, a few cause damage. Root-knot nematodes can infect just about any sort of root. The larval form penetrates root tissue to feed, triggering abnormally large growth in surrounding cells. Initially, the roots look bumpy, but as the population grows, scablike growths or galls form. Eggs are expelled through cracks in the root epidermis and the larvae travel through the soil solution to new roots.

Populations are highest in sandy soils and warm climates. But one species, *Meloidogyne hapla,* is moving north. Only 20 years ago, it was restricted to greenhouses. Now field growers as far north as New York State are reporting incidences of this nematode.

A general stunting and lack of vigor are the first observable symptoms of root-knot nematodes. Pull a few plants to check their roots. If there are unusual bulges and cracks, nematodes may have come in on soil, aged manure or transplants from another greenhouse. Any laboratory can detect nematodes, but only trained people can positively identify species by the characteristic lines around the anal openings.

Preventing nematode problems depends upon good soil management. Crop rotation helps because some species starve rather than change their preferred diet. Beneficial fungi that attack nematodes have been identified. Several products on the market stimulate these naturally occurring organisms: Greenhouse BioCast and Pent-A-Vate are available from the Necessary Trading Company (see Appendix A: Sources of Seeds and Supplies). In the near future you will be able to purchase these fungi separately to add to nematode-infested soil. But since the same fungi live in your compost pile, you may never need to buy them.

Besides these beneficial fungi, compost contains great numbers of bacteria, soil animals and even other nematodes that prey on destructive species. You greatly minimize the chances of infestation when soil mixes contain a good proportion of compost.

Predatory nematodes are available from suppliers to organic growers. I've never had occasion to use them, but assume that the supplier gives accurate rates and methods of application.

When plants are bothered by nematodes, many growers find that the best solution is to throw infected soil into a really hot compost pile. Even after composting, don't return the soil to the greenhouse or a garden area.

Commercial growers kill harmful nematodes by heating soils with special steaming equipment. At temperatures of 120°F or above, both eggs and larvae are destroyed. A home version of this commercial treatment won't completely eradicate nematodes, but it will decrease the population. Start by removing all plants, including most of the roots. Let the soil dry, stirring it to expose the lower depths. After a few days, level and cover it with a sheet of clear plastic. Stick a soil thermometer through the plastic to check temperatures as the soil heats. After it reaches the peak temperature (at least close to 90°F), remove the plastic, stir the soil to mix the layers and repeat. Add compost to the mix before replanting to replenish populations of beneficial soil microbes. Freezing, or alternate freezing and thawing, is also effective against all root-knot species except *Meloidogyne hapla*.

Some vegetable varieties are resistant to specific nematodes. Check with the local extension agent and other growers for a list of appropriate varieties for your region.

Cyst nematodes live in most of the United States, southern Ontario and British Columbia. Species in this group make small cysts on roots. Taproots on infected plants are usually stunted, and the plants react by making more lateral roots than normal. The topgrowth looks unhealthy, wilts easily and dies prematurely.

Other destructive species are less common or attack only certain crops. Again, the local extension agent is your best source of information about nematodes and resistant crop varieties for your region. Southern growers are well advised to look for this information *before* planting. In the North there's much less need to do this. In all my years of greenhouse gardening, I've never had a nematode problem.

Slugs and Snails

Slugs and snails usually come into greenhouses on soil. You aren't likely to have many, but just one slug can wreak havoc. These pests eat holes in leafy crops and take nibbles out of low-hanging tomatoes.

Both slugs and snails are night feeders. During the day they rest in moist, hidden areas. To find them, take flashlight in hand and check bottom leaves in areas where there's been damage. Boards left on the bed surface are good traps; check under them in the early morning. Meanwhile, protect plants with a mulch of crushed eggshells. The rough surface repels these soft-bodied creatures.

If you shrink from handling slugs, "salt" them. Ordinary table salt kills slugs by drawing out their fluids. I consider this remedy far more repulsive than simple squashing, but some people prefer it. Obviously, salting won't work for snails. Instead, drop them into a bucket of water and kerosene.

Sow Bugs and Pill Bugs

These oval, half-inch creatures are common to garden soils. When they're disturbed, sow bugs curl up into a ball, while pill bugs run away. It's almost inevitable that some will make their way into the greenhouse via a load of topsoil or compost.

Sow bugs and pill bugs are almost always in compost because their preferred diet is decaying organic matter. Don't be alarmed if you spot a few in the soil mix; small populations concentrate in areas rich in compost. But when there are more than one or two to a bed, begin eliminating them by handpicking or using pyrethrum for heavy infestations. They'll eat living roots when the compost runs low.

ꗃ CHAPTER 12 ꗃ
PLANT DISEASES

Fungi, bacteria and viruses cause plant diseases by invading and feeding on tissues. It takes a tremendous amount of study to know and understand every plant disease. But you don't need more than a rudimentary background to run a small greenhouse. Growers aren't diagnosticians or doctors; they practice preventive medicine, so problems are less likely to develop.

Prevention is the best approach. Plants, unlike animals, don't develop internal antibodies against particular organisms. Because certain individual plants and varieties have more natural resistance to particular diseases than others do, breeders have selected these as genetic stock. But resistance is not the same thing as a developed immunity. To the best of current scientific knowledge, plants don't have immune systems analogous to our white blood cells and lymphatic system. On the occasions when a plant contracts and overcomes a disease, it's likely that the disease organisms died as a result of changing environmental factors.

Plants do have a defense system—the protective organisms that live in the soil. Each virus, bacterium or fungus is food for something else. In a thriving soil community, protective organisms are numerous enough to keep destructive ones in balance. But they may be largely absent in a sterile or "dead" soil. In the absence of good natural controls, an invading pathogenic organism is more able to build to damaging populations. The good soils used by practiced growers are an essential feature of their ability to prevent disease outbreaks.

Balanced nutrient levels also prevent diseases. Deficiencies, especially of micronutrients, can be slight enough to escape the grower's detection but serious enough to inhibit the plant's strengthening enzyme systems. Consequently, the plant's resistance to pathogens is impaired. Foliar seaweed sprays provide protection by supplying needed micronutrients. Likewise compost contains the abundant soil life and balanced nutrients that constitute the first line of defense in a disease prevention program.

Sanitation practices, as described in chapter 10 under General Sanitation, are imperative. Disease organisms move through the air, soil and on plants, pots, tools and hands. You can minimize exposure by keeping everything in the greenhouse scrupulously clean. Here are a few tips to help you keep the greenhouse disease-free.

- Don't bring diseased plants into the greenhouse, even on a friend's request.

- When you transfer tools from the garden to the greenhouse, scrape off the soil and dip the tools in a 10 percent bleach solution.

- Keep a special pair of shoes for the greenhouse to avoid tracking problems in from the outdoors.

- Remove all diseased plants or leaves *immediately.*

- If you suspect a virus, don't include the plant material in the compost pile unless temperatures hold at 180°F for at least three days. While some viruses tolerate temperatures as high as 200°F, the majority are killed at a sustained 180°F. It's alright to compost plants suffering from bacterial and fungal diseases as long as the pile registers 150 to 160°F.

Environmental effects on diseases, particularly those caused by fungi, are enormous. Their effect is so pronounced that many commercial farmers use environmental data to predict and protect against such fungi as late blight. While farmers can't change the environment, greenhouse growers can to a certain degree. I've never known a greenhouse grower who could produce sunshine for the asking, but it's easy to manipulate temperature, humidity levels and air circulation.

The diseases covered in this chapter are only the most common, so the list is not inclusive. I've described general symptoms, but symptoms of different diseases are so similar that determining which disease is at work and distinguishing the symptoms from micronutrient deficiencies usually falls into the "best guess" category. It may be a comfort to reel off a Latin name, but in most cases, you're doing well to identify the casual organism: bacterium, fungus or virus. Even this basic identification gets muddy because one disease opens the door to others. For example, when a bacterial disease kills epidermal cells, fungi often invade. The plant ends up with two diseases instead of one.

If, despite the best of preventive measures, a disease ravishes a crop or persists from one crop or season to the next, contact a plant pathologist at the local extension agency for a diagnosis. These people are trained to identify pathogenic organisms and usually provide information about environmental control if requested.

Fungus Diseases

There are numerous fungi, each with a special niche in the ecosystem. Fungi are plants, and because they don't manufacture their own chlorophyll, they live on organic matter. Saprophytes live on dead material and are responsible for much of the action in a compost pile. Other fungi parasitize living organisms, including growing plants. Only a few of the many parasitic fungi cause diseases. But despite their relatively small numbers, they can lay waste to a crop.

For the most part, fungi are composed of a mass of threadlike structures called hyphae. The mass is called the mycelium. Most of the cells in a fungus plant are uniform, but under the right environmental conditions, specialized cells form and produce the spores (or seeds) of the fungus. Spores of some species require high temperatures to germinate, but most need only several hours of cool conditions (40 to 75°F). The consistent factor is their need for moisture. When a spore is moist and exposed to the right temperature, it germinates by growing hyphae. Fungi that attack leaves send succeeding hyphae in through the cuticle or through a stomate. Many fungi produce a corky material that seals off the invading fungus after hyphae are safely in the leaf. Once inside, the fungi is as well protected by the cuticle as the rest of the leaf. Bright light protects against fungi by stimulating the growth of tough cuticle tissue. In addition, many germinating spores are killed when leaves heat and dry in sunlight.

Some fungi can't penetrate healthy tissue. Instead, they attack bruises or lesions in cell walls of the stem, leaves or fruit. Bruises are easy to create. When you brush past plants and rub against their leaves, you may injure them. Leaves that rub against each other can also cause damage.

Fungi feed by exuding enzymes that digest and dissolve organic materials. Once broken down, these substances are absorbed by the fungus. To our eyes, the fruit, stem or leaf has "rotted."

What follows in this section is a general guide to the most common fungal diseases that you're likely to encounter in the greenhouse.

Damping-Off

Damping-off is not a single disease with a single symptom. Seeds may rot in the ground before or during germination; seedlings may suddenly rot at the soilline and fall over; or they may suffer wire stem, a girdling of the stem at the soilline. Wire stem is the most disastrous since it often goes unnoticed. Diseased plants are transplanted but, due to the wire stem, never demonstrate the vigor or yields of a healthy plant.

More than 30 different organisms, both fungal and bacterial, cause this disease. Fortunately, most of the causal organisms require high humidity levels and don't reproduce well under bright light. Damping-off is easy to prevent. You can sterilize seeds or spray seedlings with chamomile tea.

The most common damping-off fungi are *Pythium* and *Phytophthora*. Both are killed or inhibited by antibiotics contained in peat moss and hardwood bark compost. They both require stagnant, moist air to reproduce. Growers rarely lose crops to these fungi if they are attuned to the environmental needs of germinating seeds. But other damping-off organisms must be combated directly. Many come on the seed itself. Seed purchased from a good company has probably been treated against disease. But "homegrown" seed saved from affected plants needs treatment.

Seed sterilization is effective only against organisms carried by the seed itself. It doesn't protect against damping-off organisms in the air and soil. I don't bother to sterilize unless I'm planting seed from a crop that could have been infected with a bacterial or fungal disease.

Numerous organisms are killed when seeds are quickly dipped into a solution of 1 tablespoon of 5 percent vinegar to a quart of water or into a 10 percent bleach solution. Plant seeds immediately after dipping. This type of sterilization isn't 100 percent reliable, but it's certainly better than nothing.

Hot-water treatment also works. Many companies, especially those selling to commercial growers, prepare seeds this way. With an accurate dairy thermometer, you can treat with hot water at home. (When you're saving seed from cabbage family plants, use this system, since it's the most effective with them.)

Make a "bouquet garni" by placing the seeds on a square of cheesecloth and tying the corners together with strong string to make a bag. Leave plenty of space in the bag so seeds are fully exposed to the hot water. Place a wooden rack or an upside-down bowl on the bottom of a pot, fill the pot with water and turn on the heat. The rack or bowl keeps seeds from touching the bottom of the pot. Wait to add the seeds until the water has reached the desired temperature. Keep seeds of tomatoes, most cabbage family crops, eggplants and spinach for 25 minutes in water that is consistently 122°F. Immerse cauliflower seed for 20 minutes and carrot seed for 15 minutes. Celery seed requires 118°F for 30 minutes. Beware that unless a particular seed is mentioned here, hot-water treatment may damage it. At higher temperatures or longer exposures than recommended, seeds will also be damaged.

Chamomile tea is often used after damping-off has begun. It may not kill the causal organisms, but can inhibit reproduction and reduce their spread. If you spray seedlings with this tea, look very carefully for signs of wire stem before transplanting. Frankly, I would rather lose a flat of seedlings than inhibit the disease, because of the possible and irreversible damage it may have created. Remember, with good starting procedures, you shouldn't see much damping-off, anyway.

Gray Mold

Gray mold, or *Botrytis cinerea*, is fairly common on greenhouse plants, especially cucumbers, tomatoes and lettuce grown in low light and high humidity. It's also the curse of many soft-tissued ornamentals, such as geraniums. The many different kinds of *Botrytis* fungi all enter through wounded or dying tissue. The wound needn't be extensive; gray mold is happy to take up residence on slight bruises, old flower petals or aging leaves. It thrives at humidity levels close to 90 percent. This requirement would seem to limit the chances of gray mold appearing in your greenhouse. But often the boundary layer around plants is at least that moist.

Before *Botrytis* really takes over, you may have trouble making the diagnosis. Leaves often turn pale green and then brown before cracking to allow the gray mold to show. Other signs of injury include root and fruit rots, spots on leaves and softened, rotting areas on stems.

Botrytis spores can live for several years in soil. Once gray mold has appeared, some people try to get rid of it by changing the soil mix, but that's largely a wasted effort. The fungus is so widespread that almost all moisture-laden air carries it.

There are no vegetable varieties resistant to gray mold. Nonetheless, you can take preventive measures. Don't splash water on leaves or stems; space plants widely and prune well enough so that leaves don't touch; pick off old leaves, spent blossoms and injured plant parts; ventilate well and keep air moving. If some gray mold appears, immediately pick off the infected leaves.

Downy Mildew

At first downy mildew looks like a mosaic virus; areas between veins change to light green and then yellow. If you look at the undersides of affected leaves and see a purplish, white or even black fuzzy growth, that tells you it's downy mildew.

In cool winter greenhouses, lettuce and cabbage family crops are especially susceptible to strains of this fungus. It thrives in moist conditions at day temperatures of 70 to 75°F and night temperatures under 60°F. It also appears when phosphorous supplies are low. The fungus is most destructive to cabbage family crops, causing blackened spots on flower heads of both cauliflower and broccoli. The leaves of cabbage and other leafy crops develop sunken spots.

In moist conditions, downy mildew fungus produces a tremendous number of spores. The preventive advice given earlier for *Botrytis* also applies here. In addition, night temperatures of 60°F or higher may inhibit reproduction. Between hosts, this fungus lives on old roots in the soil, but also travels long distances on winds. If any fungus growth appears on leafy crops, raise night temperatures and prune off all affected leaves as well as those that touch the soil.

Late Blight

Late blight has the dubious distinction of having caused the great potato famine in Ireland. In the same family of fungi as downy mildew, it affects potatoes, peppers, tomatoes and eggplants as well as weeds and ornamental plants in the solanaceous family.

The first signs are water-soaked spots on the edges of the upper sides of leaves. Within a few days, white spores, growing in circular patterns, appear on the bottom of the leaf. The disease spreads from leaves to petioles, stems and fruits, eventually killing the plant. On tomatoes, dark, obviously rotting spots appear. The rot spreads rapidly. If the fruit cracks, a white mold grows on the lesion.

Southern strains require temperatures lower than 75°F for germination and reproduction, so the disease wanes during midsummer. Northern strains aren't inhibited by lower temperatures, but like most other fungi, even northern late blight is extremely dependent upon humidity. Maintaining low humidity is the best control. I've also inhibited the disease by frequent spraying with a half-strength solution of liquid seaweed.

Late blight also causes root rot on cabbage family plants. Good drainage is the best defense against this problem. If roots begin to rot, you have a choice of pulling the crop or trying to save it. Allowing the soil to dry until the plants begin to wilt is sometimes effective. When you resume watering, give only enough to sustain the plants. After you've harvested the crop, improve drainage in the beds and add compost to the soil mix.

Powdery Mildew

Strains of powdery mildew attack many plants. The disease is noticeable as a light powder on the upper sides of mature leaves on lettuce, cucumbers and cabbage family plants. On tomatoes, the powder shows on the undersides of leaves while the corresponding upper sides are yellow.

Powdery mildew can't survive cold winters. However, each spring winds carry the spores north. Since high humidity isn't necessary for this fungus, it can be a persistent problem. Once powdery mildew shows up, it's important to prune infected leaves immediately.

Early Blight

Early blight is an *Alternaria* fungus that can attack all of the solanaceous crops at any stage of growth. The most common symptoms are girdling of the seedling stem and concentric brownish spots on leaves. As the disease progresses, affected leaves turn brown and fall. Rotting spots appear on immature fruit, while white rings with no associated rotting show on mature fruit—unless, of course, another fungus follows.

Early blight usually strikes plants with nutrient deficiencies. Plants in a rich, balanced soil are less vulnerable. However, as always, it's important to maintain a good greenhouse environment as a safety precaution.

Other *Alternaria* fungi affect various crops. All the cucurbits are susceptible midway to late in their growth, when nutrient supplies are low or when plants begin to lose vigor. To bolster their stamina, give these plants biweekly foliar sprays with liquid seaweed throughout the season to keep trace element content high. Compost or manure teas supply major nutrients.

Fusarium Wilt and *Verticillium* Wilt

Fusarium wilt, most common in the midwestern states, grows best at temperatures consistently above 65°F. However, it can also prosper in northern greenhouses due to the artificially warm environment. The first sign of *Fusarium* wilt is drooping or wilting of the petioles. Leaves begin to yellow. Eventually the whole plant wilts and dies. Both immature and ripe tomato fruits are susceptible. To protect against this and other causes of fruit rot, don't let tomatoes rest on the soil. Rot may also start on fruits that touch each other. Thin immature fruit if there's been any rotting. Keep the soil moist at all times, but be careful not to overwater.

Verticillium wilt strikes many vegetable crops as well as wild plants and cultivated ornamentals. Of greenhouse crops, eggplants and tomatoes are the most susceptible. This soilborne fungus usually enters through broken root hairs. Plants are stunted, and as they age, leaves yellow and wilt easily.

Good seedling care does much to prevent *Verticillium* wilt. Start plants in peat or plastic pots and transplant before roots break through. Other preventive measures include keeping nutrient levels high and maintaining good environmental conditions. And for the first line of defense, take advantage of the many varieties resistant to both fungi.

Anthracnose

Anthracnose strikes beans, peas, cabbage family crops and, most often, cucumbers and melons. Water-soaked spots appear on the foliage, turn yellow, brown and then dry. As the disease spreads, leaves drop.

Immature fruit of cucumbers and melons develop sunken rotted spots. Even if the *Anthracnose* fungi don't penetrate, they weaken the skin, allowing other rot-causing fungi to invade. In response to an attack by *Anthracnose*, ripe fruit may grow bumpy calluses. This toughened skin prevents other fungi from entering the wound.

Like their host plants, *Anthracnose* fungi prefer plenty of moisture and temperatures between 70 and 80°F. For this reason environmental control is not an effective deterrent. Instead, try to prevent problems from the start by using resistant varieties. Since the fungus can be carried over on seeds, don't save seeds from infected plants. Avoid working among plants while the foliage is wet; under these conditions the disease spreads rapidly. Once *Anthracnose* has struck, don't grow susceptible crops in the same soil for three to four years.

Bacterial Diseases

Bacterial diseases are transmitted by pests and through moist air, soil, water and roots. They overwinter in plant refuse, the soil, hibernating insects and seeds. Though some bacteria depend upon environmental conditions for their best growth, manipulating the environment as a method of control isn't as effective as it is for fungus diseases. In the discussions of bacterial diseases that follow, I've given other means of control that you can try.

Bacterial Wilt

Bacterial wilt affects more than 60 different cultivated plants. Among greenhouse crops, tomatoes, peppers and eggplants are most susceptible to the bacterial wilt caused by *Pseudomonas solanaceanum*. Cucurbits are affected by *Erwinia tracheiphila*.

On solanaceous crops, the first symptoms are wilting of young leaves and/or yellowing of mature leaves. The roots of infected plants look water-soaked, and after the disease has progressed, a broken stem exudes muddy-looking sap.

Plants usually become infected through broken root hairs during transplanting into a soil that contains the bacteria. The disease does the most damage when available nitrogen is low and both soil temperatures and moisture levels are high.

To protect plants, make certain that the soil mix drains well, and remove all solanaceous plant residue, including most of the root system, at crop change. Also be sure to keep nutrient levels high.

The bacterial wilt that infects cucurbits begins with leaves of any age. As the bacteria travel through the vascular bundles, petioles wilt, fruit and lateral branches shrivel and wilt and the disease spreads to the rest of the plant.

These bacteria don't overwinter in soil. Instead, both the striped and two-spotted cucumber beetles are their winter hosts. As they feed on plants in the spring they transmit the diseases. With screens, you'll never see them in a greenhouse.

Bacterial Canker

Bacterial canker strikes tomatoes. Like *Fusarium* wilt, drooping petioles are the first symptoms in young plants. When you snap an upper leaflet off an infected plant, the sap is brown. Older plants first show the disease on top leaves. Beginning at the margin, the leaf dies, then the disease spreads along the stem to the rest of the plant. In severe cases, white circular spots with a red center appear on the fruit.

I've seen only one case of bacterial canker in greenhouse tomatoes. They were a hydroponically grown crop, raised in a soilless medium and fed with sterile chemical fertilizers. I imagine that the bacteria came in on the seed. They also live on old tomato refuse and in the soil. Researchers can't agree about bacterial canker's life span in the soil, so there really is no hard-and-fast rule about controlling the disease by crop rotation. Instead, if soilborne bacterial infection does strike, dig up each plant with as much root mass as possible and sterilize the mix as described under Nematodes in the previous chapter. Sustained temperatures of 125°F or above kill the bacteria.

Bacterial Spot and Bacterial Speck

Bacterial spot and bacterial speck also attack tomatoes. Both diseases cause spots on foliage and fruit. You may also find bacterial spot on peppers. As with most other bacterial diseases, fungi follow the bacteria and cause rotting.

Both of these bacterial diseases strike when the soil is especially wet. In general, they operate the same way as bacterial canker. A healthy soil rich in compost with good drainage should be adequate protection.

Bacterial Soft-Rot

Bacterial soft-rot can infect roots, stems and fruits of almost every plant. You've certainly seen this disease on fruits or vegetables in the garden or even in the refrigerator, when a carrot or pepper was left forgotten on the back of a shelf. The first symptom is a water-soaked spot. Rotting spreads rapidly, producing a foul odor.

In the garden or greenhouse, the bacteria enter plants through bruised or broken skin. However, in high humidity and at temperatures of 75°F or above, soft-rot can penetrate uninjured tissue.

Preventive practices include controlling humidity levels through ventilation and air circulation, maintaining excellent drainage in all growing areas and taking care not to bruise plants. You can stall soft-rot of harvested produce by immediately chilling it after picking.

Angular Leaf Spot

Angular leaf spot strikes greenhouse cucumbers and melons. It gets its name because water-soaked spots on leaves are irregularly shaped rather than round. The spots die, sometimes leaving holes. In high humidity, drops of fluid containing the bacteria form around the water-soaked spots. A white or gray residue is left after the fluid evaporates. On fruit the spots are rounded and permit entry of other rot-causing organisms.

The bacteria that cause angular leaf spot overwinter on seeds and in old, uncomposted vines. The disease is transmitted by cucumber beetles, tools and the unsuspecting hands of the gardener. The bacteria can also be splashed onto leaves during watering.

Prevent the disease through careful sanitation and gentle watering. If angular leaf spot appears, pick and compost affected leaves. Since the disease doesn't move through the vascular system, pruning is an effective control.

Blight

Blight, sometimes called black rot, affects most cabbage family crops. It causes a darkening along the leaf margin. As it progresses, the leaf wilts, dies and drops. This disease also travels through the vascular system. Veins look suspiciously dark. If you slice through the stem, vascular bundles are noticeably darker than the rest of the tissue.

This bacterium, like so many others, overwinters on plant refuse and seeds. Good composting practices, healthy soil and uninfected seed should keep your greenhouse free of black rot. If an outbreak occurs, remove all infected plants, including roots, immediately.

Bacterial Rot

Bacterial rot is a general term given to diseases caused by many different bacteria. Lettuce and cabbage family crops are most susceptible. Whenever you spot rot without evidence of fungi, you can ascribe the damage to bacterial rot. Of course, you may be wrong, but sometimes it feels good to give the problem a name.

Most bacterial rots first appear as spots on leaves. Sometimes there's a yellow margin around the dying area. Other bacterial rots attack the area along the midribs. Fungi usually follow right behind the bacteria, softening the tissue. In the cases where fungal growth doesn't take place, the affected tissue dries and becomes papery.

Preventive measures are very straightforward: Don't splash water on leaves when you water, provide plants with ample nutrients and provide excellent drainage in containers and beds.

Virus Diseases

Virus diseases affect all cultivated food crops as well as many wild plants. Most viruses overwinter on perennials and plant refuse. In the spring they're transmitted to annuals by insects, especially aphids. If for no other reason, you should control greenhouse aphids as a preventive measure against viruses.

Tobacco Mosaic Virus

Tobacco mosaic virus is probably the best-known virus disease. In addition to tobacco, it infects tomatoes, peppers and petunias among domesticated plants. Aphids and people who handle tobacco carry it. Smokers should wash their hands in hot, soapy water before entering a greenhouse. A rinse with skim milk is even more effective.

Disease symptoms vary. The most characteristic sign, a yellow mottling between leaf veins, often leads people to mistake the virus for a magnesium deficiency. Generally tobacco mosaic produces a cupping of the leaf. However, a single virus strain rarely infects a plant. Normally more than a virus is present, so diagnosis is complicated. The tobacco mosaic virus can cause leaves to be so narrow that they're called "shoestrings." Or affected plants may have leaves that grow in rosettes. Cracks may appear along the main stem, or the vine may wither. Occasionally the fruit shows strange, irregular streaking.

Tobacco mosaic virus can live only four months in soil, but it overwinters in perennial hosts and plant refuse. Don't plan to compost plants infected with tobacco mosaic virus because home compost piles rarely heat to 200°F, the minimum temperature needed to kill the virus.

Tomatoes are also susceptible to other viruses. But since they interact with each other, it's almost impossible to distinguish one virus from another. Any kind of leaf roll is likely to be viral. While tobacco mosaic virus causes margins to turn up, many others make margins turn down.

"Streak," the name given to a particular set of tomato symptoms, is often caused by a tobacco mosaic virus strain in combination with the potato X virus. To complicate matters even more, cucumber mosaic virus can cause streak when it attacks tomatoes. The disease shows itself as a downward rolling and eventual browning and dying of the leaves. Streaks may appear on the stems, and fruits ripen late and look blotchy.

Because the two viruses are so commonly associated, wash your hands between touching potatoes and tomatoes. Daytime air temperatures near 95°F may kill the disease. This method of control also works well for several other viruses. But remember that high temperatures can inhibit fruit set. Don't continue the practice for more than a week or so.

Spotted Wilt

This virus disease can visit any of your greenhouse crops. It produces small orange, brown or black spots on lower leaves. The spots dry and the leaves droop before dying. When young plants contract the disease, their yields are drastically reduced.

Lettuce is very susceptible to spotted wilt. Watch for dwarfed, yellowed leaves. Sometimes brown spots appear on both upper and lower sides of the foliage.

Spotted wilt is transmitted by thrips, which are tiny, winged, spindle-shaped insects. Adults lay eggs on leaves, and feeding larvae ingest the virus. As adults, thrips no longer pick up the disease, but they do pass it on.

Thrips are uncommon in most small greenhouses because they don't live or reproduce well in high humidity. The symptoms of thrip damage are easy to recognize—leaves take on a silvery look. Without a hand lens, you may not see the thrips themselves. To control thrips, try forceful sprays of clear water, insecticidal soap or botanical pesticides. Lacewing larvae also control thrip populations very well.

Virus Ring Spot

Virus ring spot is aptly named. When a plant is infected, one or more concentric rings form on the fruit. The center of the ring may look normal, but the perimeter rings are brown and sunken. On leafy crops, rings appear on the foliage. Although this virus affects most common crops, you won't see it often in a greenhouse. Aphids and other small insects can't carry the virus, and the primary vectors, grasshoppers, are easy to keep out with screens.

Lettuce Mosaic Virus

When leaf lettuces come down with mosaic virus, they become dwarfed and show the characteristic mosaic mottling. Head lettuce, on the other hand, doesn't mottle. Instead, it appears stunted and makes very loose heads, or in severe cases, no head at all.

The disease overwinters in the seed and in wild lettuce and related plants. Aphids spread it from one plant to another. Some companies sell seed guaranteed not to carry the virus, but "mosaic indexed" seed is very expensive to produce and thus costs more. In a small greenhouse, control is as simple as pulling and disposing of weak-looking seedlings, and controlling the aphid population.

Cabbage Family Mosaics

Several viruses cause mosaic diseases in cabbage family crops. The symptoms to watch for include mottled, malformed leaves; stunting; warty-looking growths on leaves and black spots on foliage. If any of your plants display any of these symptoms, pull them immediately, roots and all. A compost pile that heats to 180°F should safely destroy the virus.

Cucumber Mosaic Virus

The virus responsible for cucumber mosaic affects most other greenhouse vegetable crops as well, but it causes the most trouble with cucurbits. Some greenhouse ornamentals, especially petunias, snapdragons, stocks, marigolds and geraniums, are also susceptible.

Affected cucumber leaves show a mottled coloration. Tomato leaves often grow as narrow "shoestrings." Fruits on cucumber, squash, tomato and pepper plants may simply show rings, but more often have large, irregular, blisterlike lumps under the skin.

Needless to say, virus complexes on cucurbits show other symptoms, too. Distorted leaves, dark green areas on both sides of major veins, leaf blistering and stunting are all danger signals. Aphids are the principal carriers of this group of viruses. By controlling aphids, you take a giant step in preventing cucumber mosaic.

Words of Encouragement

Writing about plant diseases depresses me. But I should point out that in all my time working in greenhouses, I've had only one case of *Botrytis* and a few inconsequential cases of late blight. The *Botrytis* happened in arid Montana, where I didn't expect humidity levels to be as high as they were, and consequently, hadn't pruned a cucumber bed well enough. My late blight hasn't ever been serious enough to cut yields. I've seen diseases in other greenhouses, of course, but very few in small, well-managed organic operations. Please don't conclude that the foregoing chamber of horrors is fated and inevitable; prevention really does work.

CHAPTER 13

WARM-WEATHER VEGETABLES

As a northerner, I never doubted the worth of a greenhouse during June, July and August. After all, in our part of the country, July is the only month when frosts are unlikely. To get decent yields outside, warm-weather crops have to be coddled along under plastic covers, even during the day in the beginning and the end of the season. I've never enjoyed this routine: it's too time-consuming for my normal schedule. So I looked forward to my first summer greenhouse, and I wasn't disappointed. The reliable environment gave me huge yields of early tomatoes, eggplants, melons and fancy peppers. And the thunbergia and tuberous begonias never looked better.

But greenhouse growers in warm climates don't always look forward to midsummer. With good shading, moderate temperatures can be maintained, of course, but many people choose to do the bulk of their vegetable gardening outside and use the summer greenhouse for heat-loving ornamentals and European seedless cucumbers. Or they turn their greenhouse into a solar dryer. Very often they also close it up for several weeks and let it overheat to kill pest and disease organisms.

But no matter what the climate, both northern and southern greenhouse growers can raise extra-early crops of warm-weather vegetables in spring and early summer.

Tomatoes

Tomatoes lead the list of favorite summer vegetables. Along with cucumbers and melons, they also head the list of the most time-consuming greenhouse vegetables. But both the flavor and yields of greenhouse tomatoes are worth the time.

Tomato Varieties

Which varieties you choose depends upon the season, environmental conditions and personal preference. Many people select specific greenhouse varieties, but surprisingly, some regular garden tomatoes do as well or better.

When choosing varieties, look for resistance against *Fusarium* and *Verticillium* wilts, nematodes and tobacco mosaic virus. Unless you're devoted to a particular long-season variety, choose early-bearing plants because they save space in the long run. Use indeterminate varieties (those that grow from the top all through their lives) for all crops grown in beds. By training them vertically, you can plant them closer together. Their long bearing season also guarantees a higher yield for the work.

Determinate varieties are self-topping; they grow only a few feet tall and the lateral branches bear the fruit. Most set the majority of fruit within a 2½-month period and then lose vigor. This growth habit makes determinates most useful for commercial field growers, who want a condensed harvest period. If you grow these varieties in a green-house, plant them in tubs. However, keep tubs widely spaced so that leaves from adjacent plants don't touch. Their bushy growth crowds a bed with so much foliage that it's difficult to protect against fungus diseases. To increase air circulation, prune off leaves as they age.

The following is a list of varieties commonly used in home green-houses. This listing is by no means complete. So many good tomatoes are available that it's hard to try them all. If a particular variety has done well in your garden, try it in the greenhouse. It's always fun to sample other people's fruit, too; you might find a new favorite.

Michigan-Ohio series (hybrid): Species in this group, bred es-pecially for greenhouse culture, are probably the most common commercially grown spring tomato. All Michigan-Ohio varieties yield well in areas with moderate to high light intensities and long photoperiods. But they don't do well as a fall crop because day-length and light levels aren't appropriate. In low light these in-determinate plants have a poor fruit set and are especially sus-ceptible to fungus diseases. Even in spring they're not a good choice for northern New England or other low-light areas.

Vendor: Vendor is used as a fall tomato by growers in a wide range of climates. In the North it's often used as a spring crop, too, because it grows well with low light and shorter photoperiods. The fruit is medium-size, with good color. These indeterminate plants are quite susceptible to fungi. It's important to provide good soil drainage and excellent ventilation and air circulation, especially during the cool, humid days of spring and fall.

Spring-planted Vendors aren't vigorous enough to produce well through the summer. Top plants by pinching off the growing tip after the fifth or sixth truss (cluster of fruit) has set. Pull when the last cluster turns light orange. This procedure fits into the tomato schedule given in chapter 9 under Fall Crop Scheduling. With staggered starting dates, Vendors can provide fruit all through the growing season.

Tuck series (hybrid): Tuckcross, Tuckcross 533 and Tuckqueen are the most common in this series. They've been bred for low-light conditions. The indeterminate plants are vigorous and bear large fruit. Since they don't suit all environments, try only a few plants at first. As a personal note, I'm not crazy about their flavor but recognize that other greenhouse environments may produce a better taste.

Jumbo (hybrid): Jumbo is one of the most popular greenhouse varieties. The large fruit has a deep red color. It's resistant to cracking, and a spring-planted crop yields heavily into late July. This strong indeterminate plant has a great deal of heavy foliage: prune leaves as well as suckers to maintain good air circulation. In areas where sunburn is a problem, Jumbo's heavy foliage works to your advantage by shielding the fruit from light.

Moira: This determinate variety is justifiably popular. The medium-sized fruits are extremely uniform, deep red and firm. They have good texture and flavor, too. Moira performs well in cooler temperatures (70 to 75°F during the day) and is generally disease resistant.

Earlirouge: If you're looking for a determinate variety that's quite early, tolerates cool temperatures and low light and is somewhat disease-resistant, Earlirouge is a good choice. However, the fruit is often only 4 to 5 ounces and, to my taste, inferior to Moira.

Gurney Girl: This little-known indeterminate variety has performed quite well for me. Fruits are exceptionally large and full flavored for an early tomato. The plant bears prolifically through a long season, too. It puts out lush growth, so prune leaves periodically and make certain to support it well.

Sub-Arctic series: These are extremely early determinate varieties. Their size ranges from 1½ inches in diameter for the Sub-Arctic Early to 3 inches for the Sub-Arctic Maxi. They're supposed to be susceptible to early blight, but I haven't had this trouble, even in low-light conditions. However, I don't like their taste or texture. They're still available, so somebody must like them.

Sweet 100 (hybrid): This is my favorite cherry tomato. It's superb on every count: flavor, yields and disease resistance. Some people grow it in a 12-inch basket, but the plant can reach 6 feet high, so I prefer to give it more room in a big tub or even a bed. I've had the best yields by letting two or three stems grow per plant, supporting each separately. The only problem with Sweet 100 is that the fruit cracks easily. To avoid cracking, keep soil moisture consistent and pick the tomatoes as soon as they turn orange. Wait until they're bright red to eat.

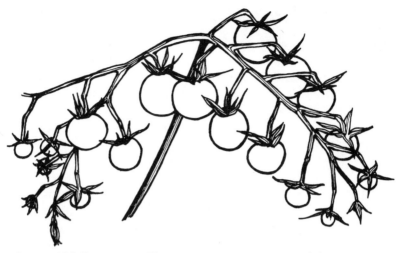

Sweet 100 Tomatoes: *These tomatoes are some of the sweetest you'll ever taste. The plants are prolific, so you'll have an abundant supply.*

Tiny Tim: This old-fashioned, determinate cherry tomato is still a favorite. The small plants do well in 10- or 12-inch hanging baskets. They bear large numbers of 1-inch fruit with an acid, rather than sweet, flavor. The plants are particularly sturdy.

Nova: This is an early-bearing, determinate paste tomato. Each plant produces numerous very firm, pear-shaped fruits. Because the plant is smaller and bears earlier, I prefer it to Roma or Chico Paste, other popular paste varieties.

Tomato Culture

Tomatoes are consistently the most popular vegetable among home gardeners. The basics of greenhouse tomato growing are easy to master, as long as you follow the guidelines given in this section.

Light Levels and Temperature

Light intensity, photoperiod and quality are important to tomatoes. Seedling plants tolerate light intensities as low as 2,500 footcandles when they're grown at 65 to 70°F during the day and 55 to 60°F at night. But as plants approach bearing age, they need at least 3,000 footcandles to yield well. Remember that outdoors, light intensities are as high as 10,000 footcandles.

Daylength should gradually increase from the 12 hours given to seedlings to the natural midsummer photoperiod. By June, northerners have a strong 16-hour day. Midsummer daylength is slightly shorter in much of the United States, but never too short for good greenhouse production.

Natural light quality varies with latitude as well. It's comforting for northern growers to know that our "bluer" light hastens maturity, making up for our shorter season.

For maximum production, try to maintain daytime temperatures of 70 to 75°F and nighttime temperatures of 60 to 65°F. At temperatures above 85 to 90°F, pollen may become sterile. High temperatures can also prevent fruit from developing a deep, rich color. At low temperatures, growth slows and flowering and fruiting are delayed.

Cold Treatment

I was educated to believe that a cold treatment would increase a tomato plant's vigor and productivity. After testing this procedure for a few years, I now think that cold treatment works well only on indeterminate varieties kept for a long bearing season. The delayed fruiting is offset by higher total yields.

Begin by germinating seeds as normal, at a soil temperature between 75 and 85°F. After the seed leaves have enlarged, grow plants at daytime temperatures of 60°F and nighttime ones of 50 to 55°F. Maintain this regimen for two to three weeks. This time coincides with the plant's most sensitive period, when the first flower clusters are forming. (They're still undetectable at this point.) After the cold period, increase both day and night temperatures by 5°F for a week, and then bring them into the normal range of 70 to 75°F days and 60 to 65°F nights.

In the North it's relatively easy to control temperatures this closely. The weather is generally cool enough so it's only a matter of regulating heaters and manual vents and fans. But since tomatoes receiving a cold treatment are started about two weeks earlier than usual, most southern growers can practice this technique.

Cold treatment is most effective with high levels of light and carbon dioxide. In cloudy regions, use artificial lighting during the seedling stage to increase future productivity, but don't exceed the 12-hour limit.

Although I don't know of any controlled experiments, fall tomatoes, usually started in the long days of June, may profit from artificial shading in the late afternoon. Keep them as cool as possible during their first month or six weeks of growth.

Soil and Nutrients

Tomatoes require a pH between 6.2 and 7.0. As seedlings, they like moderate nitrogen and high phosphorus levels. Add a scant cup of steamed bone meal to every 3 cubic feet of tomato-starting medium. Excess nitrogen is insidious; the resulting sappy foliage is very attractive to aphids, and the soft fruit is unusually susceptible to fungal and bacterial rots.

When you start tomatoes in a mix containing compost, don't add more nitrogen. With a nutrient-free mix, feed with fish emulsion or compost or manure tea. You can use liquid seaweed on plants in any kind of growing mix. Tomatoes are most vigorous when given a foliar seaweed feeding every two or three weeks, beginning when the seed leaves develop. I also use a root drench of seaweed–fish emulsion blend at both early and final transplanting stages.

In general, I fertilize tomatoes carefully, adding compost tea to mature plants only when the leaves look slightly pale. Commercial tomato growers often apply potassium and magnesium when the first fruits are beginning to swell and again a month to six weeks later. In the home greenhouse, use a solution of liquid seaweed and Epsom salts or a Sul-Po-Mag tea.

Transplanting

Healthy tomato seedlings are as wide as they are tall. By six weeks they should be about 7 inches high with short distances between branches. Their stems should be sturdy and at least as thick as a pencil, their leaves shouldn't curl and their color should be a uniform, forest green. Be firm with yourself; transplant only the best seedlings and compost the rest.

Always transplant tomatoes into permanent positions before the flowers open. Normally a seedling's buds visibly swell at six weeks, so this timing works well. If you have to hold them longer, transplant seedlings into large, soil-filled plastic bags to avoid crowding their roots (put one plant per bag). Shield the bags from light on all sides. When you transplant, lower a bag into the planting hole, cut it away and gently pull it free. In this way there is minimum root disruption.

In a new or refurbished soil mix, phosphorus and calcium levels should be high enough for tomatoes. But when you're following a spring crop and don't have a chance to add more compost, dig about a quarter cup of steamed bone meal into every planting hole.

Tomatoes need a deep root system for good growth. You can encourage this with good watering practices. Don't water transplants so frequently that roots form near the surface. Let the top inch dry between waterings while plants are getting established, but make certain that lower depths are consistently moist.

Mulching

In the garden, many people mulch around tomatoes to suppress weeds and maintain cool, moist soil conditions. Light-colored mulches are useful in a greenhouse because they reflect light back to the fruit.

Just as you do in the garden, wait to mulch until the soil temperature exceeds 60°F and bottom leaves are well suspended above the soil surface. If you have it, use straw for mulching material. Peanut hulls are often suggested as a mulch, but if you don't know their source, avoid them. Peanuts are often grown in rotation with cotton and consequently carry a tremendous pesticide residue.

Both black and clear mulches heat the soil during early spring and make early planting possible. But in a greenhouse, don't leave plastics in place all summer because soil will be too warm for healthy tomato growth.

Training Vines

Vertical training is the only practical system for vining crops such as tomatoes in the greenhouse. It saves space, minimizes some diseases and maximizes fruit quality and yield.

Training a Tomato: *To coax a tomato vine upward, gently wind the young stem around the supporting twine. Wind in a clockwise direction.*

Supporting arrangements were discussed earlier in chapter 4 under Plant Supports, but the job doesn't stop with the technology. Most crops won't obligingly climb up a string—they need help. If you use twine or heavy cord, tie it loosely around the stem under the bottommost leaves.

Young stems are flexible enough to wind around the supporting twine. Always wind stems in a clockwise direction since they grow this way naturally. But don't make the stem look like a corkscrew! Leave 6 to 8 inches between windings. Winding helps to keep the stem upright, but bearing plants are often too heavy to be supported without ties. Strips of soft cotton fabric or twistie ties hold stems close to the twine without injury. Always attach the tie under a petiole to keep the plant from slipping. Ties placed at 6- to 8-inch intervals are enough to secure most plants.

On trellises or other rigid supporting structures, tomato plants need help as well. Train them in an upright position by tying stems at convenient spots no farther apart than 8 inches.

Single- or double-leader tomato plants can be trained to a V system of trellising. This technique is most commonly associated with cucumbers. (See the following section for more details.) In a V trellis system, overhead cables are spaced 3 to 4 feet apart. Plants are not positioned directly under the cables, but between them. When trained up their strings, the stems form a V pattern. For greatest air circulation, train every other plant to each cable. When you have double-leader plants, train leaders to opposite cables.

Within a few months, tomatoes grow to the top of their support. With vigorous plants, you can train them over the horizontal wire and down another piece of twine. If they're at the end of their season, pinch off the growing tips and let the last fruits color slightly before pulling the plants.

Pruning

Tomatoes require pruning, otherwise their dense growth creates a stagnant, humid environment. Light can't penetrate the mass of leaves, and fruits overripen before they're noticed. If you do a little every day, pruning doesn't become a major, time-consuming task. I often water with one hand while pruning with the other.

Each plant has a characteristic growth pattern that helps determine how it should be pruned. Tomatoes would like to be bushes. On indeterminate varieties, secondary branches grow at junctures between the stem and each branch. These "suckers" elongate, flower and produce a new crop of lateral branches if undisturbed. To keep indeterminates under control, remove suckers at the inch-long stage. Push them off at the base with a fast sideways motion of your thumb. They'll snap off, leaving a clean break. Don't do this sort of pruning on determinate plants. When you break off a lateral branch, you're removing one of a fixed number of fruit-producing sites, which ultimately reduces your harvest.

Some growers train indeterminate plants into double-leaders by letting the first sucker just beyond the first flower cluster grow. They train this second stem to its own support. If you plan to use double-leaders, leave 30 inches between plants.

Growers who use the double-leader system claim increased yields. Single-leader proponents counter by pointing out that the double-leader plants require more bed space and they end up giving the same yields on a per square foot basis. The fact is that both systems work well. Experiment to see which system works better for you.

Old leaves invite pests and diseases. Snap off bottom leaves as soon as they lose vibrancy. Don't worry about the bare stem at the base; it

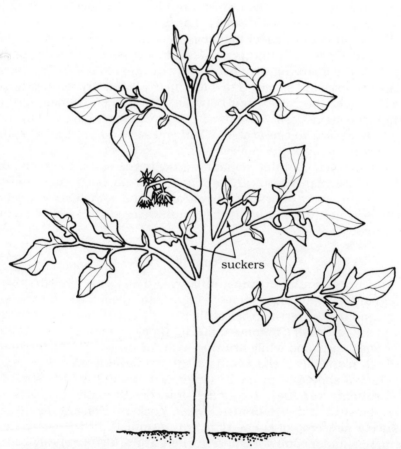

suckers

Tomato Suckers: *Between the stem and each branch, secondary branches called suckers grow. Prune suckers to keep growth under control.*

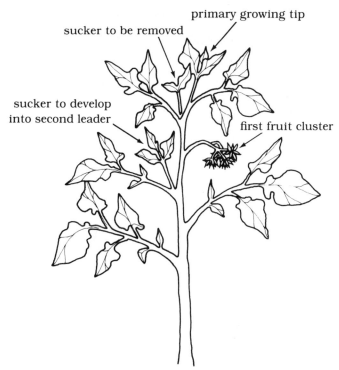

Double-Leader Tomato Plant: *To train a plant into the double-leader shape, let the first sucker after the first flower cluster grow. Prune off all others.*

helps protect against fungus diseases. I also snap off young leaves that touch another plant part. My tomato plants would never win a beauty contest, but they don't get sick, either. By the way, if whiteflies' predatory wasps, *Encarsia formosa*, are in the greenhouse, pile pruned leaves on the soil surface. It would be a shame to throw out the mature wasps that emerge from parasitized larvae on bottom leaves.

Winter Tomatoes

Winter tomatoes are healthiest when nighttime temperatures average 58°F or higher and daytime temperatures are 70 to 75°F. Fruit ripens, albeit slowly, when light levels are a minimum of 2,500 foot-candles for six hours a day. Yields are higher under brighter light and longer photoperiods, of course. It's important to keep carbon dioxide levels high by frequent ventilation.

But no matter what, fall and winter tomatoes never yield as well as spring and summer crops. They're also more susceptible to pests and diseases. Watch plants closely and pull if problems seem uncontrollable.

Ending the Season

Indeterminate tomato plants continue to set fruit and make new growth until they die. Several weeks before the plants are to be pulled, pinch off growing tips, blossoms and newly set fruit. The plants will put their energy into ripening the immature fruit on the vine, and you can clear the bed earlier. Incidentally, there's no need to wait until fruit are bright red before picking. As long as they've reached the orange stage, they'll taste vine-ripened.

Keep fully ripened tomatoes in a moderately cool place—which doesn't mean the refrigerator. Under refrigeration, some cells in the fruits collapse slightly, changing the texture. They'll stay more appetizing in a cool, dark pantry.

Common Problems with Greenhouse Tomatoes

Tomatoes are my favorite crop. They're not my favorite food, but I love raising all solanaceous plants, so I find them easy to grow. But not everyone shares this affinity; some people get along better with broccoli or lettuce.

New greenhouse owners often come to me with tomato problems. If it isn't a fungus or a magnesium deficiency, they usually have a poor fruit set. In most cases, poor pollination can be traced to high humidity around the plants, low light levels, high or low temperatures or pollination that occurs too early or late in the day. Correct these problems before ascribing the difficulty to the variety or to the soil mix.

A minor but annoying tomato problem is cracking fruit. Just as the tomato nears maturity, the skin cracks open, setting the stage for rapid fungal attack. Cracking is usually caused by uneven watering. When bearing plants are under moisture stress, water moves from the fruit to the leaves. Then, once soil water is available, the fruit takes it up quickly and the skin cracks from the sudden pressure. If you let a bed dry too much between waterings, pick fruit earlier than usual to sidestep the problem.

When plants are calcium deficient, uneven watering can also contribute to blossom-end rot, a disease characterized by a brown, rotting spot at the blossom end of the fruit. Adding bone meal to the hole at transplanting time lessens the risk of this disease. However, if it does occur, sprinkle about an eighth of a cup of bone meal around each plant, dig it in slightly and water. Use a foliar seaweed spray as well. Make another light application of bone meal in several weeks.

If the growing medium contains compost and the tomato plants receive supplementary fertilization through the season, nutrient deficiencies are rare. But just in case, the following chart, Nutrient Deficiencies in Tomatoes, may help you diagnose nutrient problems. Remember that "eyeball" diagnosis isn't 100 percent reliable. When

Nutrient Deficiencies in Tomatoes

Nutrient	General Deficiency Symptoms
Nitrogen	Lower leaves turn pale green to yellow; roots are stunted; stems are thin and weak.
Phosphorus	Lower leaves take on a purple hue, may curl down; leaflets and branches are stunted; maturity is delayed.
Potassium	Lower leaves turn brown or yellow on the tip and margins and sometimes curl; be aware that low temperatures combined with high soil water content can also cause these symptoms; tomatoes show green shoulders when ripe.
Calcium	Terminal shoots and root tips are stunted or die; tomatoes develop blossom-end rot.
Magnesium	Lower leaves develop yellow areas between green veins; margins are distorted; whiteflies are attracted to deficient plants.
Sulfur	Leaves and veins are light green; maturity is delayed.
Iron	Leaves are pale yellow near the petiole and margins; fruit doesn't redden.
Manganese	Small yellow spots develop along midribs of young leaves; veins remain green.
Boron	Leaves droop, eventually entire plant droops; leaf margins curl and brown; stems are brittle near terminals; tomatoes have corky areas, ripen unevenly.

problems are serious, it's wise to get a tissue test. Contact your local extension agency for sampling and mailing directions.

Cucumbers

In northern areas, garden cucumbers are available only for a month or two. That has always made me sad because I don't enjoy the rubbery, waxed facsimiles from the supermarket—they're as bad as cardboard tomatoes. But with a home greenhouse, you'll be savoring cucumber sandwiches from May to November.

Two kinds of cucumbers are grown in the greenhouse. Standard varieties are those that normally grow in the outdoor garden. They have both male and female flowers and must be hand-pollinated.

European seedless varieties produce the long, skinny fruit that you find individually shrink-wrapped in the gourmet produce section. They're relished for their mild flavor, thin skins and the fact that they're "burpless." These varieties are gynoecious, meaning that they produce only female flowers. (A few may produce a couple of male blossoms here and there along the vine.) Because female flowers produce the fruit, these varieties are very prolific. European plants are self-pollinating in the sense that they've been genetically altered to produce cucumbers without the standard process of pollination. This is the reason why European varieties can't be grown outdoors; the fruit becomes distorted when the flowers are pollinated.

Cucumber Varieties

Cucumbers are available with two basic growth habits—vining and bush. Vining varieties are the best choice for a large greenhouse crop. Cucumber yields per square foot, and even per plant, are higher when you train vines vertically. Upright plants receive more light and, if well pruned, better air circulation and thus more carbon dioxide. All of this contributes to better disease resistance. And when fruits hang down, fewer are misshapen from running into an obstruction. Vertically grown plants make picking easier, too.

For your first greenhouse cucumber venture, it's wise to start with the less temperamental standard varieties. Choose one that bears heavily in your garden because it's likely to do even better in the greenhouse. Victory Hybrid, Marketmore, Straight Eight and Burpee Hybrid are all known for high productivity.

If you don't eat or pickle huge numbers of cucumbers, consider growing one or two bush plants. A 3- to 5-gallon container per plant provides ample root area. Spacemaster is my favorite of the high-yielding bush varieties because the fruit quality is quite good.

After gaining experience with standard cucumbers, try a couple of European seedless varieties. Seeds used to be available only through commercial suppliers, but recently more companies are featuring them, probably in response to the growing number of home greenhouses. Listed here are some of the more common varieties.

Kosura F1: This seedless hybrid is particularly tolerant of low light levels and cool temperatures. It sets fruit at daytime temperatures as low as 60°F. This is a good variety for late-summer growing in all climates. In the North it's particularly dependable.

Pandex: This hybrid cucumber tolerates low light and cool temperatures as well as Kosura F1 does. It does well in all climates and is a good choice for northern growers.

Sandra: You'll harvest a bounty of cucumbers from this variety as long as you provide the high light levels and temperatures of midsummer.

Cucumber Culture

Cucumbers take a good bit of care, but respond lavishly to good care. A friend of mine considers cucumbers to be too aggressive. I just think of them as tropical rather than temperate plants and provide the rich soils, high temperatures, bright light and fresh air they love.

(For simplicity, both standard and seedless varieties will be discussed at once here. Any important differences between them are noted.)

Starting the Seeds

Despite the cucumber's fast growth and resistance to transplanting, most people save space by starting in pots. There is a way to do this with minimal disruption to the sensitive roots. Sow seeds in 4-inch peat pots or 4- to 6-inch plastic pots, and transplant them only once into their final containers.

Use a starting mix that is moisture-retentive but able to drain well. All cucurbits, not just cucumbers, require high oxygen levels in the root zone, particularly as seedlings. My normal mix is composed of 2 parts peat moss, 2 parts sand or perlite, 1 part compost, 1 part loam and 1 part vermiculite.

Cucumber seeds have such a high germination rate that it's easy to overplant. Besides, seeds for European varieties are expensive, so there's really no good reason to plant more than one seed per pot. Push the more pointed end toward the bottom of the pot, and bury the seed about $\frac{1}{2}$ inch deep. For cucurbits, an overnight soak in liquid seaweed makes a difference in both germination speed and seedling vigor.

Heating cables are mandatory for the spring crop unless there's a really warm niche in the greenhouse. European seedless varieties germinate best at soil temperatures between 85 and 95°F, while standard plants do well at temperatures between 70 and 85°F. Keep the medium consistently moist; cucumbers use great quantities of water.

After soaking, cucumber seeds germinate in three to five days. Seedlings must emerge into a warm, bright world. Unlike tomatoes, cucumbers won't produce well if they're exposed to cool temperatures as babies. Daytime temperatures of 75°F and nights no lower than 68°F are best during their first weeks of growth. Standard varieties can tolerate slightly lower temperatures. If the greenhouse is still cool at the time the cucumber seedlings are developing, place them in a heated propagating chamber as described in chapter 4 under Propagating Equipment.

Long days hasten the growth of cucumber seedlings. In early spring, use artificial lights to create a 16-hour day. This photoperiod gives plants such a boost that they're ready to transplant four weeks from seeding. Without lights, it may be six weeks before they've grown three or four true leaves, their optimum transplant stage.

Spray seedlings with liquid seaweed once they emerge or when the first true leaves appear. At transplanting, water them with a seaweed–fish emulsion blend to help them become established.

Transplanting

As a consultant, I see the same problems many times in many different greenhouses. With cucumbers, one of the most common is transplanting into beds with cold soil. The plants just stop growing until the soil warms up, but meanwhile, they're very susceptible to diseases.

Bed soil temperature should be at least 65°F for standard varieties and 70°F for European seedless types. To warm the soil lay down plastic mulch a week to several days before planting; vigorous cucumber plants are well worth the trouble. You can plant right into the plastic or remove it from the beds. I take it off. Bare soil is not only easier to side-dress later in the season, but it also "breathes" better, allowing more oxygen into the root zone.

Air temperatures are important, too. Days should average 75°F but shouldn't exceed 80°F at this stage. Nighttime minimums much lower than 58°F set back growth. Drape the bed with a night cover if temperatures threaten to dip that low. By the time plants are in full production, most seedless varieties grow well at 80 to 85°F days and 65 to 70°F nights. Keep standard varieties at the lower end of the seedless range, day and night.

Soil in planting beds must have the same good drainage and moisture-retention qualities as the starting mix, but should be much richer. Decrease the peat moss fraction and increase the proportion of compost and loam. Add a quarter to half a cup of bone meal and a handful of compost to every planting hole if you have any doubts about nutrient content.

During transplanting be extremely careful of cucurbit roots. If the plants were started in peat pots, the roots will be pushing through the pot at the three- or four-leaf stage. There's no need to split a peat pot for these strong roots since they have no trouble pushing through it. Place the pot in the hole and gently firm the medium around it. Don't bury seedlings any deeper than they grew in the pots.

When you use plastic pots to start plants, tap out the root ball and, handling only the soil or bottom leaves if absolutely necessary, set it into place. Again, don't bury the stem. Water plants right away to firm the soil around the roots.

Spacing

Commercial growers give cucumbers plenty of space. With vertical trellising they place European seedless varieties about 30 inches apart in 3½-foot rows. In the V trellising pattern (described later in this section), they set cucumbers 20 inches apart in 5-foot rows.

In my experience, home growers can plant standard cucumbers more densely as long as air circulation is good and plants are kept well pruned. A spacing pattern of 18 inches apart in 2- to 2½-foot rows is usually adequate in traditional greenhouses. But without north light, this spacing is too dense; try a 20-inch by 3-foot pattern instead. When access to light or air circulation is restricted, the plants won't produce as heavily and they'll be more susceptible to fungus diseases. No matter what the spacing, pull alternate plants if they start to look shaded or the atmosphere begins to feel like a jungle.

European seedless plants can yield 40 to 50 fruit per plant over a six-month season. Because these are used fresh and not pickled, one or two plants are enough for most families. They do well in either beds or individual containers. But they need space to bear well; put two plants in a 3- by 5-foot bed, three in a 3- by 8-foot bed.

Individual containers should be about the size of an old washtub or half a cider barrel. Be certain to drill and screen drainage holes directly in the bottom and low on the sides. Place the container where plants can get light without shading the rest of the greenhouse.

Trellising

Cucumbers begin their vertical growth three weeks to a month after transplanting. Support the vines as described earlier for tomatoes or train them into a V pattern.

Commercial growers use the V pattern for European seedless plants. Standard cucumbers and melons can benefit from this pattern, but they don't require it. It's a good trellising system that allows more light and better air circulation around leaves. I admit liking it on aesthetic counts—it's pretty.

To get the pattern started, plant cucumbers in a straight row, about 18 inches away from the two overhead cables. As they grow, train alternate plants to strings attached to each cable. Train the first plant to cable A, the second to cable B, the third to cable A, the fourth to cable B and so on. Looking down the row, you'll see that the plants make a V formation. Even with only two or three plants, this system promotes better health in bed-grown plants.

Pruning

Cucumbers need intensive pruning if they're to grow and bear a bumper crop. This applies to both standard and European seedless

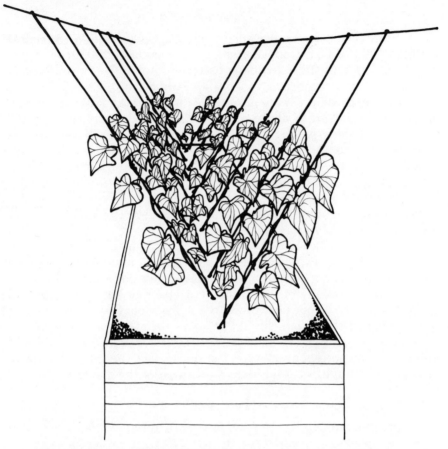

Cucumbers in a V Pattern: *This training method is nice because plants receive more light and circulating air. Melons and tomatoes can also be trained this way.*

varieties. The manner in which you go about pruning these two does differ a bit, as you'll see. But their basic growth pattern is the same. They grow by sending a flower and a new branch from the axils between stems and leaf petioles. Each leaf axil, whether on the main stem or a lateral branch, grows a flower and a new branch. Outside, all these branches reach for light in every available direction, but greenhouses don't give them room to ramble. Careful pruning ensures that each leaf has access to light.

Train standard cucumbers upright on a rigid trellis or a piece of suspended twine. Remove the first three to six bottom leaves, flowers and lateral shoots after the leaf above has fully enlarged but before the lateral shoot elongates. Beyond the lowermost 12 to 18 inches, leave each leaf and flower that grows from the main stem. Pollinated female flowers set fruit. (Refer to the illustration of male and female cucurbit

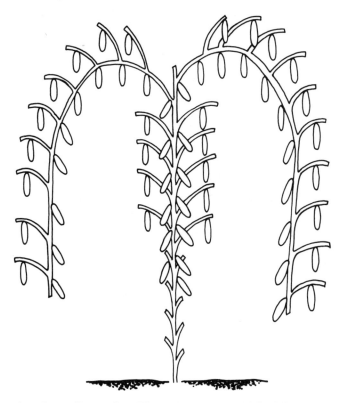

Pruning for a Cucumber Plant: In very simplified form, you can see how to prune a cucumber that's trained to a cable or trellis. Leave the bottom 12 to 18 inches of stem bare, and limit the plant to one to three leaves and fruit at every juncture off the main stem. When the plant reaches the cable or trellis top, pinch off the growing tip and let one or two laterals below the tip develop.

flowers on page 160.) If the flower is male, allow one lateral leaf and flower to grow from the axil of the first leaf. Continue this pattern, limiting the plant to one to three leaves and fruit at every juncture off the main stem. This restriction doesn't decrease yields; it forces the plant's energy into forming fruits and new, upward growth.

When the cucumber reaches the overhead cable or top of the trellis, pinch off the terminal growth, but allow one or two laterals just below the tip to develop. Train these laterals over the wire and treat them as main stems. Incidentally, more than one grower has discovered the hard way that melons and cucumbers die when all their growing tips are pinched.

Leaves age as fruits mature. Pull them, as described earlier for tomatoes, when their color fades. Old leaves and dense growth of cucurbits are particularly appetizing fare for fungi.

European seedless cucumbers are pruned in much the same way I've described for standards, only more intensively, since all (or nearly all) of the flowers are female. Commercial growers prune off all fruit for the first 18 to 36 inches of growth. In a home greenhouse with a small planting, 18 inches is certainly sufficient. For the next 2 to 3 feet, keep only one fruit and leaf per axil. Beyond that, allow two leaves and two fruit per branch. When the vine hits the top of the cable, treat it as you would a standard cucumber. Remember to pinch out the growing tip of the central stem. Allow the hanging laterals to form two leaves and fruit at every branch.

Fertilizing

Cucumbers are heavy feeders. In a rich soil mix, they don't need special attention until the first fruits begin to form. At that point, water with a weak solution of compost or manure tea to which you've added Epsom salts or Sul-Po-Mag. Afterward maintain a normal fertilizing schedule that includes foliar feeding with liquid seaweed. Watch the color of the leaves; if they look pale, apply compost tea or another general fertilizer more frequently.

Harvesting

Cucumber plants, even European seedless varieties, begin to bear about 50 to 75 days after planting. Harvest fruits before they fatten up or begin to pale. Cucumbers are tastiest while they're still young. To protect against rotting during storage, leave about $\frac{1}{2}$ inch of stem attached to the fruit. Store in a dark, cool place such as a root cellar or pantry. The crisper drawer of the refrigerator is usually too cool. Standard cucumbers keep for a week or more without losing their quality, but European seedless varieties have thin skins prone to moisture loss. The plastic wrap that surrounds them in the produce section of the supermarket is not merely decorative. If you plan to store them for more than a day, wrap them in a moisture-retentive covering.

Common Problems with Greenhouse Cucumbers

Cucumbers can give a commercial grower quite a headache. In mass plantings they're the most difficult of all vegetable crops to manage. They transpire like crazy, creating a very humid microclimate. And, of course, their soft tissue is susceptible to fungus diseases.

Pests can also be a problem. Spider mites and whiteflies love cucumbers. In large plantings you can control mites with predatory mites, but *Encarsia formosa*, the whitefly parasite, doesn't like hairy leaves, so it's not always reliable. If Encarsia wasps seem to be avoiding the whiteflies, use an insecticidal soap or botanical poison. You may find that the hairy leaves obscure your view of young whitefly scales. A ten-power hand lens will help in the search. A hanging basket of fuchsias near the plants can alert you to the presence of whiteflies, but it could also draw them to the area. Fuchsia is their very favorite food.

Cucumbers have other problems, too. If they taste bitter, it's likely they got too hot or too dry. Try to regulate growing temperatures and keep soil moisture stable.

As far as vegetables go, cucumbers are very flexible. If they hit an obstacle while growing, they'll develop a weird shape. See that fruits hang straight down, without interference, and you won't end up with any misfits. And remember the story I told earlier about the woman with the peculiar-looking European seedless cucumbers; routinely remove any male flowers that may develop to prevent pollination.

Both standard and seedless plants show stress by aborting fruit. The cucumbers start to develop and then shrivel up. The stress could be due to a nutrient deficiency, or there could be too many fruit developing at once. When you start to see shriveling fruit, check everything you can think of and prune a bit more than usual. Also watch for double fruiting. Occasionally two or more cucumbers form in the same axil. Don't regard this as a gift—it's overtaxing the plant's resources. Select the better-looking of the pair and remove the other.

Very slow growth in a cucumber vine is usually a sign of low temperatures or shading. Add heat if necessary, prune more rigorously and try to brighten the shaded spot. If you can't shed more light on the shaded plant, pull it.

Every so often I get an inquiry about the feasibility of growing European seedless cucumbers for sale. It's not a bad idea, as long as you have a market and have gained enough assurance with them to work with a large planting. I always offer a bit of caution, though. It's relatively easy to grow a few plants, but a whole greenhouse of these delicacies is sometimes a major challenge.

Muskmelons

Muskmelons, or cantaloupes, are close relatives of cucumbers and are grown in much the same manner. For greenhouse culture, choose short-season, small-vined varieties. The Israeli melons, such as Ogen, produce particularly well in confined areas. They produce about ten melons per plant in a season. Vedrantais is flavorful and well suited to trellising, and ripe melons don't slip from the vines. You have to cut them off when they smell ripe. Minnesota Midget is a prolific bush variety, giving 4- to 6-inch-diameter cantaloupes. Grow it in a tub, don't prune and support each vine as it grows over the edge.

For pointers on seed starting and transplanting, refer to the preceding section on cucumbers. Melons need plenty of room. In beds,

space plants about $2\frac{1}{2}$ to 3 feet apart. Because of their space requirements, I prefer using individual tubs in small greenhouses and set
them in bright corners. Once the plants start to grow, you'll want to
begin training them upward (unless you're growing a bush variety). I
train melons to a backdrop of strong nylon or plastic netting or even
metal page-wire fencing. The plants are often too heavy to do well on
single pieces of twine.

You don't have to prune melons as extensively as cucumbers. On
all varieties but bush melons, pinch off the necessary flowers so that
the first fruit forms 18 inches above the soil. Also remove leaves so this
bottom part of the vine is bare. The rest of the way up the vine, allow
one to three melons to develop at each axil. Watch both light availability
and air circulation. If either is restricted, prune some leaves. Be sure
to tie each lateral branch to the support with a piece of soft cloth.

Some melon varieties "slip" from their stems when ripe. To keep
ripe fruit from falling off vertical vines, I support each melon in a sling
made from an old nylon stocking. I also check them daily for ripeness.
Because I'm so careful, I haven't seen any fall off the vines, but I can
imagine how traumatic it is to have ripe melons plunging to the floor,
crushing other plants in their path.

Cantaloupes have the finest flavor when they're picked as ripe as
possible. Most varieties are ripe when slight pressure against the base
of the stem releases the melon. Test all "slipping" varieties after they
turn color and smell ripe at the blossom end, but let them "pick" themselves. Cut melons from nonslipping varieties when they have a sweet
melon aroma.

If you're unable to enjoy your ripe melons right away, you must
store them in dark, cool conditions. You can keep them at 70°F or room
temperature for two to three days, but then you must refrigerate. Unfortunately, they're unusually susceptible to fungi. If melon supplies
are suddenly too plentiful, try drying thin slices—they're wonderfully
sweet.

Peppers

Peppers are an easy summer crop. Like standard cucumbers and
melons, they grow well at temperatures of 80°F during the day and
65°F at night, but they'll also perform well at the slightly cooler temperatures that favor tomatoes. Given a bright greenhouse environment,
peppers grow into sturdy bushes loaded with fruit.

Pepper Varieties

Flip through a couple of seed catalogs, and you'll see the wonderful
range of choices you have among pepper varieties. There aren't any
special greenhouse varieties, but they all do well under glass. Select

peppers by taste—sweet, hot or pungent. The following are some of the more popular sweet pepper varieties.

Ace: This hybrid is a short-season, bell pepper variety. The peppers are 4 to 5 inches long. Plants do well under slightly cool conditions.

Bell Boy: This hybrid is a popular, long-season bell pepper. The sturdy, compact plants are heavy yielders.

California Wonder: One of the best stuffing peppers. Plants produce a large harvest of 4-inch-long bell peppers.

Canape: A short-season plant that grows well in slightly cool temperatures. A very prolific producer of bell peppers.

Cubanelle: One of my favorite sweet yellow peppers. Vigorous plants produce ample numbers of elongated peppers.

Gypsy: Fruit is light green and slightly elongated, not a true bell shape. This short-season hybrid tolerates slightly cool conditions.

Staddon's Select: Slightly cool temperatures don't affect these short-season plants. Large peppers are bell shaped and good for stuffing.

Gypsy Peppers: These light green, elongated sweet peppers are good for frying.

There are so many good hot and semihot varieties that I haven't tried them all, and I'm a pepper lover! I dry, freeze and pickle huge quantities of mixed sweet, semihot and hot varieties in olive oil, garlic and vinegar. Each variety has a distinctive flavor, so every pickling mix has its own character. The following are some of my favorites.

Anaheim: This is the skinny green, semihot pepper sold in small cans for use in Mexican cooking. Plants produce lots of medium to long peppers that are good fresh or dried.

Early Jalapeno: These are fiery hot peppers, so beware. The large, upright plants perform well in the North.

Hungarian Wax: A semihot type of pepper that's popular for canning. The short-season plants bear plenty of waxy yellow peppers.

Long Red Cayenne: This pepper is even hotter than Jalapeno; one plant a year satisfies my needs. The plants are vigorous and spreading.

Zesty Hybrid: This plant is good for timid hot pepper eaters— the peppers are merely pungent.

Pepper Culture

Peppers are slow growers at first. Start them eight to ten weeks before you want to transplant seedlings into permanent positions. For germination, soil temperatures should be 75 to 85°F.

Pepper roots aren't particularly sensitive, so you can transplant them several times if space demands it. But they do like warm temperatures. If you start peppers when the greenhouse is cool, give them a shelf in the propagating chamber. Group peppers with the tomatoes because they, too, like a 12-hour day.

When the time comes to transplant, space peppers a foot apart in each direction in the bed. At this spacing, most varieties will cover the bed by fall. Interplant only fast-growing crops such as corn salad or leaf lettuce, so you can harvest them by the time the peppers are three months old. In long-season climates, it might be wise to increase the planting distance to 16 or even 18 inches because peppers have time to become so much larger.

According to a seed company that specializes in peppers, the plants are stronger and bear more prolifically when planted two to a hole. I haven't tried this, but assume that spacing would have to be doubled between planting holes.

I use bone meal to feed peppers, since the phosphorus it contains encourages flowering and fruit formation. If it's not already in the mix, add a scant quarter cup to the transplanting hole. Peppers are reputed to be especially sensitive to excess nitrogen, so most growers are careful not to put them in a bed containing large amounts of compost or aged manure. In my experience, however, compost doesn't interfere with them, while aged manure may inhibit fruit set.

Supplementary fertilizing begins when the first blossoms open. I give a foliar feeding of liquid seaweed and, depending on the look of the plant, water with a Sul-Po-Mag tea. If the nutrient level in the medium is low, I give plants some extremely dilute compost tea about once a month. Watch the leaves and fruit; if leaves begin to pale, plants are probably nutrient deficient. When leafy growth seems too luxuriant and few peppers form, nitrogen may be excessive. Leach the bed thoroughly and discontinue using compost teas.

Harvesting

Harvest the first peppers while they're still small to stimulate higher overall production. I always pick the first one or two peppers long before they've reached full size. After the plant is bearing heavily, it's fine to leave them on until full-sized. I prefer the taste of fully mature green peppers, which are actually red, and I've learned to let only the last flush of bell peppers redden on the plant.

Peppers picked at their immature green stage continue to ripen. Ripening speed is determined by storage temperature. To keep them green, store in a cool (35 to 40°F) place, but to hasten reddening, put them on a windowsill. They won't rot unless there's already a bruise, but nonetheless, I'm careful to leave space between them.

Incidentally, peppers are easy to freeze because they don't need blanching. To prepare them for the freezer, all you need to do is remove seeds. For stuffing peppers, cut a slice off the top, scoop out the seeds and pack bottoms and tops, stem included, in the same freezer bag. For soups, stews, sauces and casseroles, slice, dice or mince the peppers and label bags appropriately. Frozen peppers lose their crispness but not their flavor.

Eggplants

Eggplants are among the most beautiful of plants. If they were perennials, I'd use them as foundation plantings. Of all the members of the solanaceous family, they look most like their exotic cousin, the deadly nightshade. Northern growers rarely see eggplants in their full glory; it takes heat, light and four or five months before they're really filled out. But in the greenhouse they're a showstopper.

Eggplant Varieties

Greenhouse growers can choose between long-season, large-fruited varieties and smaller, faster ones. Here are a few of the more commonly grown eggplants.

Blackjack: This hybrid is very quick to bear. Six- to 8-inch-long eggplants appear in only 60 to 70 days after transplanting.

Burpee Hybrid: These tall, vigorous plants produce medium-sized, oval eggplants. This variety takes longer to mature than others.

Dusky: A short-season hybrid, this plant produces slender, oval eggplants. It is resistant to tobacco mosaic virus.

Early Black Egg: A very dependable variety for short-season growers. Eggplants are long and slender in shape.

Ichiban: This oriental variety produces a long, slender, elegant-looking eggplant that is more delicate in flavor than standard varieties. The plants are prolific.

Morden Midget: A sturdy, compact plant that produces a harvest in short order. This is my favorite for harsh climates. Eggplants are medium-size.

Eggplant Culture

Eggplants germinate best at soil temperatures between 75 and 85°F. Once they're up, the seedlings grow slowly. Even at good temperatures and high light levels, plants require about nine weeks to reach transplanting size. If space is limited, I transplant to 4-inch plastic pots where they'll grow until they're as much as ten weeks old.

Don't, under any circumstances, let seedling eggplants get cold. Keep daytime temperatures at 75°F and nights at 60°F. When young, eggplants like a 12-hour photoperiod.

When you transplant seedlings into their permanent beds, provide a tomato soil mix. As the eggplants grow, fertilize as recommended for tomatoes. Be sure to feed as the first fruits are forming.

Some varieties, Morden Midget in particular, produce a few double flowers. I pollinated the first two or three doubles I saw because I was curious to see what they'd produce. Now I pinch them off immediately; the resulting fruit is semicircular in shape and too heavy for the plant to support.

Harvesting

Eggplants are at their best while still young. If you wait too long before harvesting, both seeds and skin become bitter. Once you've picked them, eggplants don't store particularly well. Immediately after picking, set eggplants in a moderately cool, dark place like a pantry, but don't put them in the refrigerator. Cold temperatures cause cells to collapse slightly. Even under the best of conditions, don't expect fresh eggplants to stay in good shape for more than a few days.

Few northern growers know how to preserve an abundance of this crop because we are rarely faced with the need to do so. But eggplants do freeze well if prepared correctly. Bread them and fry or bake before freezing for winter casseroles. If you want them to come out of the freezer bag in separate slices, freeze them on a cookie sheet before bagging them.

Common Problems with Greenhouse Eggplants

Aphids and whiteflies love eggplant leaves. But because the leaves are hairy, *Encarsia formosa* are reluctant to parasitize resident whiteflies. Instead of using these wasps, turn to botanical or soapy sprays to control whiteflies. Lady beetles, syrphid flies and *Aphidoletes aphidimyza* control aphids as long as no insecticidal soaps or botanical poisons have been used in the greenhouse within the preceding week to ten days.

Eggplants are prone to many of the same diseases as tomatoes. They're particularly susceptible to blights and tobacco mosaic virus. Make certain that air circulates freely around each plant, never water them late in the day, avoid splashing soil onto their foliage and observe good sanitation practices. Routinely prune and compost old leaves.

ᴄ❦ CHAPTER 14 ❦ᴐ
COOL-WEATHER VEGETABLES

Cool-weather crops are generally easy to grow. The stalwarts of greenhouse food crops, most grow well in three greenhouse seasons: fall, winter and spring. Even though seasons are moderated in an artificial environment, differences are great enough so that you must adapt cultural techniques accordingly.

Every passing fall day shortens the photoperiod and lowers light intensity. Nights are cooler and interior humidity is usually on the rise, especially in the early morning and just after dark. Clear days may bring high temperatures, but still, there are more and more cool days.

The fall environment hastens the end of heavy bearing for the last of the fruiting crops such as tomatoes and cucumbers. Once light intensity and photoperiod are lowered, plants can't photosynthesize at their summer rate. Disproportionately high temperatures only bring problems because a fast respiration rate puts a stress on the plant's nutrient supply. Add high humidity in semilit conditions and it's easy to understand why late fruiting crops are so susceptible to pests and disease.

Although it seems contrary, work to keep temperatures fairly low during the early fall. Highs of 75°F are usually a good goal. Plants won't respire heavily, and evening condensation will stay within manageable limits. High interior air circulation, even when it's cool, is essential to plant health during fall days and sometimes in the evening. If late-afternoon humidity seems excessive, use the exhaust fan to drive it off.

Fall pest and disease watches must be thorough, particularly on old summer crops and tiny seedlings. Use a ten-power hand lens to search for aphids hiding in nooks and crannies, and check both the undersides and tops of leaves for fungi. Believe it or not, sometimes your nose detects a fungus before you can see it; don't ignore what your nose tells you. Pull affected plants at the first sign of trouble. A couple of extra tomatoes aren't worth a troublesome fall season.

But happily, fall is also one of the best growing times. The summer vegetables may be slightly tattered, but the fall crops look terrific because the environment suits them.

226

Seed early-fall crops in mid- to late summer, and transplant into beds as fruiting crops are pulled. Plants started at this time of year grow very quickly. Late-August plantings of lettuce are mature by early November, for example. This rapid fall growth requires moderately high fertilization and frequent watering.

Through most of the country, seedlings don't grow well in natural light if planted after mid-October. With artificial lights, they can be started at any time of the year, depending upon germination temperatures. But even a quick-growing seedling slows down once it's in the bed and under short days of low natural light. Don't expect a 60-day lettuce planted in early October to mature before late December. As you gain experience with the performance of different varieties in your specific environment, fall scheduling becomes easier. Most people experiment with fall planting dates for the first few years. Good records are invaluable planting tools.

Despite higher greenhouse temperatures during August and early September, southern schedules don't differ much from those of the North. If possible, schedule fall crops to mature just after frost has touched the garden vegetables. For example, if heavy frost comes to your area in late November, plant the first lettuces in mid-September, keeping them as cool as possible through Indian summer. You might need to shade them during the hot part of the day.

But sooner or later winter does come. For most people it's the most gratifying season. Few small pleasures compare with the comfort of looking out to a snow-covered world while puttering around a warm greenhouse.

Midwinter plants don't have enough light to produce much new growth. They simply stay alive. Unless the greenhouse is fitted with artificial lights, try to have large, nearly mature plants in all beds by early December. Harvest through the winter by pulling a few outer leaves at a time from lettuces, oriental greens and kale. Remember to leave at least five leaves on each plant. Venting is crucial; carbon dioxide levels have to be replenished daily. Water infrequently and eliminate most fertilizing. Pests aren't likely to be much trouble if they've been controlled through the fall. But fungus spores are still kicking around, so keep interior air circulation good.

Some people in northern regions close down from early December through mid-February, the darkest, coldest period of the year. This plan is certainly practical if your greenhouse isn't energy conserving; utility bills during this season can be formidable! If you do close down, clean all areas, as described in the box in chapter 9, Housekeeping Chores in the Greenhouse, before starting up again.

Spring comes early. By mid- to late February, both light levels and photoperiod are good enough to promote beginning growth. Days are warmer, too, and insects are often stimulated to crawl out and resume feeding. Evening condensation increases in proportion to the fluctuation between day and night temperatures. Again, venting and interior air circulation are important.

You can start an early-spring crop of cool-weather vegetables under lights as early as January. They'll be ready for transplanting just as the photoperiod increases. But in cloudy regions, an early crop may still be retarded; later sowings will give healthier crops.

Without artificial lights, mid-February is the first sensible planting date in most regions. Even if most of the greenhouse area is to be used for garden seedlings, fresh cool-weather crops are well worth a last planting. In northern Vermont, for example, a late-February planting of greens can be harvested in late April and early May, several weeks before the garden plants are even seeded. I like to keep a succession of cool greenhouse vegetables going until the garden begins to yield.

There are many choices among cool-weather vegetables for the greenhouse. An amazing variety of plants grow during cool months, so there's no fear of getting bored with either the work or what you harvest for the dinner table. And most cool-weather crops are surprisingly easy to grow.

Lettuce

Lettuce is the most popular greenhouse crop by far. It's relatively easy when everything is going fairly well. But be prepared for a few challenges over the years. In adverse conditions, lettuce can develop a bewildering number of problems.

Lettuce Varieties

One year I grew 32 different varieties. Some sort of obsession impelled me: I intended to find out which kinds of lettuce performed better under various environmental conditions. By the end of the season, I had *some* useful data. But my overriding conclusion was that insanity was the probable outcome of trying to keep track of 32 varieties under three or four different environmental conditions. Since then I've been more sensible. Each year I grow only one or two new lettuces.

Once you become a serious lettuce grower, my peculiar behavior will become more understandable. Lettuce varieties just don't stop. Some are bred for low-light, cool conditions, some tolerate heat and some claim to be good in any season. Some are looseleaf; some form solid heads; others form loose heads; and some are romaine type, with cylindrical, dense heads. The color can vary, too, from pale green to bronze.

Read catalog descriptions carefully. The best fall and winter varieties are described as suitable for low-light and/or cool conditions. In general, looseleaf kinds perform the best, followed by loosehead varieties. Of the lettuces available from North American seed companies, Arctic King (looseleaf), Capitan (loosehead), Hilde (loosehead), Winter Density (intermediate between loosehead and romaine), North Pole (a cross between looseleaf and loosehead) and Parris Cos (romaine) have given me the best fall and winter performance. But don't ignore European low-light lettuces; more research has gone into their development, and as a consequence, they generally outperform North American varieties in flavor, texture and disease resistance. Val d'Orge (loosehead) and Quatre Saisons (loosehead) are two of these lettuce imports. (Sources of European seeds are listed in Appendix A: Sources of Seeds and Supplies.)

Almost every lettuce does well in early-spring conditions. Light, humidity and temperature combine to give a very tender, sweet leaf. But once the weather turns, you should grow specific hot-weather varieties. I prefer Boston Bibb (loosehead), Grand Rapids (looseleaf), Salad Bowl (looseleaf), Slo-Bolt (looseleaf) and Green Ice (looseleaf) during hot weather. Each is resistant to bolting, but more important, these varieties stay sweeter under hot conditions. If day temperatures average 80°F or higher, try Kagran or Ostinata (both loosehead).

Lettuce Culture

As I said earlier, lettuce can be either a relatively foolproof crop or one that gives you a series of problems. You can lay the groundwork for a successful harvest by understanding the optimum conditions for healthy lettuce growth and the best cultural techniques to use.

Starting Seeds

Sow lettuce four weeks before it is to be transplanted. Use a starting mix containing nutrients, place the seeds at least an inch apart on a vermiculite surface, and mist. Cover flats with clear plastic during germination. Lettuce seed must remain quite moist, and many varieties need light to germinate.

Transplant seedlings into their permanent positions at the fourth and fifth leaf stage or when they're about $2\frac{1}{2}$ inches tall. They are least likely to be set back at this stage. Transplanted earlier or later, their wide and shallow root system suffers unnecessary stress.

The growing mix should contain a high proportion of good quality compost. Don't use unfinished compost or manure that isn't well aged, even though it works in the outside garden. It's true that lettuce needs lots of nitrogen, but if too much becomes available at once, potassium supplies may become tied up, leading to a deficiency. This makes the plant more susceptible to fungus diseases.

Most varieties make the best growth when greenhouse temperatures average 55 to 70°F during the day and 50 to 55°F at night. Heat-

dard cauliflower I've used in a greenhouse. Mini-Snow is a dwarf variety recommended for fall culture, but despite the recommendation, I've had success with it in early spring under cool conditions.

Start broccoli and cauliflower six weeks before transplanting into permanent beds. Transplanting more than once is a waste of labor unless they're growing too leggy. Start them in deep flats or 4-inch pots. They germinate best at soil temperatures of 70 to 75°F, so it may be necessary to use a heating cable or propagating chamber. After germination, maintain air temperatures that average 60°F during the day and 50°F at night. If cauliflower is exposed to temperatures much lower than 50°F, it bolts prematurely. Broccoli does well at 45°F nights. In a cool environment, choose to grow broccoli over cauliflower.

Despite the moderate temperatures, these seedlings require lots of light. You'll know immediately if they're light deficient—their stems will elongate. When the natural photoperiod is still short, put them under artificial lights with a 12-hour day. Final transplanting should coincide with a minimum 11-hour natural day.

Both of these plants are heavy feeders, with cauliflower clearly the most demanding. The soil mix should contain generous amounts of compost or aged manure. If it isn't rich enough, give spring crops a feeding every two weeks once they're four or five weeks old. Compost or manure tea are both good cabbage family fertilizers.

Cabbage family crops tolerate a relatively narrow pH range. They grow best in soils with a pH of about 6.5. When soils have been over-limed, boron shortages are likely and, in acid conditions, manganese or iron deficiencies are common.

When the young cauliflower head reaches the size of a plum, gather the green leaves around it and hold them in place with a rubber band. This should guarantee a snowy white head. Harvest the entire cauliflower plant when the head is enlarged but still tight. Broccoli heads should be tight and show no signs of yellow. After you cut the central broccoli head, leave the plant in the bed for about a month. During this time most varieties produce a succession of smaller sideshoots more tender than the main head.

Problems with Broccoli and Cauliflower

Fortunately, the common scourges of garden plants—flea beetles, cabbage-root fly maggots and cabbage moth caterpillars—are rare in a greenhouse. Damage from other pests is minimal, too. Whiteflies, mites and even aphids choose other crops in preference to their tough, waxy leaves.

Diseases are equally uncommon in greenhouse-grown broccoli and cauliflower. But occasionally they suffer from a soilborne fungus disease called clubroot. Infected plants look sickly and don't grow or head well. Diagnose the disease by checking for swellings on roots. To avoid importing it into a greenhouse, don't buy seedlings from other growers or transplant cabbage family crops from the garden into the greenhouse. If plants in the greenhouse exhibit symptoms, avoid planting cabbage family crops in the same bed for at least a year.

Neither cauliflower nor broccoli gives growers many perplexing problems. Symptoms can be nicely tied to causes here. Bright light makes cauliflower heads yellow. As long as you tie leaves over the developing head, it should be nice and white. Stunted heads are usually caused by high temperatures. Leaves nestling among the curds are the result of too much heat or wide temperature fluctuations between day and night. Ricey heads, or those with a dusting of tiny white spikes, form when temperatures are too cool. Late, excessive supplies of nitrogen are also supposed to cause riceyness, but growers using compost teas aren't likely to encounter this problem. Heads go to flower prematurely if exposed to high temperatures while they're still forming. Be careful about this. Even if you cut the heads before they bolt, they're likely to be tough.

The most common nutrient deficiency in the Northeast is boron. The first symptom is a hollow area in the center of the stem. Serious deficiencies result in distorted growing tips and, specifically in cauliflower, discolored, bitter-tasting heads. Foliar feeding with liquid seaweed should prevent boron deficiencies, but if they do happen, ordinary borax corrects them. Use a solution of $\frac{1}{2}$ ounce borax in 5 gallons of water for every 5 square yards (45 square feet) of bed area that is a minimum of 2 feet deep. Be careful. Too much boron is extremely toxic. It's not an easy thing to leach out of a mix, either.

Collards, Kale and Mustard Greens

These leafy greens are good performers in most fall and winter environments. They tolerate temperatures close to freezing and continue to grow in moderate light at minimum temperatures of 40°F. This makes them invaluable for very cool environments.

Variety selection is not as challenging with these vegetables because so very few are available. I like Vates collards, Harvester kale and Tendergreen mustard, but really, there isn't a lot of difference between varieties.

These are tough plants. In the garden, they're rarely transplanted because of their rapid growth. But if space is limited in the late-summer or early-fall greenhouse, go ahead and start them in flats or small containers since they transplant easily. Despite their resilience, they need to be sown before the end of October to make good growth before midwinter.

Their soil should contain ample amounts of humus and nutrients. See the recommendations given earlier for broccoli and cauliflower concerning good soil amendments. Because they're only moderate feeders, you don't have to fertilize these leafy crops as frequently. Decrease watering and fertilizing in midwinter to take into account slowed plant growth.

Like people, aphids prefer these plants when they're young and tender. If biological controls are unavailable, use insecticidal soap sprays, being careful to mist into the new growth where aphids feed.

Harvest these greens through the winter by pulling a few outside leaves at a time. Grow enough of each crop so that you don't have to denude them to get a good supply for supper. Remember that the leaves are photosynthesizing nutrients for new growth: if you take too many at once, particularly in slow-growth periods, the plant may sicken and die.

Most people chop and steam these greens or use them in stir-fries. However, with a large crop, you're forced to discover their versatility. Sliced thinly, they're particularly good in soups and stews. Large leaves of kale stuff well; use your favorite recipe for stuffed cabbage or treat them like grape leaves. Mustard greens, cut into ribbons, add spice to a salad. And for collards and kale, you can't beat a traditional southern method of cooking: sauté onions in oil or butter, add ribbon-sliced greens and stir until they're coated. Add a quarter cup of water, pop on a lid and let simmer for a few minutes. Serve with seasonings and the pan juices.

Kohlrabi, Turnips and Radishes

These three crops make fine candidates for the spring or early-fall greenhouse. But unlike the leafy members of their family, these root crops don't grow well under poor light. They need a natural photoperiod of 12 to 13 hours minimum to grow a good root or, in the case of kohlrabi, an enlarged stem. Because I like turnip greens as well as the roots, I'll cheerfully plant them late in the season, but take it from experience—half-formed radishes and kohlrabi are disappointing.

Kohlrabi is rarely seen in the supermarket, so many people are unacquainted with it. The edible portion is a swelling of the stem, several inches above soil level. I consider kohlrabi a beautiful vegetable; the skin is unusually fine textured, and the leaves grow symmetrically from half-moon-shaped dimples on the top.

Both purple and white (really pale green) varieties are available. Early Purple Vienna is the best-known purple kohlrabi. It's gorgeous, but the light green varieties, such as Early White Vienna, taste much better. Peel one and eat it like an apple; even children like it this way.

Turnips you grow in the greenhouse are *not* the wax-covered storage roots many of us associate with the word turnip. They're an entirely different vegetable: small, tender and spicier, but less turnipy. Just like kohlrabi, my children are happy to eat them raw. Tokyo Cross

Kohlrabi: You can find varieties on the market with purple or pale green coloring. Kohlrabi has a pleasant, mild flavor and a nice, crunchy texture.

Hybrid and Yorii Spring are the fastest and, in my opinion, the tastiest of what are classed as spring turnips. But don't let the name dissuade you from an early-fall planting; late-August plantings do very well.

There are a bewildering assortment of radishes. Champion, Scarlett Globe Forcing and Cavalier work well for me. I suspect, however, that you can't go too far wrong in variety selection. Use your garden favorite with confidence.

Like leafy members of their family, these crops like high levels of humus, moderate levels of nutrients and moist soil. The secret to fine flavor is very simple: These plants must grow quickly and steadily. Otherwise, they develop a slightly bitter aftertaste. Air temperatures can range between 55 and 75°F during the day, and settle to 45 to 55°F at night.

With all three of these crops, harvesting couldn't be simpler—just pull the entire plant. Pick them according to their size and proximity to other plants. Take out the smallest plants when you thin, but remove the biggest when you harvest. Like greens, these plants are harvested as needed. But if they're getting woody or the bed is being cleared, pull them and store in a dark place at about 34 to 40°F. Under cool, dark conditions, such as a pantry, root cellar, unheated basement or refrigerator, they'll keep for several weeks. Those people who plant all of the radishes or turnips on the same day regret their haste. Plant in succession to avoid a glut.

You can steam or boil peeled turnips and kohlrabi and serve them as a side vegetable, but I like them better grated raw into salads or sliced thinly for stir-fries or vegetable stews. And when I'm feeling particularly self-indulgent, I grate them and bring out their sweetness by gently frying in butter. Add some seasonings and crisp the edges just before serving.

Few pests bother these plants in a greenhouse, but flea beetles can take a fierce toll. Fortunately, they aren't common in greenhouses unless they've come in on infested soil. I don't envy a grower with this problem: flea beetles are hard to control under any circumstances! Adults overwinter in the soil where they can't be frozen. Root-eating larvae are equally hard to detect or freeze. In fact, only feeding adults are vulnerable. Rotenone is effective, but if you've got other beneficial insects in the greenhouse and don't want to jeopardize them, try a gardener's trick: Tie a rectangle of cardboard on a stick and coat it with Tanglefoot or Ced-O-Flora. Hold the cardboard at an angle under the leaves while jostling stems. Flea beetles will jump onto the cardboard and get stuck. Repeat the process several times a day until populations are minuscule. Be persistent. It's important to kill adults before winter to prevent a spring population boom. With a bad infestation, you may be forced to dispose of the top few inches of soil mix.

Oriental Greens

A few years ago a knowledgeable friend told me that the government of China had passed legislation prohibiting long-distance truck or rail transport of vegetables. Even in the frigid northern part of the country, produce must be grown close to the distribution point.

While legislation of that sort would cripple the American produce system, I understand why the Chinese accept it. Some of their acceptance can be attributed to attitude, but two other factors probably play a part: good winter techniques and hardy crops.

Chinese farmers are exceptionally skillful in the use of season-extension technologies. Unheated glass or plastic structures are quite common, even in winter. At night straw mats over the glazing retain daytime heat. And Chinese farmers grow a wealth of cold-tolerant greens, which we in North America are only beginning to know. I love these greens; they are so good that I feel pampered by using them for my staple winter crops.

The majority of what we refer to as oriental greens are in the cabbage family and exhibit the characteristics of that group. They have superb nutritive value and are relatively resistant to pests and diseases. Many have been developed to grow well in cool, low-light conditions. And best of all, they have marvelous and diverse flavors. You won't get bored with them.

To date, only a few domestic seed companies offer a wide selection of oriental greens. However, over the past few years, both the companies supplying oriental vegetables and the selections offered have increased dramatically. Additionally, independent research groups and seed houses have begun trials to determine which varieties are most suited to various climatic conditions. The varieties mentioned here represent only a small sample of those available from domestic sources. Keep watching; offerings are sure to increase. (For a listing of oriental variety suppliers, please see Appendix A: Sources of Seeds and Supplies.)

Chinese Cabbage

Chinese cabbage is the only oriental green commonly available at the supermarket. Most stores carry just one type, a cylindrical head with prickly leaves. But Chinese cabbage doesn't end there. Other varieties are rounder, referred to in catalogs as barrel-shaped or Napa-type, and have crinkled to savoyed leaves without the prickles. Still others are loose or semiheading. I agree with aphids—Napa and other prickle-free varieties are nicer raw.

Most varieties of Chinese cabbage prefer cool weather but refuse to form a tight head as days lengthen. This makes them rather touchy to grow in the spring. If the catalog doesn't mention season, assume the variety does better in the fall, when days are getting shorter. The following is a listing of varieties that I've found to work fairly well in the spring.

Hakucho: A hybrid that forms a barrel-shaped head. One of the earliest-maturing varieties.

Kashin: This plant develops a loose, cylindrical head. It's an early-maturing variety.

Santo: You'll harvest a nice loose head from this variety, which is well adapted to cool growing conditions. The heads are 20 inches high, with creamy-colored inner leaves and light green outer leaves with wide ribs.

Seoul Cabbage: Plants produce loose, cylindrical heads. According to catalogs, you can plant it in the fall as well as in the spring.

Spring A-1: A hybrid that produces a cylindrical head, with outer leaves that measure 8 to 10 inches tall.

Sow these plants as early as possible for a spring crop and place them in moderate light. A temperature range averaging 55 to 65°F during the day and 45 to 50°F at night produces good growth and flavor. Transplanting is tricky. Start them in small peat pots for the least disruption to their delicate taproots. Bed spacing depends on the variety; you can find this information in catalogs or on seed packets. To prevent bolting and to clear beds for summer crops, spring crops are normally harvested before they reach full size. If the variety is new to you, space plants 10 to 12 inches apart in all directions. Cylindrical varieties should go toward the north side of the greenhouse because they're taller than Napa types and more likely to shade neighboring crops. In early spring apply a weak manure tea or liquid seaweed solution twice a month.

Fall varieties are so numerous that it would be foolish to name them all. Some of the most popular varieties, along with their distinguishing characteristics, are given here.

Chihfu: This variety is extremely tolerant of cool conditions. Planted by mid-October, it continues to grow through the worst of the winter. It's a good choice for unheated cold frames because it survives frosts so well. Space plants 12 to 14 inches apart.

Market Pride: This plant produces a cylindrical head that matures in about 75 days. It's a good late variety if planted by mid-September. Space at 16-inch intervals.

Nozaki Early: In about 70 days after transplanting, you'll be able to harvest a tight barrel-shaped head. Space plants 10 to 12 inches apart.

South China Earliest: This is a small plant that matures in only 45 days. Plant it any time from midsummer to early October. It makes an unusually succulent tight head. Space at 8- to 10-inch intervals.

Wong Bok: This is the variety that first appeared in this country. It forms a prickly leaved cylindrical head that becomes enormous. More than one plant of mine has weighed in at 10 pounds or more. It matures in about 85 days when planted in mid-July, but won't grow as large if started in mid-September. Space 16 to 18 inches apart.

Other than the directions for spacing and timing, follow the growing directions given above for spring varieties.

Other Oriental Greens

When you're stocking your cool-season greenhouse, don't stop at Chinese cabbage. Explore some of the other exotic greens to perk up your winter meals. In general, these greens can be treated as Chinese cabbage. Differing cultural directions are spelled out.

Garland Chrysanthemum

This plant goes by a number of different names: garland chrysanthemum, edible chrysanthemum, shungiku. It's a beautiful plant that grows to 3 feet tall in as many months. You can use the leaves and flowers in soups, stews, stir-fries or steamed dishes. Because it's so large and the flavor is so strong, plant only one or two the first year. Give fall plants a 12-inch hanging basket and sow in early October; within 60 days, outer leaves will be ready for harvest. Spring plants bolt quickly. Space them only 4 to 6 inches apart and harvest when they're about 6 or 7 inches tall.

Komotsuna

Komotsuna is a Japanese green that is best cooked in stir-fries or lightly steamed. It's a bit bland on its own, but works well with any flavoring. Crops mature in about two and a half months in fall conditions. You can harvest spring plants two months from the date you sowed the seeds. Komotsuna has an open growth habit.

Mizuna

This is a large plant that, left to itself, grows into a very pretty, bushy shape. Its serrated leaves drape gracefully from hanging pots. Mizuna is truly a fall plant, which takes 65 days to mature. If you want to try it in the spring, seed as early as possible. Harvest spring plants at 50 to 60 days. You can eat mizuna leaves raw or cooked. They taste a bit spicy, leaning a little toward the bitter side.

Osaka

Osaka is an oriental mustard, and my favorite green. There are both green and purple varieties. The plant has rounded leaves that stand out from the stems. Use it raw in salads or lightly steamed as a side dish. Be forewarned—it's pretty spicy. Osaka germinates slowly; don't assume that something's wrong for at least two weeks after planting. This is another beautiful plant. Display it in a 12-inch pot or in the back of a bed.

Pac Choi

Pac choi is, in my opinion, the most versatile of all the oriental greens. Alone, its flavor is almost spicy, but it readily takes on other seasonings. Most of the crunchy white midribs you find in dishes in Chinese restaurants are pac choi–type greens. Pac choi plants stand upright with dark green, glossy, spoon-shaped leaves. Taisai, Burpee's pac choi offering, and Johnny's Selected Seeds' Chinese Pac Choi stand well through the spring. But they grow well in the fall, too, maturing in only 50 days under a shortening photoperiod. Other varieties that I've tried have bolted under spring conditions. Experiment with each new type to determine its best season.

Use pac choi in stir-fries, steam it or slice thinly and eat it raw. The thick midrib is an excellent conveyer for dips; trim off the leafy part to use in another dish.

Shirona

Shirona is a mild-flavored green that can be used in salads or cooking. It matures quickly and, in my experience, is a better fall than spring crop.

Miscellaneous Greens

Besides lettuce and the leafy oriental greens, a host of other plants can keep your winter salad bowl filled. Corn salad, chard, sorrel, rocket, burnet, watercress and spinach all grow well in an early-spring or fall greenhouse and add variety to winter meals.

Corn Salad

Corn salad—or mâche, as it's sometimes known—is a substitute for lettuce in the early spring. It has a very delicate flavor. Corn salad grows quickly, maturing in only 45 days. Sow this small plant at 3-inch spacings in a bed and thin as it matures. Corn salad also transplants well.

Chard

Chard grows into an enormous plant unless you harvest frequently. A spring sowing stands well into summer without bolting. A fall sowing produces leaves, though slowly, throughout the winter. Transplant seedlings into the bed when they are six weeks old. Space plants just 8 to 12 inches apart and thin by harvesting alternate plants. A fully mature plant needs 16 to 18 inches of bed space.

Chard toughens with age, so be sure to pick outer leaves before they get too old. Pick only a few at a time to sustain a continuous harvest. Often touted as a spinach substitute, chard can be used in any recipe calling for spinach. Just don't expect a spinach flavor. Chard has a rich taste all its own. In my opinion, the green varieties taste better than those with red ribs and veins.

Sorrel

Relatively unknown in this country, sorrel is one of my favorites. Some domestic catalogs list it as an herb, but I consider it a staple vegetable and use it in salads, combination dishes and as the main ingredient in sorrel soup. If you like watercress, you'll like sorrel, too. It has a pleasing, peppery taste.

Outside, sorrel is a perennial. It also lives for many years in the greenhouse if you manage it well. Started in large pots, spring plants yield in only a few months. Pick outer leaves as the plant grows. Unless the temperature averages 80°F or above, sorrel yields all summer. Pick off flower stalks as they form. When growth begins to slow down, let the plant rest. Gradually decrease watering and put it in progressively cooler areas. In February when the greenhouse begins to warm up, sorrel resumes growth.

In a small greenhouse, you may want to treat sorrel as an annual. Sow as usual in spring and let the plant grow through most of the summer, taking leaves as you need them. At summer's end, transplant to an outside garden space or compost. Start a new greenhouse crop in mid- to late summer. These new plants will produce through the winter.

Rocket

Rocket may very well be an acquired taste. When young, add the piquant leaves to salads. But older leaves are much too strong for anything other than pot greens. Rocket serves as both a spring and fall crop and holds through the winter. Try only a few plants at first, since not everyone likes it.

Burnet

Burnet is supposed to taste something like cucumbers, but my imagination doesn't stretch that far. To me, it tastes like burnet and only burnet. A pretty little perennial plant with fernlike foliage, it's often mistaken for an ornamental. Crimson flowers that appear in midsummer strengthen that impression. Depending on greenhouse space and plant vigor, you may decide to treat it as an annual. Plant in 6-inch pots placed in a cool, bright location. Pick leaves when they're young and tender to use in salads and vinegars.

Watercress

Watercress is surprisingly easy to grow in a cool greenhouse. Plant seeds in hanging pots or containers filled with a rich soil mix with very good drainage. Despite the need for constant moisture, watercress also needs ample oxygen. Flood the pots at least once a day. Fertilize them regularly with a compost tea or a liquid seaweed–fish emulsion blend and place in bright light.

Spinach

Because it thrives at cool temperatures, spinach is a spectacular fall and early-spring crop. Seeds germinate in soil as cool as 35°F although 45°F gives surer results. Plant from early September through mid-October. Resume planting again in early February. Direct-seed spinach but if you must transplant, use peat pots. Experiment with varieties to see which work best in your greenhouse. Melody is a good choice for spring crops, while Winter Giant stands well through fall and winter if you harvest only outer leaves.

Beets

Make room for beets in both spring and fall. When you sow them in the early spring, the plants have a chance to make good roots. But fall plantings produce only leaves because light intensity and photoperiod are too low for good root production. Beets interplant well with cabbage family crops because their soil requirements are similar. But watch nitrogen levels—an excess produces woody roots. In acid conditions, beets suffer from nutrient deficiencies. Misshapen roots indicate too little phosphorus, while dark corky areas on the roots signify a lack of boron. A light watering with a borax solution, as recommended earlier for cauliflower and broccoli, is sometimes beneficial.

Peas

Peas offer such a low edible yield per square foot they aren't cost-effective. But an early spring planting may cheer the heart if not the pocketbook. Choose an edible-podded variety to get the highest yields.

Even dwarf varieties must be planted on the north side because greenhouse peas climb much higher than those grown outside. If the soil hasn't grown peas before, use a bacterial inoculant to stimulate nitrogen fixation.

Even dwarf varieties yield more when given vertical support. Pea vines don't need tying; their tendrils cling to supports. I certainly wouldn't bother hanging strings for each and every plant. Instead, screw posts to both sides of a bed and staple chicken wire across the area. Plant the peas about 4 inches away from the wire on both sides. When plants reach 4 inches, hill up the soil on the outside of the row to force them toward the wire. Their tendrils do the rest.

Keep the vines picked. To conserve bed space, pull plants after the first flush of pods. The second picking won't be large enough to warrant bed space.

ᕀ CHAPTER 15 ᕙ
WINTER FLOWERS

A daisy can seem prosaic in July, but never in January. Plant a few flowers to brighten winter days. Even if you prefer vegetables to pansies, sprinkle some flower seed in the odd pot or hanging basket. If you wish, rationalize that they're habitats for beneficial insects. But more likely, you'll find that they're good medicine, an antidote to the February doldrums.

Many of the best winter ornamentals are good cut flowers. But even those that don't cut well, such as calceolaria, are decorative. Wait until the plant is in full, glorious bloom, and then move it, pot and all, into the house. With some experience, you'll be able to schedule flowers so that something is always in bloom, all through the year. And don't neglect plants that add fragrance; they smell even better during the winter.

A surprising number of ornamentals can bloom in a cool winter greenhouse. As a rule, winter blooms result from forcing spring flowers or delaying summer- and fall-blooming plants. Winter-flowering varieties of some plants, such as pansies and snapdragons, have also been developed.

Most annual ornamentals have fairly simple needs. To bloom well, they need full winter sun, minimum night temperatures of 50°F and daily temperatures that range between 55 and 75°F. Exceptions to these rules and specific guidelines for perennials are noted in the individual plant descriptions that follow in the chapter.

Flowering plants require high phosphorous supplies. Routinely add a cup of bone meal to every 4 or 5 cubic feet of soil mix. If the plants are to be kept in the same pot for longer than three months, add a few pieces of activated charcoal to every pot. The charcoal absorbs some of the excess salts, keeping the soil in good condition longer. You can also add activated charcoal to a soilless mix or water where plants are rooting.

Flowering plants don't grow or mature as rapidly during the fall and winter as they do during warm months with high light levels. But cool temperatures do have a nice side effect: they prolong the blooming period and help the flowers stay fresh longer.

With only a few exceptions, once an annual plant has stopped blooming, it's finished. Consign it to the compost heap. You can hold over perennials, of course, for many flowering seasons.

To save bed space for vegetables, grow both annual and perennial ornamentals in pots or large tubs. Pots give you greater flexibility as well. You can move them around, in and out of beds or high-light areas, and they're easy to dump after the plant is finished.

Control both pests and diseases on ornamentals as you would on vegetables. During the winter, aphids are usually the most prevalent pests. But a warm environment will also support whiteflies. This is the season when biological controls are least effective; in response to short photoperiods and cool conditions, many beneficial insects are in diapause. You'll probably have to resort to soapy sprays or botanical poisons during winter.

Fungi are the major disease problems during the cool months of the year. It's imperative to keep air circulation high. Don't overwater any plants, ornamental or edible. Those with tender foliage, such as geraniums, snapdragons and stocks, are especially susceptible. Pick off old leaves and faded blooms to deprive fungi of a winter haven.

The plants discussed in this chapter bloom well during the winter with very little fuss. But this listing is by no means complete. Other favorites of yours may do as well. The only way to find out is to try. To experiment, start flats of summer-flowering plants under natural light from midsummer to early fall. Pot them up, give them the best possible environment and see how they do through the winter. You can start spring-blooming plants late in the fall or in early winter with artificial lights. When in doubt, use a 12-hour day; most plants do well with this photoperiod.

I've listed plants in alphabetical order under their common names. I've also included their Latin names in parentheses because these are sometimes used in catalogs. Whenever it's appropriate, I've also mentioned particularly good varieties.

AGERATUM (*Ageratum* spp.)   Annual

When you sow seed in September, ageratum blooms during the winter, adding blue, white or rose to the border of a bed or to a row of pots on a shelf. The seeds require light and warm temperatures (about 75°F) to germinate. After germination, keep the seedlings somewhat dry and ensure good air circulation. Young plants are particularly prone to damping-off. But once they're a few inches tall, ageratum become sturdy. Full light guarantees the best bloom. I've never tried to cut them; I just move blooming pots around.

ALYSSUM (*Lobularia maritima*)   Annual

Alyssum is a very easy ornamental for winter culture. Plant seeds in early September. Like ageratum, germinating alyssum seeds need light and soil temperatures of about 75°F. Be on guard against damping-off during the early stages of seedling growth. Pot seedlings in groups for a pretty display. I use six in a 6-inch pot, eight in an 8-inch pot and so on. They'll form a dense mat and then drape attractively over the sides.

The massed white, rose and purple flowers give off a wonderful pervasive perfume. Bring blooming pots into the house for a real mid-winter treat.

BABY'S BREATH (*Gypsophila elegans*)   Annual

Sow baby's breath in September and, if you have artificial lights, every two weeks thereafter through the winter. Each sowing blooms about two months after planting. Plant baby's breath in groups to show these plants to their best advantage. Roughly ten seeds per 10-inch pot grow into a 2- to 3-foot "bush" covered with tiny, delicate flowers. In addition to the traditional white baby's breath, varieties are also available in shades of rose and red.

Baby's breath doesn't bloom well in rich soil. Use a light, sandy soil mix that contains a small fraction of compost. As buds form, foliar-feed with liquid seaweed but don't give them a general fertilizer unless the leaves look pale. These plants require full light during the winter.

Compost annual varieties after the show closes. Perennial varieties (*G. paniculata*) are best left in the outdoor garden.

Florists use sprays of baby's breath to lighten arrangements of carnations, roses and other strong flowers. One of my favorite mid-winter arrangements is a mix of baby's breath, forget-me-nots and sprays of asparagus fern—it's as light as spring itself.

BACHELOR'S BUTTONS (*Centaurea cyanus*)   Annual

For a winter's bouquet of bachelor's buttons, sow seeds in August. Cover the flat with a piece of thick black plastic or a magazine to provide darkness until germination occurs.

Most varieties are tall, with far-reaching roots. I've had the best luck potting several seedlings in a tub 12 to 14 inches deep. Dwarf varieties do well in a regular 12-inch pot. The soil mix must drain well; add extra perlite and/or vermiculite, and keep nitrogen levels a bit low for the most prolific blooming.

Bachelor's buttons hold well at the worst of times, but in cool conditions they are spectacular. Their flowers stay crisp and vibrant, day after day and their color is more intense than in the summer. I prefer the blue, single-flower varieties. Single or double, blue, pink or mauve, winter bachelor's buttons add a touch of elegance to your green-house or living space.

BROWALLIAS (*Browallia speciosa*)   Perennial

Browallias aren't well known, and that's a pity because they're so lovely. They have a nice, compact habit; lustrous leaves; and bright little blue or white flowers. Best of all, they're ideal for the winter greenhouse. But don't let them live there year-round. Move them to a cool, somewhat shaded spot in the house during the summer.

For blooms the first winter, start seeds in July. Browallias require light and warmth during germination. Place three or four seedlings in a 6-inch pot and place in moderate light. With the exception of the variety Troll, browallias must be pinched frequently to encourage branching. If night temperatures don't go below 60°F, July-sown plants will bloom by late December. At lower temperatures, blooms are delayed for at least a month. Once established, browallias flower during the darkest winter months.

To whet your interest even further, you can take cuttings in the early spring to root and then transplant to a shaded, outdoor spot. These plants will bloom all summer, but don't bring them back into the greenhouse—you'd be importing pests.

BRUNFELSIA (*Brunfelsia pauciflora* and *B. calycina*)   Perennial

Brunfelsia is a houseplant that has, unfortunately, gone out of fashion. Look for it in European seed catalogs or in fancy domestic plant shops. It grows several feet tall over a few years and has lovely lilac-blue flowers that give off a light fragrance.

If you can find seeds, start them in midsummer. The soil mix should be somewhat acid with excellent drainage. Place brunfelsia in moderate light, and water sparingly during the winter. This plant doesn't need frequent fertilizing while it's cool. Feed each summer and then take cuttings from new growth. If the greenhouse is too warm during summer months, move brunfelsia plants to the house until temperatures stay below 80°F.

BULBS   Perennial

Hardy, spring-blooming bulbs are easy to force for an early show of color. The most common and least demanding are crocus (*Crocus*), daffodils (*Narcissus*), tulips (*Tulipa*), hyacinths (*Hyacinthus*), glory-of-the-snow (*Chionodoxa*), snowdrops (*Galanthus*), snowflakes (*Leucojum aestivum*), grape hyacinths (*Muscari*) and Siberian squills (*Scilla siberica*).

Pot bulbs in the fall or early winter. Use a rich mix containing about half a cup of bone meal to every cubic foot of soil. Add a high proportion of drainage material, and put gravel or pot shards over the drainage holes.

Plant small bulbs (crocus, glory-of-the-snow, snowdrops, snowflakes, grape hyacinths and squills) so their noses are just barely covered with soil. Pot in groups; use six to eight in every 6-inch pot.

The noses of tulip bulbs are also placed just below the soil. Plant three or four in a 6-inch pot, placing the flat side of the bulb toward the rim of the pot. As the bulbs grow, the foliage will drop toward the flat side, an arrangement that allows better air circulation and is more pleasing to the eye, as the leaves frame the flowers.

Daffodils need their noses right at soil level. Again, plant three or four in a 6-inch pot. You must pot hyacinth bulbs with about half an inch of bulb showing above the soil surface. Be sure to firm the soil thoroughly around the bulbs. Use three in a 6-inch pot, and give each one a small stake.

After potting, place in a dark, cool spot such as a cellar or cold frame. Keep the soil moist and don't let them freeze. Ideal temperatures are 35 to 40°F at night and 40 to 45°F during the day. Check the drainage holes on the pots often for signs of root growth. Once roots appear, bring pots into the greenhouse. (This will take only six to eight weeks from planting for small bulbs and three months for large bulbs.) Start by placing them on the floor where they will receive some light and slightly higher temperatures than they were getting in cold storage. Once shoots show, move them onto well-lit benches or shelves.

For best blooming, plants shouldn't be exposed to temperatures much above 60 or 65°F. They tolerate nighttime lows between 40 and 50°F.

When the petals finally drop, snap off the developing seed heads to save the plant's energy. Bulbs need good moisture levels while in bloom, but once flowering has stopped, gradually decrease watering. The foliage stays green for some weeks while making nutrients for storage. But eventually, the leaves brown and die back. At this point let the soil dry and then lift the bulbs.

Store dormant bulbs in a paper bag or open container. They must stay dry so that fungi can't get a foothold. Put them in a dark, dry spot until fall and then plant the bulbs outside. If you're likely to forget them, plant them in the spring once the soil has warmed. But don't try to force the same bulb twice. Forcing is hard on bulbs because it causes them to draw heavily upon their stored food supplies. Even when they're planted outside afterward, they often refuse to bloom the following year. Instead, their foliage collects nutrients to strengthen the bulb for the next season.

CALENDULAS (*Calendula officinalis*)   Annual

Calendulas are one of the easiest and most satisfying of winter flowers to grow. They're trouble-free and produce many cheerful orange, yellow or cream-colored flowers through the winter. The flowers make good, long-lasting arrangements.

Plant seeds in August, and cover flats to keep them dark until germination. Pinch growing tips after the seedlings are a few inches high, and again when new shoots have two or three leaves. This encourages a bushier plant and more flowers. Night temperatures of 45°F are quite to their liking. Keep the soil mix moist, and give them full sun. Unless you're going to plant in deep tubs, choose the dwarf varieties and set them in 8- to 10-inch pots. To prolong the bloom period, pinch off developing seed heads as petals drop.

CALIFORNIA POPPY (*Eschscholtzia californica*)   Annual

Cheerful and summery, California poppies can look incongruous on a dark winter's day. But they might make you feel like singing. They come in lovely shades of white, pink, crimson, salmon, orange and yellow.

To start poppies, surface-sow the seeds in the pots where they are to grow. These flowers do not transplant well at all. Cover germinating seeds with cardboard or black plastic. A late-June to July planting gives you a supply of fall flowers.

Poppies do well in a fall and winter greenhouse only with good light. They don't like rich soil, so include half the normal amount of compost in the mix. The soil mix should drain well, and plants should be kept slightly dry. Once they've finished blooming, compost them.

CAPE PRIMROSES (*Streptocarpus × hybridus*)   Perennial

Cape primroses are spectacular. In the same family as gloxinias, they have some of the same lushness, although their blooms are smaller and more restrained. Cape primrose flowers are tubular, flaring at the end to form five petals. Their colors range from light pink through mauve and purple.

Plant Cape primrose seeds in the early spring for blooms the following fall and winter. They need light to germinate. Transplant into a rich mix with excellent drainage and keep cool through the summer. Each fall, expect another round of flowers.

CARNATIONS (*Dianthus caryophyllus*)   Perennial

In a cool greenhouse you'll have no trouble growing a profusion of carnations. Start seeds in late July or August for flowers through the early part of the winter. Early-spring sowings give blooms in late summer and early fall. But a spring schedule has inherent drawbacks unless your greenhouse averages 75°F or lower during the summer. To get fall flowers, you must keep plants cool during their seedling life and pinch off all buds until mid-August. To avoid overheating, many people set carnations outside during the summer. But even if I spray the foliage with a soap solution before bringing the pots back in, aphids always come along.

Unstaked carnations make winding, twisting stems. If you don't want flowers for cutting, this habit is quite beautiful. But carnations for formal arrangements should have straight stems. Stake the plants in pots while they're still young. Commercial growers produce large blooms by pinching all but one bud on each stem. I let my carnations flower freely.

Fertilize carnations with compost tea or fish emulsion every two weeks during their period of rapid growth. Place pots in full sun when buds are forming, and ensure very good air circulation around each plant. For healthy plants make sure that night temperatures don't go below 45°F.

CHRISTMAS CACTUSES (*Schlumbergera bridgesii*)   Perennial

Seeds are available for the Christmas cactus, but it's much easier to get a cutting from a friend. Kept in moderate light, cuttings root easily in damp sand, vermiculite or perlite. Pot rooted cuttings singly in 2-inch pots or place several in a 4-inch pot. Increase pot size as the plants grow. Within a few years, plants easily fill a 12-inch hanging basket. The flowers appear at the tips of the stems and have several tiers of petals. Colors include white, crimson, mauve, pink and purple.

Christmas cactuses need long nights to initiate flowers. In homes, people sometimes have difficulty getting flowers; even an incandescent bulb in a nearby room can inhibit the plants. An unlit greenhouse is ideal, but if light from the house filters through a window, move the plant to a dark corner, or shade the window or the plant.

CHRYSANTHEMUMS (*Chrysanthemum* spp.)   Annual

Annual varieties are better suited than perennials to greenhouse conditions because they're smaller. But perennial varieties can work well if you plan to keep them inside for only one season. Spring-sown seeds or cuttings are still small when they come into fall bloom. After they've flowered, put the mums in a cool, moderately bright spot through the winter, and transplant them to permanent positions outside in the spring.

Plant seeds of annual mums in the spring and early summer for blooms the following fall and winter. These are tough plants; they'll survive heat and continue to bloom well into the winter as long as you pick spent blooms and seed heads.

Chrysanthemums require good light and frequent fertilizing during their period of rapid growth. When buds begin to show color, stop fertilizing but continue to keep plants moist. For a nice, bushy shape, increase branching by repeatedly pinching terminal shoots on both annuals and perennials during early growth. Stop pinching in July; otherwise, you might inhibit flowering. Night temperatures of 50°F are ideal for chrysanthemums, although they bloom well at 40°F if buds are already well developed.

ENGLISH DAISIES (*Bellis perennis*)   Perennial

These daisies thrive in very cool environments. Night temperatures can average 40°F without injuring them in the least. They'll still manage to put forth a display of single or double flowers in shades of white, pink or crimson.

Plant seeds in July for bloom during the winter. It's best to put several plants in a 10- to 12-inch pot. Give them good air circulation, only moderate fertilization and bright light. After the bloom period, hold them in a moderately bright spot until spring. Then divide the crowns and set the plants into permanent spots in the garden. Some people repot for another year in the greenhouse, but second-year plants tend to get very large.

FLOWERING MAPLES (*Abutilon* spp.)   Perennial

Start flowering maples—or abutilons, as they're sometimes called—from seeds or cuttings. Seeds can be hard to germinate. And despite the catalog description, they don't always come true. That is, plants may revert to characteristics of a great-grandparent rather than the desired characteristics listed in the catalog. Usually the surprise is a different flower color. If you want a specific variety, work with cuttings.

Abutilon seeds need minimum soil temperatures of 80°F. Use a heating cable under flats or wait until July to plant them. Summer-started plants flower the following spring. February sowings begin blooming in late summer and keep going through the fall and early winter.

Take cuttings from new growth in the fall and root them in a soilless mix. While they're rooting, water with a 10 percent vinegar solution every week to ten days. Maintain high humidity. Once roots form, set the cuttings in 4-inch pots and move them to larger quarters as they grow.

Flowering maple likes full sun. Day temperatures can go as high as 75 to 80°F, but night temperatures shouldn't dip below 50°F. Provide exceptionally good soil drainage and air circulation. Add only well-aged compost to the mix, and don't use manure. It's too high in nitrogen, which inhibits blooming. During rapid growth, water with weak compost tea once a month and a foliar-feed biweekly with liquid seaweed. If the foliage gets too lush, cut down on the compost tea. Within a couple of years, you'll have a shrub about 3 feet high and 2½ feet wide. The crepe papery, translucent blooms are similar to Iceland poppies, but abutilon blooms are pendulous. They don't last well as cut flowers. Abutilons survive summer greenhouse temperatures well, but if space is restricted, you can move the pot into the living room.

FORGET-ME-NOTS (*Myosotis* spp.)   Annual

A pot full of forget-me-nots in bloom looks like a delicate blue cloud. You can also find white- and pink-flowering plants. Annual, early-flowering varieties of forget-me-nots bloom during the winter if you start them in early to mid-August. Keep the seedlings cool and partially shaded during hot weather. Even in full bloom, forget-me-nots like lots of light. Pot in a moisture-retentive mix, and maintain good air circulation.

GAZANIAS (*Gazania* spp.)   Perennial treated as an annual

Gazanias don't enjoy the popularity that they deserve. In or out of bloom, the plants are striking. Gray-green succulent foliage arises in a rosette from a central crown. During the seedling stage, leaves are almost blade shaped. After about six weeks of rapid growth, new leaves are deeply toothed. The daisylike flowers have bands of yellow, orange, red and mahogany.

Although it's classed as a perennial, gazania acts more like an annual in all but the mildest of climates. Even in the greenhouse, gazania won't bloom all through the winter. High light and warm temperatures stimulate budding. But long after garden plants have succumbed to frost, spring-planted gazanias carry on. Place pots in maximum light and fertilize infrequently. Keep their slightly sandy mix somewhat dry.

GERANIUMS (*Pelargonium* spp.)   Perennial

Geraniums will bloom in the late winter, although they are never as vigorous or free-flowering as they are during the summer. Sow seeds or take cuttings from established plants in the early summer. Pot rooted cuttings in a rich, well-drained soil mix.

If your geraniums aren't doing well, check soil moisture and pot size. Geranium roots don't like soggy conditions. Restricted roots stimulate flowering; that's why florists' plants always look too big for their pots. Keep geraniums in a well-lit, warm area, and move them into the main house if night temperatures go below 55°F.

Geraniums' soft tissue is extremely attractive to fungi. Pick off faded blooms, including petals that may have dropped onto lower leaves. Seed-started geraniums can be a nuisance since their blooms "shatter" easily. That is, several flowers of the cluster open and drop more quickly than the rest. I prefer the firmer blooms of varieties that must be propagated by cuttings, especially in humid conditions.

GERMAN VIOLETS (*Exacum affine*)   Perennial

The German violet, also called the Arabian violet, is a dainty little pot plant. Small blue flowers with yellow centers cover the plant for months at a time. Sow the seeds in August, and cover them only slightly with vermiculite. Plant one seedling to a 4-inch pot, and move up as necessary to a larger size. Keep the soil moist and fertilize moderately. German violets do well in full light at night minimums of 50°F. They will grace the greenhouse for many years. Take cuttings from fresh growth in the spring. Move the plants into the house if summer temperatures go above 85°F.

IMPATIENS (*Impatiens wallerana*)   Annual

In a moderately cool and bright spot, impatiens flower through most of the winter. They come in a delightful range of colors: red, crimson, salmon, pink, orange and white.

For winter bloom, sow seed or take cuttings from established plants in July or August. Impatiens seeds require good light for germination, so press them into the surface without covering. Pot young plants in a moisture-retentive mix that contains moderate levels of compost. Aphids are especially attracted to impatiens: prevent an infestation by keeping nitrogen levels a bit low and watching plants carefully through the fall and winter. For the best growth and flowering, impatiens shouldn't be exposed to night temperatures below 55°F. During the worst of the winter you may want to move them into the house.

When spring comes, move the impatiens outside to a spot with filtered or moderate light. Despite their listing as annuals, they can live for several years with good care. But they do lose their neat, mounded habit with age. If aphids aren't a problem, take cuttings from established plants each summer for another round of winter greenhouse plants.

KALANCHOES (*Kalanchoe blossfeldiana*)   Perennial

Kalanchoes are succulents with brilliant orange and red flowers. Seeds you plant in spring should produce blooming plants by winter.

To germinate, seeds need full light, so don't bury them with starting mix. The potting mix for transplants should contain a high proportion of sand and drain well. Don't let plants dry out during periods of vigorous growth. After the plants have finished flowering, decrease the frequency of watering. Never allow the soil to dry completely. Kalanchoe thrives if night temperatures don't go below 55°F.

LOBELIAS (*Lobelia erinus*)   Annual

These low-growing plants treat you to a dazzling display of many small purple, pink, white or blue flowers. To enjoy their blooms in late fall and winter, plant lobelia in mid-August. Young lobelia plants are so tiny that it's difficult to transplant them when they have their first true leaves. To compensate for this, fill a deep flat with seed-starting mix and cover it with a $\frac{1}{4}$-inch layer of vermiculite. Then sow the seeds on the surface at $\frac{1}{4}$- to $\frac{1}{2}$-inch intervals. Leave the flat in a bright spot, and mist frequently to keep the seeds and medium moist. Just as the tiny leaves begin to obscure the soil surface, cut or break the flat into 2-inch-square sections. Repot each plug into a 4- to 6-inch pot or place four plugs in a 10-inch hanging basket, spacing three toward the rim and one in the center. Despite their tiny initial size, lobelia plants quickly carpet the pot. Lobelia needs moderate light and a moist, moderately rich soil.

MARIGOLDS (*Tagetes erecta* and *T. patula*)   Annual

With coaching, marigolds can be induced to bloom in the fall and early-spring greenhouse. At these seasons the greenhouse environment isn't really to their liking; don't expect the profuse blooms of summer. But still, the plants reward you with a few perky golden flowers. Be sure to select dwarf varieties. Standard-sized marigolds are too rangy for the greenhouse. Sow the seeds in August and keep plants in a warm, bright location. Make sure the soil mix isn't too high in nitrogen;

otherwise, you'll see more foliage than flowers. Pinch off faded flowers immediately to keep marigolds blooming for as long as possible.

NASTURTIUMS (*Tropaeolum minus*)   Annual

Nasturtiums bloom well in a sunny, moderately cool greenhouse. Many people eat both flower buds and leaves in salads, and pickle immature seed pods to use as mock capers. But their greatest advantage, aside from beauty, is as a trap crop. If aphids are around, they'll head for the nasturtiums first. I grow space-conserving dwarf varieties in the greenhouse.

Nasturtiums don't transplant easily. Start them in the containers where they are to grow, but if you do want to transplant them, use large peat pots. Cover the pots with cardboard or black plastic until the seeds have germinated.

For the most impressive flowering, the soil medium should contain bone meal and about half the normal amount of compost. Don't fertilize with compost tea or fish emulsion unless the leaves begin to yellow. Too much nitrogen gets you nothing but leaves, and nary a nasturtium flower.

NEMESIAS (*Nemesia strumosa*)   Annual

Nemesia is an old-fashioned flower that blooms under cool temperatures. Most seed houses carry Carnival, an aptly named variety with masses of intense yellow, orange and red flowers on 8-inch stalks. During the summer I use it outside with Shirley poppies because the value of the colors is so similar. A friend swears by combining it with a dwarf phlox variety named Beauty Mix so that the two form a vivid carpet. Other varieties of nemesia have white, pink or light purple flowers.

July-sown seed gives winter blooms, while early-spring planting gives summer flowers for the outdoor garden. Germinate the seeds in total darkness at a soil temperature of 60 to 65°F. Nemesia is extremely susceptible to damping-off during both germination and its early life. If fungi have been a problem, plant the furry little seeds at 2-inch intervals in a flat or in individual 2-inch pots. Water every few days with chamomile tea or a 10 percent solution of vinegar. Provide good air circulation and don't overwater.

Place several plants in each 6- to 8-inch pot. As long as air circulation is high, established plants are able to tolerate cool greenhouse conditions and 50°F nights.

Nemesia dies after blooming. I plant often for a year-round supply of blooming plants to feed beneficial wasps.

NICOTIANA (*Nicotiana alata*)   Annual

Nicotiana, also known as flowering tobacco, is somewhat large for most home greenhouses. But if you've got well-lit space for a 2-gallon tub, this flowering plant is worthwhile. Tubular star-shaped blossoms come in shades of white, pink, red, purple, yellow and even green. Flowers of some varieties stay open all day, while others open only at twilight. Seed catalogs indicate which are the less common day-blooming varieties. My favorite is the white Evening Scented nicotiana.

For winter bloom, germinate the seeds in light in mid-July. Six-week-old seedlings transplant easily.

PANSIES (*Viola* × *wittrockiana*)
Perennial treated as an annual

As a child, pansies were my favorite flowers. But in Maryland, where I grew up, these cool-loving plants bloom for only a few weeks in the spring before warm temperatures cut them short. In the North, I discovered that pansies bloom from early June through August. And then, wonder of wonders, I found winter-blooming greenhouse varieties. I'd truly fallen into pansy heaven.

Pansies prefer day temperatures no higher than 70°F, but tolerate nights of 40°F with no damage. For vigorous winter plants, germinate seeds in the dark in July. Set flats under a bench to keep the soil cool.

As seedlings, pansies prefer a combination of bright light and cool temperatures. The moderately rich soil mix must allow excellent drainage. Let the top ½ inch of medium dry between thorough waterings.

Winter-flowering varieties need support. If you pick off faded blooms, pansies usually flower continuously from fall to spring. Should they stop blooming during midwinter, don't throw them out. Spring stimulates a new flush of blossoms.

If you can't find special winter varieties, don't despair. With a July sowing, all pansies bloom during early winter and late spring. Once summer comes, you can transplant outside varieties to the garden.

PETUNIAS (*Petunia* × *hybrida*)   Annual

I like the Cascade series of trailing petunias for winter color. But trailing or not, your variety choice is extensive. Single or double, frilly edged or plain, petunias come in almost every color imaginable.

Petunia seeds are quite tiny. Sprinkle them sparsely on the surface of a flat that's been covered with vermiculite and mist gently. The seeds need light and warmth to germinate. A July planting gives good fall and winter blooms.

Recently, pelletized petunia seed has become available for the home market. Coated with a claylike substance, pelletized seeds are about the size of a cabbage seed. If you've had trouble seeding and transplanting petunias in the past, pelletized seed is worth the extra cost. Crowded flats will no longer be a problem.

Petunias tend to damp off if they are mistreated during their early life. Mist them gently when they're small so you don't knock them over. If you're transplanting them when they're tiny, be careful not to bury their crowns. To encourage bushiness and prolific flowering, pinch them frequently after they begin lateral growth. Sixteen- to 18-hour days stimulate the earliest blooming, so you'll probably want to grow seedlings under lights.

To bloom, petunias require a moderately warm environment. You can guarantee full flower production with night temperatures no lower than 60°F. At a 50°F night, plants survive quite nicely but stop blooming. Growth and flowering resume when the greenhouse warms up. Remember to pick off faded blooms; petunia plants stop flowering if seeds are allowed to develop.

POCKETBOOK PLANTS (*Calceolaria crenatiflora* and *C. multiflora*)
Annual or perennial

Although few home growers try calceolarias, as these plants are also called, they aren't difficult to raise from seed. And they do put on quite a display; in March and April, they're covered with masses of pouchlike orange, yellow or red flowers. Attractive patterns of darker-colored spots speckle the flowers.

Most varieties should be planted in September in a sterile starting mix. Make sure air circulation is excellent. Fungi like these plants. Transplant single seedlings into 6-inch pots. The soil mix must drain well. Pocketbook plants like leaf mold, but peat moss does in a pinch. They're heavy feeders, so don't skimp on the compost.

Keep seedlings cool and in diffuse or moderate light. They prefer nighttime temperatures of 50°F and daytime temperatures of 55 to 65°F. Watch leaf color; if it begins to pale, feed with a weak compost tea or seaweed–fish emulsion. Fungi are a constant threat. Be careful not to overwater or let greenhouse air stagnate. Although some forms of calceolarias are technically perennials, you're better off treating them all as annuals and disposing of them after blooms fade.

PRIMROSES (*Primula* spp.)   Annual or perennial

Primroses are one of my favorite plants. In the late winter and early spring the mounded foliage is covered with multicolored blooms. Most seed companies sell special annual and perennial greenhouse varieties. Don't bother fooling around with species meant to grow outside; they don't perform as well indoors. If you've never grown primroses, try the forgiving *P. malacoides* plants first. Their star-shaped flowers come in white, pink, red or lilac.

Surface-sow primrose seeds in April and May for bloom the following winter. September sowings give flowers in the early spring. Mist the seeds into a covering of vermiculite, and place flats in filtered light at about 75°F. After germination, don't let temperatures exceed 65°F. Transplant young primroses into a fairly humus-rich soil mix. Leaf mold is an especially good addition. Transplant into progressively larger pots, ending up with a 6-inch pot at maturity. During the summer, give the primroses increasing amounts of light, but keep them as cool as possible. You may need to keep a fan on them. Feed every two weeks with a weak compost tea until the early fall. By this time they'll be budding. Begin foliar feeding with liquid seaweed every two weeks. Don't revert to a general fertilizer unless the foliage begins to yellow.

If you're growing perennial primroses, hold them over the summer in a cool and shaded spot. Dispose of annuals after they're done blooming.

SALPIGLOSSIS (*Salpiglossis sinuata*)   Annual

Salpiglossis flowers are incredibly beautiful. The velvet blossoms range in color from yellow through mauve, red, blue and bronze. Many varieties have golden veins, and all display gradations of color.

Salpiglossis is not a tidy little plant. It grows at least 2 feet tall with sparse foliage. In the summer garden I make up for the rangy appearance by massing plants. But in a container, crowded plants are unhealthy. Don't worry about how it looks in the greenhouse—it is meant to be used as a cut flower.

For winter bloom, plant seeds in August. Keep the flat absolutely dark during germination. You don't have to sow seeds in final pots; seedlings transplant easily. Use several plants in a deep pot that contains a moderately rich mix with excellent drainage. Outdoor plantings are usually placed to receive light shade during midday. However, fall and winter greenhouse plants require full sun. If the soil mix is low in nutrients, fertilize about once a month with a good general fertilizer. For the most abundant flowering, you must induce branching. Pinch back growing tips repeatedly. Every new branch produces flowers. Outside, salpiglossis doesn't require staking. But in a winter greenhouse with its lower light levels, tie the plants loosely to bamboo sticks.

SCHIZANTHUS (*Schizanthus* spp.)   Annual

Schizanthus is often called the butterfly flower, presumably because its small, clustered blooms reminded someone of hovering butterflies. My four-year-old daughter calls it a "fairy flower." Despite breeding advances, schizanthus is not as common today as it was a generation ago. Consequently, it always draws compliments and questions.

You can sow schizanthus in July for midwinter bloom or in mid-October for early-spring flowers. Sprinkle seeds directly on the surface of the medium or on a vermiculite covering, and place black plastic or cardboard over the flat until germination. Because young seedlings are very small, I start them in a deep flat where they can grow for several weeks. Afterward, each seedling can go into a 4- or 6-inch pot.

Pinch young schizanthus at every opportunity. Without pinching, plants get too top-heavy and produce very few blooms. In a cool environment, the flowers last for weeks. Once flowers fade, compost the plant; it won't bloom again.

SNAPDRAGONS (*Antirrhinum majus*)   Annual

The same snapdragons that grace your garden with their colorful spikes can be forced to bloom in early-spring or late-fall greenhouses. Snapdragons make lovely cut flowers, and are available in crimson, pink, white, orange and yellow. Start spring plants in midwinter under artificial lights with a 12-hour day. In late February to early March, move seedlings into full sun. They should begin blooming shortly. With this regimen, snapdragons flower well for a couple of months. For fall-blooming plants, start seeds in natural light in late July and August.

Conventional garden snapdragons are never as vigorous as a green-house winter-forcing variety. Look for the greenhouse variety Goliath in seed catalogs; it's fairly common. Start seed in late July or August with natural photoperiods.

All snapdragon seeds need light for germination. To encourage branching, pinch back terminal shoots during the plant's seedling life. Be particularly careful not to wet the foliage when you're watering; snapdragons are quite susceptible to fungus diseases. They need evenly moist soil, but give them less water during cloudy weather. For further protection, provide snapdragons with good air circulation. Although they can survive lower temperatures, all varieties perform best at night temperatures of 50°F and day temperatures between 55 and 75°F.

STOCKS (*Matthiola bicornis* and *M. incana*)   Annual

The evening-scented stocks that were a focal point of your grand-mother's garden open only in the evening and are *M. bicornis* varieties; *M. incana* varieties open during the day. No matter when they open, both deserve their nickname of perfume flower. Their long flower spikes come in shades of white, blue, purple, yellow, rose and dark red. Dwarf varieties grow only a foot high, but standard stocks reach 2 feet at maturity. The flowers hold exceptionally well when cut.

Plant stocks in August and give them light during germination. Plants require full light, rich soil and good air circulation. The extensive roots require deep pots. Like snapdragons, stocks are prone to fungus diseases; otherwise, they're easy to grow. Try several varieties; you won't be disappointed.

SWEET PEAS (*Lathyrus odoratus*)   Annual

Sweet peas are a delight to have in the greenhouse, with their delicately fragrant, flower-laden vines. The ruffled flowers are available in crimson, salmon, pink, blue and white. Winter-flowering sweet peas will bloom from midwinter into early spring if you plant them in late August or September. Start these in peat pots if you plan to transplant; sweet pea roots are very fragile. Seeds require absolute darkness for good germination. Soak the seed for 24 hours in a liquid seaweed solution, plant about $\frac{1}{2}$ inch below the soil surface and cover with black plastic or cardboard. If you've had trouble starting them in the garden, try both presoaking and covering; it really helps.

Sweet peas started in 2-inch peat pots must be transplanted into a bed or deep trough in about two weeks. You can hold seedlings in 4-inch pots about a month before transplanting. But don't let them sit around. As soon as roots begin to break through the pot, move seedlings into a deep container full of rich growing mix.

If bed space isn't available, plant groups of sweet peas in doubled heavy-duty black plastic garbage bags filled with a rich soil mix. Poke drainage holes in the bottoms of the bags, and shield them against light to keep the soil cool. I like the flexibility of this system; a row of sweet peas can take up temporary lodging beside a permanent bed or against the back water barrels.

If you've chosen a standard variety, the plants will need to be supported, since they grow 5 or 6 feet high. Dwarf varieties grow only 2 or 3 feet high and don't absolutely require support. However, even these shorter plants are healthier and have straighter stems when they're given support.

WAX-LEAVED BEGONIAS (*Begonia semperflorens*)
Annual treated as a perennial

No one can accuse a semperflorens of being stingy. An August sowing of wax-leaved begonias gives continuous bloom from midwinter to spring. Once the weather's settled, pinch them back and transplant into an annual garden bed or window box. Within a couple of weeks they'll start blooming again.

These seeds certainly qualify as tiny. In your palm they look like nothing more than dust. Sprinkle them on the surface of a vermiculite-covered flat, mist with liquid seaweed, cover with clear plastic and set them in a warm, bright spot. Once plants have their first true leaves, transplant groups of three or four into 4-inch pots. After several sets of leaves have formed, encourage branching by pinching back the growing tips. Begonias need occasional pinching throughout their lives or they'll become ungainly. You'll have to move them into progressively larger pots every so often, too. Plants usually end up dripping over the sides of a 12-inch hanging basket.

Begonias need good light. If it's shady, they become leggy and refuse to bloom. Keep their nighttime temperatures at 50°F or above to promote flowering. Wax-leaved begonia flowers come in shades of white, rose, pink or red. Some varieties have bronze-colored foliage. Begonias are not a cut flower; bring a blooming pot into the house.

It's hard for me to list these particular begonias as "annuals." I've never had one that didn't live for years and years. When plants get rangy, I root cuttings from fresh growth. Then I give them to friends or pass the cuttings around the neighborhood. Eventually, I'll try keeping one into old age, just as an experiment.

APPENDIX A
SOURCES OF SEEDS AND SUPPLIES

De Giorgi Company Inc.
P.O. Box 413
1411 Third Street
Council Bluffs, IA 51502

This company's offerings include many unusual seeds for both ornamentals and vegetables at reasonable prices.

Dr. Yoo Farm
P.O. Box 290
College Park, MD 20740

A source of a wide variety of oriental vegetables. The catalog is quite descriptive.

Epicure Seeds Ltd.
Box 450
Brewster, NY 10509

This company imports European seeds. The lettuces are particularly good. Overall, the quality of the seeds is superb.

Joseph Harris Co., Inc.
Moreton Farm
3670 Buffalo Road
Rochester, NY 14624

Commercial growers often favor Harris, which has a good selection of proven varieties. The catalog is descriptive and quite helpful.

Le Jardin du Gourmet
West Danville, VT 05873

This company imports some seeds from France, but it also sells domestic stock. The 20-cent herb packets are a good value because you get just enough seed for a season's planting without having a lot left over.

Johnny's Selected Seeds
Albion, ME 04910

An excellent source of northern varieties of most vegetables. The catalog is as outstanding as the seeds.

Meadowbrook Herbs & Things, Inc.
Whispering Pines Road
Wyoming, RI 02898

Biodynamically grown herbs are the stock-in-trade of this company. The quality of the plants is uniformly superior.

Necessary Trading Company
P.O. Box 305
Main Street
New Castle, VA 24127

This company offers a selection of environmentally sound products to control pests and diseases, fertilize plants and build good soil. You can also order garden and kitchen equipment, as well as useful books.

Nichols Garden Nursery
1190 North Pacific Highway
Albany, OR 97321

An organically oriented company that offers some excellent and unusual herbs, ornamentals and vegetables.

Redwood City Seed Co.
P.O. Box 361
Redwood City, CA 94064

This company specializes in unusual seeds. It has a good selection of oriental vegetables and cool-weather varieties.

Stokes Seeds Inc.
P.O. Box 548
737 Main Street
Buffalo, NY 14240

This company offers an incredibly wide selection. Many of the varieties are suitable for greenhouses. The catalog is informative, but the seed packets are a treasure trove of information!

Thompson and Morgan, Inc.
P.O. Box 1308
Jackson, NJ 08572

The prices in this catalog tend to be a little high, but the company carries some vegetables and ornamentals for which I gladly pay. The catalog is impressive and offers many European seeds.

Tsang & Ma International
P.O. Box 294
1556 Laurel Street
Belmont, CA 94070

This is a good source for seeds of oriental vegetables. The company also sells great kitchen equipment.

Vesey's Seeds Ltd.
York, Prince Edward Island
Canada C0A 1P0

You won't find a wide selection in this catalog, but it does offer excellent short-season varieties. The tomatoes are exceptionally good.

William Dam Seeds Limited
P.O. Box 8400
Dundas, Ontario
Canada L9H 6M1

This company offers some unusual varieties, and the prices are quite reasonable. You'll find some good short-season, warm-weather crops.

APPENDIX B
MONITORING THE GREENHOUSE

Good records help you develop good greenhouse skills. By looking back on last year's seedling production, for example, you'll be able to see which crops were over- or underplanted, which were planted at the right time and which were ahead or behind the season.

Notes usually teach you something. For example, slow-ripening crops are easy to explain by a prolonged period of cloudy weather, especially in low-photoperiod times. But if it's been sunny and the crops are still slow to ripen, you might decide that a planting date is too early for a particular variety.

Records also give clues to help manage pests and diseases. What was the climate like, both inside and out, for the week before that horrible *Botrytis* attack? Could you ventilate and heat more carefully the next time such a pattern occurs? Or perhaps lady beetles shipped in early March were killed by cold weather in transit. An insecticidal soap might be the best choice at the same time next year. When did you find indigenous aphid predators? Was it just after the apples bloomed? By planning for this infusion of free predators next year, you might be able to avoid having to buy them. In short, notes taken over the course of the year can jog your memory and spur you on to greater success the following year.

For many people, record keeping is an onerous job. I would much rather weed a 500-foot bed of carrots than count and record the number of tomatoes in a bed. The best solution is to keep all records as simple and as relevant as possible. The Daily Record worksheet is designed for those who don't enjoy taking notes. If you fit the category, try this form, adapting it to your own purposes as time goes on. This record, which is the one I use every day, takes about three minutes to fill out on the busiest day and only a minute on a day when watering and harvesting are the only jobs. Even I find it tolerable.

More specific records serve other purposes. If you start a great many seedlings for both the garden and greenhouse, a separate Planting Record is almost mandatory. Not only will next year's planting be more organized, but current records help to keep track of all those shifting

Daily Record

Date: _____ Time: _____

Temperatures: Min _____ Max _____ Ambient _____

Yesterday's Sunshine: (Low, Moderate, High)

Yesterday's Relative Humidity: (Low, Moderate, High or %)

Yesterday's Photoperiod: _____

Heater Thermostat Setting: _____

Fan Thermostat Setting: _____

Vents Opened, Times: _____

Seedings, Quantities and Locations: _____

_____

Harvested Crops and Amounts: _____

_____

Insect Sightings and Locations: _____

_____

Disease Sightings and Locations: _____

_____

Tasks Done: (for example watered beds 4 and 5; pruned tomatoes in bed 4) _____

_____

General Comments: _____

_____

_____

flats. Without this sheet, I'm likely to forget what's been planted and how it was treated.

The Harvest Record keeps track of the vegetables you harvest. After reviewing it, you might decide, for example, to reduce the area given to lettuce the next year, substituting other cool-weather crops.

Just as horticultural skills improve year by year, record-keeping skills become more refined. Begin by keeping the basic information about plants and the greenhouse environment. Continue to develop a system that suits your needs. But whatever you do, develop a record-keeping habit early, and give it the same allegiance you give to brushing your teeth.

Planting Record*

Crop (Variety name)	Date Sown	Date Trans- planted	Final Position	Comments
Tomato (Vendor)	1/3	1/17–2/23	Bed 2	Lights/heat; 2 flats; good germination
Petunia (Velvet Flash)	2/28	3/21	Garden	Half-flat
Broccoli (Premier Crop)	3/28	4/28	Garden	Lights; no heat; 3 flats

*I've given you a couple of entries from my own planting record to serve as examples of information to record.

Harvest Record*

Date	Crop (Variety)	Location	Amount
4/1	Beet greens (Long Season)	Bed 3	3 bunches
4/1	Lettuce (Buttercrunch)	Bed 5	6 heads
4/2	Chard (Lucullus)	Bed 4	Final harvest, 3 plants

*I've given you a couple of entries from my own harvest record to serve as examples of information to record.

BIBLIOGRAPHY

Abraham, George (Doc), and Katy Abraham. *Organic Gardening Under Glass.* Emmaus, Pa.: Rodale Press, 1975.

Borror, Donald J., and D. M. DeLong. *Introduction to the Study of Insects.* 5th ed. New York: CBS Publications, 1981.

Brady, Nyle C. *The Nature and Properties of Soils.* 8th ed. New York: Macmillan Publishing Co., 1974.

Brooklyn Botanic Garden. *Gardening Under Artificial Light*
Greenhouse Handbook for the Amateur
Handbook on Propagation
Handbook on Soils
Handbook on Biological Control of Plant Pests
These small booklets are published by the Brooklyn Botanic Garden, 100 Washington Avenue, Brooklyn, NY 11225. *Handbook on Biological Control of Plant Pests* has gone out-of-print, but check with your local library and gardening friends to see if you can locate a copy.

Bubel, Nancy. *The Seed-Starter's Handbook.* Emmaus, Pa.: Rodale Press, 1979.

Carr, Anna. *Rodale's Color Handbook of Garden Insects.* Emmaus, Pa.: Rodale Press, 1979.

Clegg, Peter, and Derry Watkins. *The Complete Greenhouse Book: Building and Using Greenhouses from Cold Frames to Solar Structures.* Charlotte, Vt.: Garden Way Publishing Co., 1978.

Davies, J. *A Guide to the Study of Soil Ecology.* Scarborough, Ontario: Prentice-Hall Canada, 1973.

Fichter, George S. *Insect Pests: A Guide to More Than 350 Pests of Home, Garden, Field and Forest.* New York: Golden Press, 1966.

Fisher, Rich, and Bill Yanda. *The Food and Heat Producing Solar Greenhouse: Design, Construction, Operation.* Santa Fe: John Muir Publications, 1976.

Gilkeson, Linda, and Miriam Klein. *A Guide to the Biological Control of Greenhouse Aphids*. Prince Edward Island, Canada: The Ark Project, 1981.

> This booklet is available from The Memphremagog Group, P.O. Box 456, Newport, VT 05855.

Hartmann, Hudson T., and Dale E. Kester. *Plant Propagation: Principles and Practices*. 4th ed. Englewood Cliffs, N.J.: Prentice-Hall, 1983.

Hills, Lawrence D. *Fertility Without Fertilizers*. Essex, England: Henry Doubleday Research Association, 1975.

Jacobs, Betty E. M. *Profitable Herb Growing at Home*. Charlotte, Vt.: Garden Way Publishing Co., 1976.

> This book has gone out-of-print, but check with your local library and gardening friends to see if you can locate a copy.

Jeavons, John. *How to Grow More Vegetables Than You Ever Thought Possible on Less Land Than You Can Imagine*. Palo Alto, Calif.: Ecology Action of the Midpeninsula, 1974.

Jordan, William H., Jr. *Windowsill Ecology*. Emmaus, Pa.: Rodale Press, 1977.

> This book has gone out-of-print, but check with your local library and gardening friends to see if you can locate a copy.

Klein, Miriam. *Biological Management of Passive Solar Greenhouses—An Annotated Bibliography and Resource List*. Butte, Mont.: National Center for Appropriate Technology, 1979.

―――. *Horticultural Management of Solar Greenhouses in the Northeast*. Newport, Vt.: The Memphremagog Group, 1979.

> For a copy write to The Memphremagog Group, P.O. Box 456, Newport, VT 05855.

McCullagh, James, ed. *The Solar Greenhouse Book*. Emmaus, Pa.: Rodale Press, 1978.

Mastalerz, John W. *Bedding Plants*. 2d ed. University Park, Pa.: Pennsylvania Flower Growers, 1976.

> For a copy of the book, contact the Pennsylvania Flower Growers, 103 Tyson Building, University Park, PA 16802.

———. *The Greenhouse Environment.* New York: John Wiley & Sons, 1977.

Nearing, Helen K., and Scott Nearing. *Building and Using Our Sun-Heated Greenhouse.* Athens, Ga.: Social Science Press, 1979.

Ott, John N. *Health and Light.* New York: Pocket Books, 1983.

Philbrick, Helen, and John Philbrick. *The Bug Book.* Charlotte, Vt.: Garden Way Publishing Co., 1974.

Savigear, Elfrida. *Garden Pests and Predators.* Wellingborough, North-amptomshire, England: Thorsons Publishers, 1980.

Shapiro, Andrew. *The Homeowner's Complete Handbook for Add-On Solar Greenhouses and Sunspaces.* Emmaus, Pa.: Rodale Press, 1985.

Smith, Shane. *The Bountiful Solar Greenhouse.* Santa Fe: John Muir Publications, 1982.

Stephenson, W. A. *Seaweed in Agriculture and Horticulture.* Edited by Bargyla and Gylver Rateaver. Pauma Valley, Calif.: Bargyla and Gylver Rateaver, 1974.

Suffolk County Extension Service. *Lead in the Soil, A Gardener's Handbook.* Boston: 1980.

> Order a copy from the Suffolk County Extension Service, Urban Gardening Program, University of Massachusetts, 100 Arlington Street, Boston, MA 02125.

Sussman, Vic. *Easy Composting.* Emmaus, Pa.: Rodale Press, 1982.

> This book has gone out-of-print, but check with your local library and gardening friends to see if you can locate a copy.

Swan, Lester A., and Charles S. Papp. *The Common Insects of North America.* New York: Harper & Row, 1972.

Wolfe, Delores. *Growing Food in Solar Greenhouses.* New York: Doubleday/Dolphin Books, 1981.

Yepsen, Roger B., Jr. *The Encyclopedia of Natural Insect and Disease Control.* Emmaus, Pa.: Rodale Press, 1984.

INDEX

Page references in italics indicate illustrations.
Boldfaced page references indicate charts and tables.

A

Abutilon. *See* Flowering maple
Acetic acid, for soil pH adjustment, 100, 101
Acid soil, pH adjustment of, 100, 101
Actinomycetes, 81, 82
Aerobic respiration, 9
African violet, 158
Ageratum, 244
Air, 13–15
    boundary layer of, 13, 34
    composition of, 14
Air circulation, equipment for, 68–69
Air temperature. *See* Temperature
Alfalfa, 116–17
Algae, 82
Alkaline soil, pH adjustment of, 100
Alternaria, 192–93
Alyssum, 244–45
Amblyseium californicus. See Mites, predatory
Anaerobic respiration, 9
Angular leaf spot, 196
Anthracnose, 193–94
Ants, 85, 166
Aphidoletes aphidimyza, as aphid predators, 173–74, *174*, 225, 231
Aphids, 165–66, *165*
    ants and, 166
    Aphidoletes aphidimyza and, 173–74, *174*, 225, 231
    checking for, 161
    control of, 167–76
    eggplant and, 225
    lacewings and, 171–72
    lady beetle and, 169–71, 231
    lettuce and, 231
    lettuce mosaic virus and, 198–99
    life cycle of, 166–67
    "mummies" of, 175–76
    repellent plants for, 148–49
    syrphid flies and, 174–75, *175*
    tobacco mosaic virus and, 197
    trap plants for, 145
Aphtis melinus, 182, 184
Apical dominance, 4
Apical meristem, 4, 5
Arabian violet. *See* German violet
Arid climate, watering methods for, 11
Ashes, wood, as a fertilizer, 111, 116
Attached greenhouse. *See* Greenhouse, solar, attached
Auxin, 4, 12

B

Baby's breath, 245
Bachelor's buttons, 245
Bacteria, 81, 108, 113
Bacterial canker, 195
Bacterial diseases, 194–97
Bacterial rot, 196–97
Bacterial soft spot, 195–96
Bacterial speck, 195
Bacterial spot, 195
Bacterial wilt, 194–95
Beans, 159
Bed clearing, 101–2
Bed design, 51–58
    benches, 56–58, *57, 59*
    deep beds, 54–56, *56*
    troughs, 51–54, *53*
Bedding plants, crop scheduling of, 142
Bed layouts, 143–49
    companion planting, 145–49, *148*